Capitalism, Democracy, and
Ralph's Pretty Good Grocery

*

Capitalism, Democracy, and and Ralph's Pretty Good Grocery

*

JOHN MUELLER

PRINCETON UNIVERSITY PRESS

PRINCETON AND OXFORD

Second printing, and first paperback printing, 2001
Paperback ISBN 0-691-09082-3

The Library of Congress has cataloged the cloth edition of this book as follows

Mueller, John E.
Capitalism, democracy, and Ralph's Pretty Good Grocery / John
Mueller.
p. cm.
Includes bibliographical references and index.
ISBN 0-691-00114-6 (cloth : alk. paper)
1. Capitalism. 2. Democracy. 3. Entrepreneurship. I. Title.
HB501.M83 1999
330.12′2—dc21 99-17412

British Library Cataloging-in-Publication Data is available

This book has been composed in Baskerville

Printed on acid-free paper. ∞

www.pup.princeton.edu

Printed in the United States of America

3 5 7 9 10 8 6 4

To JAM and ESM,

to Karl, Michelle, Karen, Erik, Susan, Kraig,

and now Timothy,

and in memory of

Ernst A. Mueller, capitalist

Contents *

* *Acknowledgments* *

For invaluable advice, information, and pointed commentary at every step, I would like to thank Stanley Engerman with his encyclopedic mind and equally encyclopedic library. I also received beneficial comments and suggestions from Zoltan Barany, Edward Bird, William Bluhm, Randall Calvert, Henry Carey, Ian Fried, James Johnson, David Landes, Eric Larson, Christopher Lasch, Michael Mandelbaum, Henry Manne, Mira Marody, Karl Mueller, John Nye, Normand Perreault, Ronald Resnick, Richard Rosecrance, Andrew Rutten, Edward Schleh, Kenneth Shepsle, Randall Stone, and David Weimer.

I also benefited when portions of the argument were presented to conferences and seminars at Skidmore College; Ohio University; Harvard University; the University of California, Los Angeles; the University of California, Irvine; the University of Warsaw; the Hungarian School of Public Administration; Comenius University, Bratislava, Slovakia; the Civic Education Project Conference at Košice, Slovakia; the Bucharest Social Science Center; the Bratislava Symposium; the Universidad Nacional Autónoma de México; the University of Rochester; the University of South Florida; the Council on Foreign Relations, Washington, D.C.; the University of Alberta; the Brookings Institution; the University of Texas; and the RAND Corporation. I am grateful to Michael Mandelbaum for guidance in publishing an earlier version of parts of the argument. Elements have appeared as well in *American Journal of Political Science* and are recycled here with permission. And thanks as well to Malcolm Litchfield and the crew at Princeton University Press for their wise care and help.

It is customary to excuse others, such as those listed above, from responsibility for the excesses and errors in the text, and I, of course, do so now. However, there is an important sense in which it could be said that the lapses in this book are the fault of William Riker. In the early stages I was able to bounce my ideas off him, but because of his death in 1993 I have had to flail on without his immeasurably valuable counsel. I miss it, and him, greatly, and so, I'm afraid, will the readers of this book.

Capitalism, Democracy, and
Ralph's Pretty Good Grocery

*

INTRODUCTION

*

Capitalism and Democracy

IMAGES AND IMAGE MISMATCHES

Dᴇᴍᴏᴄʀᴀᴄʏ and free-market capitalism seem to suffer from image problems—opposite ones, as it happens. Capitalism is much better than its image, while democracy has turned out to be much worse than its image.

Although capitalism is generally given credit, even by its many detractors, for generating wealth and for stimulating economic growth, it is commonly maligned for the deceit, unfairness, dishonesty, and discourtesy that are widely taken to be the inevitable consequences of its apparent celebration of greed. But capitalism actually tends, all other things being equal, systematically, though not uniformly, to reward business behavior that is honest, fair, civil, and compassionate, and it inspires a form of risk-taking behavior that can often be credibly characterized as heroic. Under capitalism, as it happens, virtue is considerably more than its own reward.

Meanwhile, democracy is often compared to an ideal image which envisions citizens actively participating on an equal basis and entering into a form of enlightened, or at any rate informed, deliberation about the affairs of governance. By contrast, actual democracy, notable chiefly for discord, inequality, apathy, hasty compromise, political and policy ignorance, and manipulative scrambling by "special interests," is found to be disappointingly wanting.

These disconnections can have significant, and often detrimental, consequences. The mismatch of capitalism with its image can damagingly impede economic growth and development, particularly if people in business misguidedly embrace the negative stereotype. The democracy mismatch can enhance cynicism about the process—even to the point of inspiring a yearning to scrap the

system entirely—and it can rouse minorities into misguided rebellion, lead to an undue pessimism about the prospects for
democracy's growth and acceptance, and facilitate the efforts of
tyrants to postpone or avoid political change.

CAPITALISM

The negative image of capitalism has been propagated for centuries—perhaps forever—not only by communists and socialists,
but by the church, popular culture (including capitalist Hollywood), intellectuals, aristocrats, and often by capitalists themselves—particularly those who have lost out in the competitive
process. Swindlers and moral monsters sometimes do become rich
(in both capitalist and noncapitalist systems), but contrary to the
popular image, capitalism by its nature rewards many important
values that are highly regarded. Of course, capitalism generally inspires business behavior that is industrious, prescient, diligent,
and prudent. But modern business has also found that such slogans as "Honesty is the best policy; it's also the most profitable," "A
happy employee is a productive employee," and "The customer is
always right" are not only sound advice, but are part of a broader
set of self-effacing moral principles that are, on average, wealth-
enhancing.

This is not to say that capitalists necessarily and always behave
virtuously. Many, indeed, have lied, cheated, behaved shabbily, and
let themselves be dominated by arrogance and ego. But such behavior is, on balance, on average, in general, and in the long run,
economically foolish.

Nor does the existence of the capitalist virtues mean that there
is no room for government or that capitalism can be entirely self-
regulating. Societies may find it useful, usually for noneconomic
reasons, to use tax policy and regulation to redistribute wealth, to
aid the unfortunate, to enhance business competition, to provide
for public health and safety, and to control undesirable side effects
or externalities such as air pollution. They may also consider it desirable to ban or inconvenience the propagation of certain goods

and services for which there is profitable demand, like drugs, pornography, prostitution, cigarettes, liquor, and gambling. And it should be emphasized that capitalists do not pursue virtue to the point of stupidity—the virtues do not require one to cut an unfavorable deal, keep open an unproductive factory, trust a swindler, or retain excess workers when business slackens.

But virtue is, on balance and all other things equal, essentially smart business under capitalism: nice guys, in fact, tend to finish first. Not all successful capitalists are necessarily nice people. Some scoundrels become rich even as some heavy smokers escape cancer. But, as nonsmoking is, in general, good for your health, virtuous business behavior is, in general, good for your bottom line.

Capitalism's image mismatch causes problems. In particular, it can hamper economic development because the often unacknowledged capitalist virtues are necessary, or at least extremely helpful, for economic growth: without them, countries can remain mired in poverty. Fortunately, because it generally furnishes a business with a competitive advantage, virtuous behavior can arise from normal competitive pressures and does not need to be artificially imposed by outside authority. For that to happen, however, someone must lead—innovate—by actually behaving virtuously, and sometimes the widely accepted negative image of capitalism keeps this from coming about. Virtuous business practices may be financially beneficial in the long term, but in part because of the traditional image, this reality may not be obvious to the very capitalists who stand to benefit from them.

Democracy

Democracy suffers from the opposite image problem.

The nature of democracy has been debated for several millennia as philosophers and other thinkers have speculated about what it is, what it might become, and what it ought to be. After democracy actually came into being in large countries some two hundred years ago, however, a remarkable dilemma emerged.

On the one hand, democracy worked rather well by the values

most theorists and idealists have held to be important. When compared to competing forms of government and methods of organizing society, democracy has characteristically produced societies that have been humane, flexible, productive, and vigorous, and under this system leaders somehow emerged who—at least in comparison with your average string of kings or czars or dictators—have generally been responsive, responsible, able, and dedicated.

On the other hand, democracy didn't come out looking the way many theorists and idealists imagined it could or should. It has been characterized by a great deal of unsightly and factionalized squabbling by self-interested, shortsighted people and groups, and its policy outcomes have often been the result of a notably unequal contest over who could most adroitly pressure and manipulate the system. Even more distressingly, the citizenry seems disinclined to display anything remotely resembling the deliberative qualities many theorists have been inclined to see as a central requirement for the system to work properly. Indeed, far from becoming the attentive, if unpolished, policy wonks hoped for in many of the theories and images, real people in real democracies often display an almost monumental lack of political interest and knowledge.

Inspired by their optimal illusion and confounded by grim democratic reality, disappointed theorists, idealists, and reformers have generally taken one of two courses to deal with this mismatch. One is to retreat into the vapor and to conclude that democracy, as it turns out, doesn't really exist at all, but that it is just some sort of attractive, impossible dream. Thus, in February 1990, Czechoslovak president Václav Havel patiently explained to the Congress of the world's oldest democracy that the country it represented still hadn't made it and, actually, never would: "As long as people are people, democracy in the full sense of the word will always be no more than an ideal; one may approach it as one would a horizon, in ways that may be better or worse, but it can never be fully attained. In this sense you are also merely approaching democracy."[1]

The other recourse is to stress dilemma. For example, one analysis first notes that, "in theory, a democracy requires knowledgeable citizens," and then goes on to observe that "for the last two hundred years the United States has survived as a stable democracy, de-

8

spite continued evidence of an uninformed public." It labels this "the paradox of modern democracy."[2]

Inspired by such thinking, democratic theorists, idealists, and reformers have sought to perfect the system, attempting to refashion democratic institutions and their human constituents to more nearly approximate the qualities called for in the theories, and in the ideals that derive from some of the theories. As part of this effort, reformers have frequently tried to make the process more politically equal and to control the play of "special interests." They have also sought to elevate the human race to match such rarified images as the one projected by John F. Kennedy: "Democracy is a difficult kind of government. It requires the highest qualities of self-discipline, restraint, a willingness to make commitments and sacrifices for the general interest, and it also requires knowledge."[3]

By contrast, I will suggest in this book that the fault in the mismatch between democracy's image and its reality lies more with the ideals than with the facts—more in the stars than in ourselves, as Shakespeare's Cassius didn't put it. After all, if my theory tells me the moon is made of green cheese and then a spacepersonage inconveniently brings home a lunar soil sample composed entirely of dirt and rock, even my closest friends would be disinclined to label the resulting conundrum a "paradox." Most people would be so ungracious as to suggest that my theory has been soundly disconfirmed. And they would probably deride any effort to implant the moon with green cheese in order to make it more closely resemble my theory.

Perfect democracy, in my view, is an oxymoron, and the undisciplined, chaotic, and essentially unequal interplay of "special interests" is democracy's whole *point*. Moreover, the patent and inevitable contrast between the hopelessly ideal images of democracy—such as those so sonorously promulgated by Havel and Kennedy—and its rough-and-ready reality often inspires the very cynicism about the democratic deliberative process that the idealists continually bemoan and profess to want to reduce. Bismarck once observed that "If you like laws and sausages, you should never watch either one being made." It is a fundamental property—and perhaps defect—of democracy that citizens may watch laws being made, and when they do so they often compare democracy to its mystical, Kennedyesque image and then reject the actual process with righteous disdain, even outrage, opaquely dismissing it as bickering and correctly, but uncomprehendingly, labeling it "politics as usual." Effectively, however, politics as usual is the same as democracy in action.

RALPH'S GROCERY

Ralph's Pretty Good Grocery in Lake Wobegon, a Minnesota town invented by humorist Garrison Keillor, operates under a sensible, if rather unexhilarating, slogan: "If you can't find it at Ralph's, you can probably get along without it." (The opposite slogan, hopelessly hyperbolic, promotes Alice's Restaurant—in some other town, presumably—where "you can get anything you want"—excepting Alice.) It is a central perspective of this book that democracy and capitalism, despite their image problems, have triumphed in part because people have essentially been persuaded to accept a version of Ralph's slogan: the systems can't supply everything, but on balance, people have effectively if sometimes rather reluctantly concluded, if you can't get it with democracy and capitalism, you can probably get along without it.

For example, it is possible to create a society in which order reigns supreme, but experience suggests that society in the process loses flexibility, responsiveness, intellectual growth, and individual freedom. Although they complain about it all the time, democrats have basically decided that, even though democracy is distressingly, profoundly, and necessarily messy and disorderly, it's better, on balance, to get along without the blessings an orderly society can bring.

And capitalism revels in—indeed, seems viscerally to require—a considerable amount of insecurity, risk, and uncertainty. It may be possible, at least in principle, to design an economy in which privilege, station, prices, employment, and economic security are comfortably, reassuringly, and authoritatively preserved. Since these approaches tend to stifle the economically invigorating effects of selfish acquisitiveness, however, they lead to slower growth and to less wealth overall. Experience seems to suggest, then, that it is better to learn to get along without total security.

In addition, capitalism and democracy are in important respects viscerally unequal and unfair at the systemic level, if not at the personal level.

This condition stems naturally and inevitably from the related facts that both systems leave individuals free to pursue their interests and that some will simply do better at the pursuit than others. Thus even when everyone is equally free, some people under democracy will be more successful at manipulating the political system in a beneficial way (extracting favors from it, getting it to support their pet policy projects). And under capitalism, some will prosper because they are more successful at providing goods or services other people happen to value at the moment.

This inequality of result will often emerge because people are differently abled: differently skilled, differently capable. For some people, particularly for those who are inclined to overrate their own abilities, this condition is deeply unpleasant, even unbearable, and they can become resentful.

But inequality will sometimes also result not so much because people are differently abled but because they are differently lucky: they succeed because they just happen to know or be related to someone who can help them out at a crucial point, because they just happen to be in the right place at the right time, or because an ill-considered, even foolish, gamble just happens to pay off. In an important sense, then, freedom is notably unfair. Democracy is perhaps worse off than capitalism with regard to the issues of equality and fairness. Capitalism does not profess to make everyone equally wealthy, but the beguiling, ringing notion that "all men are created equal" has often been taken to suggest that some sort of political equality is central to democracy; the system can be seen, then, to be viscerally hypocritical.

But if capitalism and democracy can't supply orderliness, certainty, equality, security, and systemic fairness and are thus (only) pretty good in the Ralph's Grocery sense, their image mismatches make them pretty good in opposite senses. Democracy compared to its image is (merely) *pretty* good, while capitalism compared to its image is (actually) pretty *good*.

The laid-back and markedly unromantic perspective of the folks at Ralph's Pretty Good Grocery—unexhilarating perhaps, but blessedly free of misdirecting hyperbole—is relevant to the development of democracy and capitalism in another sense as well.

It seems to me that an institution is likely to be fundamentally sound if it can function adequately when people are rarely, if ever, asked to rise above the ignorance and selfishness with which they have been so richly endowed by their creator. Or, putting it a bit more gently, since human beings are a flawed bunch, an institution will be more successful if it can work with human imperfections rather than requiring first that the race be reformed into impossible perfection. Therefore, it may well actually be fortunate that democracy does not require people to be good or noble, but merely to calculate what is best for them or what they take to be in the best interest of society, and to seek to further these interests if they happen to be so inclined, while capitalism raises selfishness and acquisitiveness to dominant motivations. And it may be desirable that democracy and capitalism are about as romantic, to apply Charlotte Brontë's phrase, as Monday morning.

THE PLAN OF THE BOOK

This book traces—and celebrates—the ascendancy, the curious and unexhilarating triumph, of the pretty good over the ideal, the certain, the harmonious, the romantic, the orderly, the secure, the divine, the transcendent, and the sublime. It assesses the consequences of the image mismatches, and it also seeks to explain the remarkable growth of the political institution of democracy and the economic institution of free market capitalism over the last two centuries or so.

Fundamentally, it seems to me, capitalism will emerge if people are left free to be acquisitive, and democracy can come about if people are left free to complain and to organize complainants. Neither quality, it seems, is terribly difficult to inspire. The United

States Constitution, for example, nowhere deems it necessary to call upon people to complain or to pursue their selfish interests; rather it simply and wisely restricts the government's ability to abridge those instincts. It follows from this perspective that democracy and capitalism should not be terribly difficult to institute or to maintain, that no elaborate prerequisites are necessary for them to emerge, and that they are not fundamentally fragile.

Capitalism is considered first.

Chapter 2 begins by focusing on the individual behavior the system tends to inspire and reward—honesty, fairness, civility, compassion, and heroism. The motivation for these virtues is essentially insincere under capitalism—virtuous business behavior is inspired not by the virtues' intrinsic value but by the quest for profit. However, in practice it is very difficult for people to fake the virtues over extended periods of time, and therefore people who are genuinely nice guys tend, on balance, to finish first and to flourish. At the same time, in its rapacious desire to supply people with any product or service they happen to think they want at the moment (and can afford to pay for) capitalism can lead to a kind of cultural materialism that many people may consider unpleasant, distasteful, and even debased. It can also generate considerable economic inequality and what may be taken to be an unfairness of result. Government can be used to soften the cultural, fairness, and equality problems somewhat, but to a substantial degree they are built in.

Chapter 3 assesses the many sources of capitalism's negative image over the ages. Socialists, communists, religious leaders, storytellers, intellectuals, and aristocrats have all contributed to that image. But it also seems that the image may have been substantially built on reality because businesspeople, insufficiently unaware of the profitability of the business virtues, may often have behaved in an economically foolish manner—that is, they have behaved as if capitalism's negative image were correct.

Chapter 4 evaluates the consequences of capitalism's negative image on economic development. It argues that for growth to happen people in business need to abandon that image and to behave virtuously. However, since virtuous business behavior turns out actually to be profitable, it is generally not necessary to impose such behavior from above by establishing policing institutions: rather, it can emerge from normal competitive activity. Because the profitability of virtuous business behavior has apparently often not been obvious, however, a business innovator must discover the economic value of virtue and then act upon this important discovery. Others, out of competitive pressures, will then imitate. The chapter also suggests that a rise of business virtue may well have been an important element in the amazing economic development much of the world has experienced over the last two centuries. And it concludes that virtue-enforcing institutions are more nearly the result of the rise of virtue than its cause.

Chapter 5 proposes that the world's economic development in the future is likely to be enhanced even further because of the rise in credibility and effectiveness of the economics profession and because politicians and policymakers are increasingly willing to take the profession's often politically painful advice. Over the last century or two, economists and like-minded idea entrepreneurs seem to have substantially sold four important propositions, the acceptance of which, among other things, suggests the demise of empire as well as major (and perhaps minor) international war. These propositions are: the growth of economic well-being should be a dominant goal; wealth is best achieved through exchange rather than through conquest; international trade should be free; and economies do best when the government leaves them substantially free.

The chapter also observes that, although the rise of capitalism over the last two centuries has coincided with, indeed has importantly helped to cause, a very substantial betterment of the human condition in what we now call the developed world, happiness has failed to soar in tandem there—in fact, people seem simply to have taken the remarkable economic improvement in stride and have deftly found new concerns to get upset about. In an important sense, then, things never get better. However, the seemingly unquenchable quest for economic improvement may be useful—crucial, even—for economic advance.

A similar assessment is then carried out for democracy.

Chapter 6 defines democracy as a form of government which is necessarily and routinely (though not necessarily equally) responsive, and it argues that democracy comes about when the people effectively agree not to use violence to overthrow the leadership and when the leadership leaves them free to try to overthrow it by any other means. Much of the real stuff of what goes on in a democracy comes from petition and pressure, not from elections and legislative voting—indeed, it seems to me that it is possible, though not necessarily desirable, to have an effective, responsive democracy even without elections. Democracy is a form of government in which people are left (equally) free to become politically unequal, and it works because it is characterized not by political equality, active participation by the citizenry, and something resembling majority rule and consensus, but by political inequality and substantial apathy—effectively, by minority rule and majority acquiescence. Because of this characteristic, democracy has been able to survive a potential defect that theoreticians had previously considered terminal: democracy was able to coopt, rather than to alienate, the rich.

The chapter concludes by comparing democracy to its competitors and argues that, for all its scruffiness in practice, democracy seems superior (though, of course, far from perfect) in governmental effectiveness and in choosing leaders. It is also fairly good at protecting minorities: democracy does often persecute minorities but, unlike other forms of government, it routinely allows the persecuted to work to change things, a process that has often been remarkably effective even for tiny minorities which are regarded with disgust and contempt by the majority. There is also strength in that democracy can work quite well with real people and generally does not require a great deal from them.

Chapter 7 seeks to ferret out some of the consequences of the mismatch between democracy's image and its reality. It begins by assessing the quests for equality, for deliberative consensus, for active participation, and for an enlightened citizenry, and it concludes that these quests, while not necessarily undesirable, are substantially hopeless—there is no conceivable way, for example, that the average factory worker can have remotely as much political clout as the average industrial leader or newspaper columnist. Moreover the quest itself can inspire cynicism when citizens are continually asked by reformers to compare grim democratic reality with its idealized image.

The chapter also suggests that the overselling of equality can be profoundly harmful for democracy when that notion is extrapolated to the economic realm, because the only way economic equality can be fully achieved in a democracy is by destroying democracy itself. Another danger is that the image may inspire minorities logically to conclude that, if democracy is truly about equality and majority rule by an active citizenry, they face certain persecution in a democracy and must rebel to protect themselves. The chapter ends with some cautionary comments about the field of transitology which often holds out ideals for new democracies to seek, an approach that is not only often unrealistic, but one that can inspire a damaging short-range perspective.

Chapter 8 traces the rise of democracy. It argues that, contrary to the ideal image—an image which has often inspired a considerable pessimism about its prospects and one which can furnish authoritarian leaders with a convenient excuse for neglecting reform—democracy is really quite a simple and easily graspable form of government. As Americans should surely know by now, any dimwit can do democracy. If this is true, it follows that the chief barrier to democracy's expansion has not been any inherent technical, historical, social, cultural, economic, or anthropological difficulty, but the effective exertions of antidemocrats. Sometimes these people can be, simply, thugs with guns. But at other times they have been people projecting a different vision that can be arrestingly beguiling. Democracy's growth, it appears, has not been the result so much of broader economic, social, or cultural developments; rather, it has been the consequence of a sort of marketing process that has been characterized by product testing, by luck, by fashion leadership, by the convenient self-destruction of competing institutions, and particularly by the effective propaganda endeavors of idea entrepreneurs—politicians, writers, and organized interest groups.

At base, I suggest, democracy is merely an idea (a pretty good

one, as it happens), and about the only requirement for its acceptance is that people be persuaded to take it up. Accordingly, the
world could just as well have embraced it centuries earlier. Or the
world could have missed it entirely, and we'd still be living, like
most of the human race for most of its existence, under the capricious rule of queens and kings and eunuchs.

The concluding chapter juxtaposes democracy and capitalism
to ferret out connections between them. It argues that, while capitalism can exist without democracy as has often been noted, recent experience in some postcommunist countries demonstrates
that democracy can exist without capitalism as well. The chapter
also suggests however, that, for better or worse, democracy has
been associated of late with capitalist prosperity. This undeserved
connection could lead to destructive disillusion in some places,
but it might also help democratic development if the world is really in the process of massive economic improvement. There could
also be trouble in some areas in the casual and popular, if undeserved, connection of democracy and capitalism with crime.

While democracy may not be necessary for capitalism, democracy probably does benefit capitalist growth. It does so by furnishing property owners some potential remedy against governmental
confiscation, by establishing the rule of law, by routinely encouraging an openness and transparency of information, by allowing
all interest groups (rather than just a privileged subset of them) to
attempt to influence government policy, by providing a mechanism for removing defective leaders, and, at least in recent years,
by furnishing an atmosphere of stability and predictability. Finally,
democracy and capitalism, it seems, are similar in that they can
often work pretty well even if people generally do not appreciate
their workings very well. As human institutions, in fact, that paradoxical quality may be one of their most important strengths.

CAPITALISM

*

.

Capitalism's Image

CAPITALISM is routinely assumed to inspire in its practitioners behavior that is deceitful, deceptive, cowardly, unfair, boorish, and lacking compassion. I assess this negative image in this chapter and conclude that, however popular, the image is fundamentally misguided. On the contrary, capitalism systematically encourages and rewards business behavior that is honest, fair, civil, and compassionate, and it also encourages, and often rewards, behavior that in many cases should reasonably be considered heroic. Moreover, people who are genuinely honest, fair, civil, and compassionate are more likely to succeed in business than those who simply feign such qualities. Or, more generally, nice guys tend to finish first.

It is important to stress at the outset that I am *not* arguing that all capitalists are always honest, fair, civil, and compassionate. Rather, under capitalism, honest, fair, civil, and compassionate business behavior is, on average, economically advantageous, and those who behave in another way will generally do less well. Indeed, in later chapters I will argue that capitalists have often engaged in economically foolish behavior because they apparently have not understood the advantages of the business virtues, and furthermore, that such behavior has often hampered economic growth.

The chapter includes a consideration of the capitalist culture so many people find objectionable and of the inequality and apparent unfairness of result that competitive capitalism often fosters at the systemic level. It appends a discussion of capitalism's central dependence on the gambling instinct and thus, in effect, on business behavior that is essentially irrational and effectively altruistic.

Capitalism is an economic arrangement in which the government substantially leaves people free to pursue their own economic interests as long as they do so without physical violence (including physical theft). That is, capitalism emerges when it is possible and legal (or effectively legal) to make a profit nonviolently. Nathan Rosenberg and L. E. Birdzell suggest that capitalism can be viewed as an arrangement where economic investment is primarily carried out by individuals who will gain if they are right, will lose if they are wrong, and "lack the economic or political power to prevent at least some others from proving them wrong." Interestingly, with minor modifications, this might also be used as a definition of democracy.[1]

There has been a lively debate over the degree to which the government should intervene in the free market. By the end of the twentieth century, this debate seems substantially to have been won by those who argue that it is best for long-term economic growth if the free market is allowed to prevail and if the government moves toward reducing its hold on the economy—though there remains a wide (and sometimes reluctant) acceptance of the notion that the government will still play a notable role particularly by providing for public safety, furnishing a safety net for losers, establishing an effective legal structure, and regulating undesirable side effects like pollution. Although I will mostly not engage in that debate in this book, an appreciation for its course is a central concern of chapter 5.

THE CAPITALIST VIRTUES

In assessing the capitalist virtues, I will not assume that capitalists are saintly in any sense, but rather that they are essentially impelled as envisioned by their caricaturists: their highest goal and motivation is the acquisition of financial wealth—greed, it is often called. Moreover, although they must eschew violence under capitalism, the system does in principle leave them generally free to lie, cheat, swindle, collude, misrepresent, price-fix, engage in fraud, be discourteous, and attempt to stifle competition. I assume, however, a *long-term acquisitiveness* in all this—the concept of "short-term greed" is really quite oxymoronic after all.

From time to time some individual capitalists may be impelled as well by motivations that are generally more esteemed. But the point to be developed here is that, under capitalism acquisitiveness alone encourages certain kinds—though not necessarily *all* kinds—of behavior that are generally held to be moral, virtuous, and admirable. And, if the community generally values honesty, fairness, civility, and compassion, the sensible capitalist will, inspired by acquisitiveness, seek to furnish them—or at least seem to furnish them—in full, unambiguous measure.

Capitalists often spend a great deal of money on advertising, but as most would readily agree, the most generally effective advertisement is word of mouth. Thus the best way to get ahead (that is, to become rich) in the long term is to establish a good word-of-mouth reputation. Conversely, a wealth-seeking capitalist can be severely punished, often at little cost to the aggrieved, if the word of mouth becomes unfavorable. As a business slogan puts it, "A customer who goes away happy will tell three friends; a customer who goes away unhappy will tell ten." This phenomenon gives individual customers and fellow deal-makers a considerable enforcement mechanism. They can punish behavior they find unsuitable by refusing again to deal with, and by bad-mouthing, someone they have had a bad experience with or have heard unfavorable things about.

But virtuous business dealings often make sense even in cases where repeated dealings are unlikely. A store clerk who is civil to a one-time customer, for example, is more likely to make a sale than one who is not.

Honesty

It is impossible, or nearly so, to create a perfect written contract, and it would be wildly inefficient to require even an imperfect one for every transaction. It would be even more inefficient to have contracts regularly adjudicated in court. Therefore, in its general day-by-day dealings, business requires, and inspires, integrity, honesty, trustworthiness, and reliability in order to achieve its vaunted efficiency and growth. As the Better Business Bureau puts it, "Honesty is the best policy. It's also the most profitable." That is, although it is certainly possible to make a quick profit by cheating and lying, the best prospects for secure, long-term wealth derive from honest business practices.

Thus, in a classic study of actual business practices Stewart Macaulay found that the strong norm, "One does not welsh on a deal," is enforced because "both business units involved in the exchange desire to continue successfully in business and will avoid conduct which might interfere with attaining this goal." In consequence, each is "concerned with both the reaction of the other party" and "with his own general business reputation." Similarly, George Stigler observes that "A reputation for candor and responsibility is a commercial asset"; Donald McCloskey that "One must establish a relationship of trust with someone in order to persuade him"; and Benjamin Franklin that "Tricks and treachery are the practice of fools that have not wit enough to be honest." Or, as Gregory Kavka puts it crisply, "Time wounds all heels."[2]

The Quakers, a religious group that requires absolute honesty from its members, enjoyed a competitive advantage because of this quality: all other things equal, customers preferred a business run by Quaker because they knew they could trust the Quaker to be honest. They discovered "that if they sent a child to their shops for anything, they were as well used as if they had come themselves," and the shopper's inquiry became, "Where is there a draper or shopkeeper or tailor or shoemaker or an other tradesman that is a Quaker?"[3] Accordingly, Quakers became prosperous. But, because the image of capitalism holds that one can only become wealthy by cheating, Quakers have regularly been accused of being hypocrites: as Balwant Nevaskar observes, "although they established a reputation as reliable merchants, the Quakers were often suspected of being shrewd, conniving, sly, and dishonest."[4]

The experience of the legendary P. T. Barnum furnishes another arresting example. He is best known for supposedly having coined the phrase, "There's a sucker born every minute." Not only did Barnum never make this statement, but it would be out of character.[5] Although a few of his famous "humbugs" early in his career did have a degree of (rather good-natured) fraud about them, he became wealthy in the circus not by bilking "suckers" but by providing a good, honest show that people appreciated and were quite happy to patronize year after year.

Before Barnum, circuses were very often run by fly-by-night cheats: ticket takers would regularly short-change customers; pickpockets, working on a commission, would roam the grounds; "Monday men" would steal the wash from clotheslines or burglarize homes when the citizenry was at the performance or watching the circus parade; shows would be frauds; games would be fixed.[6] Quick profits were made this way, but soon the entire industry was on the verge of extinction because its customers, through experience, no longer were foolish enough to attend.

Barnum was one of the circus innovators who changed all that. He used honest ticket takers, hired private detectives to police pickpockets, and spent a lot of time and money creating what he (with characteristic understatement) labeled "The Greatest Show on Earth." Whether customers always fully agreed with that representation, they did find the show, and the whole experience of attending the circus, enjoyable, and they were happy to come back year after year. Accordingly, Barnum and such like-minded circus managers as the Ringling Brothers, applying their "Sunday School" approach to business, soon became far richer than the cheats who had preceded them. As journalist George Ade observes, they "found the business in the hands of vagabonds and put it into the hands of gentlemen." They "became circus kings of the world by adopting and observing the simple rule that is it better to be straight than crooked."[7]

In his spirited pamphlet and popular lecture, "The Art of Money Getting," Barnum stresses that integrity "is more precious than diamonds or rubies" and argues that "the most difficult thing in life is to make money dishonestly," since "no man can be dishonest without soon being found out" and "when his lack of principle is discovered, nearly every avenue to success is closed against him forever." Therefore, even "as a mere matter of selfishness," he concludes, "honesty is the best policy."[8]

This conclusion holds also for businesses which generally do not service the same customer repeatedly. Since a taxi driver is unlikely ever to see the rider again, it is to the driver's short-term advantage to cheat the rider. However, where this is common, the taxicab system as a whole gets a reputation for fraud, and people take cabs only when they have no other choice. Thus the industry as a whole makes much less money than it would if it had a reputation for honesty and integrity.[9] Consequently, taxi companies have often found it very much in their interest to establish industry regulations which keep their own drivers from cheating. In Mexico City, government-certified taxicabs cost *more* than other ones, and do an excellent business with visitors who are willing to pay extra for the simple favor of assured honesty.

This pressure for honesty even affects that most legendary of fly-by-night operators, the traveling salesman. The lessons of the unusually insightful musical, *The Music Man*, are instructive in this regard. The chief protagonist, Harold Hill, is a skilled con artist who descends on a town to pump up the populace, sell a decrepid line of band uniforms, and then vanish into the night before the townsfolk can discover they have been bilked. But behavior like that gives a bad reputation to traveling salesmen as a group, and another traveling salesman (a heavily laden representative of the Gibraltar Anvil Company) informs on him in an Iowa town out of a feeling that he's "got to protect the good reputation of the traveling fraternity from that swindler" because "he spoiled Illinois for me, but he's not going to spoil Iowa." Perhaps unfortunately, such self-policing, if self-interested, crusaders were insufficient to resuscitate the reputation of the fraternity, and traveling salesmen of his sort, precisely because of their soiled reputation, have largely gone, or been forced by government, out of business—something that almost happened to circuses in the nineteenth century. That is, they have made much less money than they would if they had been able to establish a reputation for honesty.

Something similar may be happening currently to telephone marketing. Because of public complaints about fraud (and also, of course, about nuisance), regulators are coming closer to banning it outright.[10] On the other hand, telephone ordering—where a customer initiates the contact—has expanded enormously. This business overwhelmingly relies on trust and honesty; if it gained any sort of reputation for fraud or unremediable misrepresentation, it could die out quickly.

The quality known as "transparency" is closely related to honesty, and it is also generally good for business sometimes even in single transactions. Suppose that two different people are selling two comparable used cars, but that one seller is evasive about the car and its repair history while the other is very open, supplying repair records and even pointing out defects, like a cigarette burn in the back seat, that the prospective buyer may have overlooked. The transparent seller will have a competitive advantage and will be far more likely to get the sale—in many cases even if the selling price is a bit higher.

Although they are often disparaged as formulaic and lacking in variety and humanity, chain and franchise stores have an even greater incentive for integrity than individual stores: a customer who feels cheated in one store is unlikely to patronize not only that one, but any other in the chain or franchise. Conversely, of course, a pleased customer will tend to venture into any store in the chain. Something similar can be said about brand-name merchandise.[11]

The principle can be writ larger. In general, as the organizers of the Better Business Bureaus strongly suggest, it is harmful to business as a whole for swindlers to be able to flourish since they taint all business, reducing sales in the aggregate. Honest business may be bad for swindlers, but it is good for business generally and therefore, as will be suggested more fully in chapter 4, for economic growth.

Honesty is also important in successfully (that is, profitably) managing a firm and in dealing with employees. For manager James Autry, "Honesty is the single most important attribute in a manager's relationship with employees and fellow workers." Management guru Peter Drucker strongly concurs, and emphasizes that integrity is "the one absolute requirement of a manager." If a manager "lacks in character and integrity—no matter how knowledgeable, how brilliant, how successful—he destroys. He destroys people, the most valuable resource of the enterprise. He destroys spirit. He destroys performance." Fellow workers "may forgive a man a great deal: incompetence, ignorance, insecurity, or bad manners. But they will not forgive his lack of integrity. Nor will they forgive higher management for choosing him."[12]

Fairness

Since people value fairness, a vendor or deal-maker who is perceived to be unfair will do less well in the long run than one who appears to be fair. Unfair treatment can also inspire the feeling in others that they have been cheated, causing the deal-maker to gain the reputation not only for unfairness, but for dishonesty—indeed, the two words are often used interchangeably.

Thus, businesspeople who acquire the reputation of being sharp operators—those who take "unfair" advantage of a situation when the opportunity presents itself—will be approached with a wariness that is not beneficial to them from an economic standpoint. In general, they will become less rich—find it more difficult to make deals—than those who have been able to create a reputation for fairness and for fair dealing.

Hence, it is to one's long-term economic advantage that the other party walk away from the deal feeling that the agreement has been fair even though this might mean cutting a deal that is somewhat less favorable or immediately profitable. Nothing riles people more than the feeling that they have been "taken." It was for this reason that, for example, John D. Rockefeller would not fight for the last dollar in forming mergers and always tried to conclude deals cordially; as he put it, he was not "so short-sighted as to antagonize" the very people he would later seek to have a close and profitable relation with. As Stigler observes, the main asset of the great merchandizing companies has been "their reputation for fair and careful dealing." Or as Barnum puts it succinctly, "Men who drive sharp bargains with their customers, acting as if they never expected to see them again, will not be mistaken."[13]

Similar observations are routine in many of the thousands of books and tracts published by businesspeople about how to achieve success—that is, about how to create and run a profitable business enterprise. For example, in his book, *What They Don't Teach You at Harvard Business School,* Mark McCormack notes that "people do not like to feel they are being conned"; that "sometimes you make the best deal for yourself by driving a soft bargain"; and that "I've often found that by recognizing extenuating circumstance and letting someone off the hook I have accomplished much more for myself and my company in the long run." Or, in his sequel, *What They* Still *Don't Teach You at Harvard Business School:* "People often agree to do things and then for reasons beyond their control are unable to do them. If you let them off the hook, are you being a nice guy or a fool? Obviously, if you intend to do business with them again, the choice is not that tough. . . . Rarely have the long-term benefits from such decisions made me feel foolish."[14]

The economic value of fairness is also seen in the curious phenomenon of price stickiness. There seems to be a nearly universal aversion to what is called price gouging, a practice that is generally considered unfair. Accordingly, even when demand clearly comes to outstrip supply, a smart business will be careful about suddenly charging the higher prices that would be myopically dictated by economic rationality. Ski resorts, for example, do not abruptly boost their prices during peak seasons because they know that "If you gouge them at Christmas time they won't come back in March."[15]

This problem can sometimes be handled by establishing list prices and then discounting from them.[16] Thus airlines may charge $1,000 to fly between Rochester and Los Angeles, discounting to $500 if the traveler buys the ticket well in advance and accepts certain restrictions, rather than announcing a price of $500 that will be increased to $1,000 if the customer waits until the last minute and wants no restrictions. Similarly, a university whose effective tuition is $18,000 might list its price at $25,000 and discount from that amount rather than advertising its price as $18,000 except for people it thinks can afford it who will be charged $25,000. The economic effect, obviously, is the same in either case, but the discounting device is generally accepted as being more fair. And airlines and universities use it even though it carries the disadvantage, to them, of sticker shock.

Relatedly, it is most interesting that in advanced capitalist economies bargaining over prices has been abandoned almost entirely in ordinary retail commerce, a phenomenon that will be considered more fully in chapter 4. This development has presumably been to the short-term disadvantage of retailers who, since they bargain all the time and obviously know the product better, have an advantage, on average, over the casual ordinary customer. Nevertheless, businesses have found they tend to do better in the long run if they handicap themselves by setting (attractive) prices for a commodity, a practice that eliminates the often unpleasant and emotionally unsettling task of haggling over a price, the fear of being unfairly taken, and the possibility, generally held to be unfair, of charging different prices to different customers for the same product.

The chain or franchise store effect shows up on the issue of fairness as it does on the one of honesty. Hotel chains in Super Bowl cities, for example, sometimes decline to hike prices on the Big Day out of fear that customers will deem the practice unfair and resentfully bypass other hotels in the chain at other times.[17]

Fairness is also important in a business's relations with its employees. At a time of downturn, it may make the most economic sense to lay off the least productive workers and to retain the most productive, but the usual approach is to fire those with least seniority instead because that policy is more likely to be considered "fair" even by those who have been laid off.

Civility

Although rudeness is hardly unknown among capitalists, the system itself rewards civil behavior: in Barnum's words, "politeness and civility are the best capital ever invested in business."[18] The philosophy that "The customer is always right" is self-effacing, even cravenly self-abnegating perhaps, but it enhances profits.

It seems reasonable to speculate that the reason McDonald's insists its employees treat customers courteously is not simply that Mr. McDonald (or whoever) is an especially nice person. Rather, the company has calculated that when salespeople are pleasant and polite, the customers will likely return to buy more. As Barnum observes, "Large stores, gilt signs, flaming advertisements, will all prove unavailing if you or your employees treat your patrons abruptly. The truth is, the more kind and liberal a man is, the more generous will be the patronage bestowed upon him."[19]

John Wanamaker, the nineteenth-century retailer, reports on an experience he had as a boy that, he says, helped him later to create the foundations of his extremely successful retail business. On a Christmas Eve around 1850 he went into a jewelry store to buy his mother a gift. He spent a long time looking at the goods on display and finally made a choice, but as the jeweler was wrapping it up, the boy changed his mind and said he would like to take another piece instead. The impatient jeweler refused, and Wanamaker recalls that he was "too abashed to protest." But as he left, he said to himself, "When I have a store of my own the people shall have what they want."[20] Wanamaker doesn't mention it, but it seems a reasonable speculation that he never patronized that store again.

Civility even makes sense for panhandlers. Although aggressive panhandling probably is more effective in the short term, it is quite unwise in the long term. Politely saying "Have a nice day" to a potential patron who has turned down a panhandler's entreaty is likely to instill a bit of guilt in the patron who may then mellow the next time. It may also get the panhandler on good—that is to say, profitable—terms with anyone who overhears the exchange. Aggressive panhandling, by contrast, is very bad for public relations because it turns customers off and inspires later avoidance behavior, and because it gives the whole industry a bad name which could ultimately lead to its being entirely outlawed.

In their exuberant, best-selling book, *In Search of Excellence*, published over a century after Wanamaker's valuable, if traumatic, experience with the foolishly boorish jeweler, Thomas Peters and Robert Waterman stress that excellent (that is to say, highly profitable) businesses "love the customers," and they have an "*obsession*" for "a seemingly unjustifiable overcommitment to some form of quality, reliability, or service." A major reason IBM became the world's most profitable company, notes Robert Cringely, was "customer hand holding." And one study found that, when customers

31

were asked why they had stopped shopping at a store, 69 percent gave poor service as their reason whereas only 13 percent mentioned product satisfaction and only 9 percent mentioned high prices. As John Templeton, head of one of the world's most effective—that is, most profit-producing—mutual funds, has put it, "If you are trying to do the most for people, if you are trying to help people the most, you'll be most successful."[21]

Similarly, employers who are considerate and courteous to their employees will tend to find them working harder for less money or doing more work for the same money—a happy employee, as they say, is a productive employee. Contented employees are also likely to be more impervious to the potentially problematic attractions of union organizers and to be less likely to steal from the company. Peters and Waterman stress "productivity through people," and they admonish, "Treat people as adults. Treat them as partners; treat them with dignity; treat them with respect. . . . In other words, if you want productivity and the financial reward that goes with it, you must treat your workers as your most important asset."[22]

For example, McCormack cites the qualities of an executive who, he suggests, "has all the earmarks of a champion CEO," and as evidence cites the testimony of a fellow worker: "No matter who you are, when you're in the room with her, she acts as if you're the only person who matters. She makes you feel like her equal. She defers to you, cares about your opinions, gives you time to present your views. If there are other people present, even if you are a secretary or minor flunkie, she treats you like the chairman of the board." And capitalists who are pleasant to work with tend to find other deal-makers willing to cut special, favorable agreements. As McCormack admonishes, "Be nice to people. . . . All things being equal, courtesy can be most persuasive."[23]

Rudeness was routine—notorious—in communist enterprises, and, more generally, it is commonly found in agencies (such as passport or driver's license offices) where two conditions prevail: supply is outstripped by demand, and the seller is unable to raise the price. Under these conditions customers become supplicants, and there is no economic disincentive to incivility, surliness, and arrogance. One Soviet citizen tells of being kept waiting by a butcher who was chatting with a friend. When she asked for meat, he turned grumpily to her and said, "Next, I suppose you'll want me to cram it in your mouth for you." Another points out the dilemma: "Where else can you go if they have what you want?" And David Landes vividly recalls how, until eventually forced to change by European Community standards, the French post office would often use several stamps on an airmail letter, enhancing its weight and boosting the cost of sending it: "One had to experience these exercises in petty tyranny," he suggests, "to understand the retardative effects of bureaucratic constipation."[24] Since enterprises like these cannot ration by price, they are inclined to ration by rudeness, by creating inconvenience or, where possible, by corruption—demanding side payments to obtain the product.[25]

The point here, of course, is not to suggest that incivility never shows up in a capitalist system, but rather that the system encourages and rewards civility. Sometimes a capitalist may feel there are qualities more important than economic gain: individual executives may like the sense of personal control over underlings and take pleasure in lording it over them, for example. Thus, McCormack relates the tale of a CEO who gathered his 100 employees in a room and then fired an executive in front of them. Such essentially sadistic behavior may have few negative consequences for the perpetrator when he is a drill sergeant terrorizing a group of conscripted recruits, but it is a distortion of sensible acquisitive behavior under capitalism, and people indulging themselves will pay an economic price. As McCormack puts it pointedly, "I leave it to you to judge how this stunt would motivate the ninety-nine survivors."[26]

Compassion

Logically, it might be expected that appropriately acquisitive capitalists would be essentially indifferent to any human suffering or inadequacy that doesn't affect their own enterprises: neither supportive nor opposed. In strict economic principle, capitalism doesn't oppress the unfortunate so much as it simply neglects them.

In practice, however, it is to the capitalist's advantage—that is to say, it is good for business—to show a sense of compassion, of community responsibility, of charity, and of altruism. People who do have money to spend and deals to make like doing business with people like that, and consequently a reputation—image—for decency and community concern is good for profits.

Barnum had something to say on this issue, none too surprisingly: "Of course men should be charitable, because it is a duty and a pleasure. But even as a matter of policy, if you possess no higher incentive, you will find that the liberal man will command patronage, while the sordid, uncharitable miser will be avoided." He carried out his various business ventures with an eye toward what he called "profitable philanthropy." For example, when managing soprano Jenny Lind's spectacularly successful tour he saw advantage in the many charity concerts she gave: bread cast on such waters, he observed, "would return, perhaps buttered; for the larger her reputation for liberality, the more liberal the public would surely be to us and our enterprise."[27]

Or, as another New England businessman, the CEO of a Boston bank, explained over a century later, his company's enthusiastic involvement with "community service" was a "win for the shareholders" in part because of "the pride that's built within our employees and the respect from our customers." As the company founders point out, people buy Ben and Jerry's ice cream in part because they "like what our company stands for," and the more the company manages to "actualize" its "commitment to social change, the more loyal customers we attract and the more profitable we become."[28]

Richard Steckel and Robin Simons begin their book *Doing Best By Doing Good* with the frank contention that "no matter how altruistic a company may look, when push comes to shove what really counts is money." But they then go on to show how putatively altruistic behavior can be managed to enhance a company's image and credibility, target markets, make it stand out from the crowd, reinforce advertising, increase consumer loyalty, create cost-effective promotions, increase retail activity, facilitate product launches and market entry, attract beneficial media coverage, reverse negative publicity, strengthen community relations, entertain clients, develop new products, lower research and development costs, improve employee morale, create inexpensive employee perks, help with employee retention and recruitment, enhance visibility, diversify the company's income base, help it gain experience in managing promotional campaigns, attract future donors and business partners, reinforce business skills, and offer an opportunity for executives to rub shoulders with people they'd like to meet such as potential customers, lobbyists, opinion makers, and policy makers. Another survey of the ways business interests can be serviced by corporate philanthropy includes attracting loyal customers ("we're giving away money, but we're doing it in a way that builds business"—American Express), building a productive workforce ("one more notch on its belt to show why it's a great organization to be affiliated with"—Merchants National Bank), supporting research that can help a firm's general economic interest (as on "innovative uses of computing and engineering applications"—IBM), and promoting probusiness public policy. It would be difficult to measure precisely the benefits that derive from such policies, of course, but the same can be said for advertising.[29]

Of necessity, however, capitalism often requires acts that can be viewed as lacking compassion: the firing or laying off of employees for cause or when business slackens, for example. Even in this case, however, the wise capitalist will seek to be as compassionate as possible—striving to ease the blow because a reputation for casual heartlessness can harm employee morale, foster hostile union relations, and pose difficulties in times of labor shortage.

Hence, the rise of the "golden handshake," a departure payment, very often not required by employment contracts or union agreements, that is generally accepted as wise business. As McCormack observes, "when people feel they have been fired 'fairly'— treated with dignity, respect, and sensitivity in what, by definition, is a demeaning experience—they will be reluctant to bad-mouth their excompany. And they just may—as has happened to us on

35

several occasions—become valued future business associates." Or, in Autry's words, "there's just one way to fire someone: with love and support and deep, deep regret." Applying a concept that is almost oxymoronic, he suggests that as far as possible firing an employee should be a "caring confrontation."[30]

Perhaps the most famous disemployer during the downsizing 1990s in the United States is Albert Dunlap, who specializes in rescuing companies in severe decline and very often finds it necessary to fire substantial portions of their workforces in the process. However, in a book that discusses his adventures in business and is bluntly entitled *Mean Business,* Dunlap points out that he proceeds with great care and consideration. He can justify firing 35 percent because it means secure jobs for the remaining 65 percent (as opposed to zero percent if the company collapses), but "when I fire people, *of course,* I feel for them." He says he is proudest of what happens in labor relations, and he works very hard openly and clearly to explain the situation and to establish trust. And he treats "those who would be let go with respectful separation packages," helping them to "leave with dignity" even though this is often quite expensive.[31]

More generally, managers who are able to show compassion toward their employees—to show they care—will have a more productive workforce and higher profits. As one corporate executive puts it, "take our family-leave policy. It costs us next to nothing. And yet the statement it makes to employees is powerful. It says to them that we care. And when employees know you care about them, they tend to be more productive. It's the same with our day care. To me, it's a no-brainer."[32]

Not all capitalists act in a compassionate manner, of course. But those who fail to do so are generally acting foolishly if their goal is to maximize long-term profits.

Heroism

In her anticapitalist play, *The Little Foxes,* Lillian Hellman wants us to believe that her capitalist characters are essentially parasitic and never actually *do* much of anything even though it is clear that they have been working on a deal for months with great skill and expertise, and that they are willing to risk their fortunes to make it a reality. Hellman undercuts the risk issue by simply positing that the business venture is certain to be a success, when in fact ventures of the sort she depicts stood at best a fifty-fifty chance of survival. The dramatically convenient omission of the crucial element of risk is particularly notable also in the traditional vilification of speculators.

However, to be successful an entrepreneuring capitalist must continually run risks. Bankers, often criticized for stodgy, conservative behavior, in fact take more risks in a single business day than many of their critics do in a lifetime. Indeed, as it is often put, "The greatest rewards are usually not far from the greatest risks." Often, in fact, entrepreneurs risk their financial futures on a venture, a large proportion of which miscarry—the failure rate for new products and services in the United States is 80 to 90 percent—often with consequent harm to the adventurer's long-term (and in some cases short-term) physical health.[33]

As historian Allan Nevins has pointed out, contrary to popular mythology, the rise of John D. Rockefeller's Standard Oil "was not meteor-like, but accomplished over a quarter of a century by courageous venturing in a field so risky that most large capitalists avoided it, by arduous labors, and by more sagacious and farsighted planning than had been applied to any other American industry." He further suggests that "the best businessmen have been great adventurers. . . . They played it with zest and gusto, they enjoyed it even when it was perilous, and they took its ups and downs with equanimity."[34]

And, of course, such risk-taking behavior will characteristically be successful only if it also benefits others by supplying or helping to supply a product or service people are freely willing to purchase.

In war or in conventional adventuring and exploring, risk-taking behavior is considered to be heroic. However, as George Gilder has pointed out, creative, risk-taking capitalists, successes and failures alike, are never given anything like the same credit.[35]

The Capitalist Virtues and the Monopolist

For the most part, even a monopolist will find it profitable to sub-scribe to the capitalist virtues. Good employee relations remain im-portant to generate productivity, and deals still need to be made with fellow capitalists. Moreover, monopolists with a reputation for honesty, fairness, civility, and compassion are more likely to be able slide price boosts past a wary public—that is, such moves are less likely to inspire angered customers to use less of the product and/ or to engender embittered protest to governmental agencies.

Hence, it is not surprising, for example, to find cable television monopolies treating their customers with civility and sponsoring public relations projects to show how responsible they are. And taxicab companies which have cleverly managed to gain a mo-nopoly in certain areas—serving an airport, for example—have sometimes come to the dawning realization that they will make more money if they are honest, fair, and courteous, because their customers will then be less inclined to invest time and effort in-conveniently arranging for alternative means of transportation. Tips will be higher as well.

The Essential Insincerity of Capitalist Morality

It should be acknowledged that the honesty, fairness, civility, com-passion, and heroism that characterize successful capitalism are es-sentially insincere, or even cynical and hypocritical. Capitalism en-courages people in business to be honest, fair, civil, compassionate, and heroic not because those qualities are valued for themselves, but because of acquisitiveness or greed. Thus businesspeople do not seem to pass Wilson's test for a "moral man": "one whose sense of duty is shaped by conscience, that is, by the impartial spectator within our breast who evaluates our own action as others would evaluate it." Similarly, a century ago Archbishop Richard Whately observed that someone who acts on the principle that honesty is the best policy is not honest—meaning, as Stigler parses it, that "he who behaves honestly because it is remunerative is simply an amoral calculator; an honest man is one whose principles of right conduct are adopted independently of their consequences for him."[36]

Accordingly, if one walks into an automobile showroom and says, "I want to buy that car over there but I demand that I be treated dishonestly and with consummate discourtesy," one can reasonably expect the dealer to evince few moral qualms in complying. A true saint, by contrast, would likely undergo a certain angst when trying to service that improbable request.

But essential insincerity can often be found in other moral systems as well. For example, the soldier may be heroic not because he values heroism for itself but because it leads to medals and admiration. Or his heroism is rewarded by the kick of exultation some combatants feel in battle (rather similar, perhaps, to the high that pious masochists received when self-flagellation was a respected and admired activity). And the common moral injunction, "Do unto others as you would have them do unto you," certainly implies that the moralizer is chiefly inspired not so much by conscience as by a cagy calculation of ultimate, if collegial, self-interest.

More importantly, however, most people find it difficult to counterfeit morality. Sam Goldwyn is alleged to have said, "The most important thing about acting is sincerity: once you've learned to fake that, you've got it made." This may well be true for acting, but not for real life: most people cannot consistently and routinely fake sincerity. And using not much more than commonsense, people very often can, at least on substantial exposure, spot pretenders. Indeed, part of the growing-up process involves the development of social skills for sizing up others for the purposes of forming, or avoiding, relationships. As Wilson observes, "A person can be fooled by a chance encounter, but during a continuing relationship he will usually form an accurate assessment of another person's character." Or, in Peter Drucker's words, "The men with whom a man works, and especially his subordinates, know in a few weeks whether he has integrity or not."[37]

As McCormack puts it succinctly, "people don't like phonies."[38] Therefore, the penalties for an act—or even to a vague suspicion—

of phoniness can be severe and immediate: customers stop coming back and bad-mouth the business to friends, fellow deal-makers fail to return telephone calls, employees become resentful and less productive. Ben and Jerry have been financially successful in part because they really do seem to believe in those uplifting causes they so exuberantly advocate; if their double-dipping customers acquired the suspicion that the company had been double-timing them, its competitive advantage, its profitability, and perhaps even its existence could vanish in a heartbeat.

Thus, a clerk or manager who actually hates people is unlikely to be successful because the customers and employees will eventually see through the act. As one manager puts it in a book pointedly entitled *Love and Profit,* "*If you don't care about people, get out of management before it's too late.* I mean it. Save yourself a heart attack and save many other people a lot of daily grief." I have an acquaintance who became a doctor only to discover that he was ill suited to the work because he had great difficulty dealing with people. Accordingly, he went back to school and became a pathologist, and is now quite happy because the only patients he has to deal with come in the form of disembodied fluids and chunks of flesh. This seems to have been an especially wise career decision. A number of studies have shown that the quality of care provided is not a major determinant of malpractice claims: that is, incompetent physicians are not more likely to be sued than competent ones. Rather, complaints tend to be registered against those who, in the view of the patient, devalue the patient, fail to understand the patient's perspectives, communicate poorly, and, in general, do not establish relationships that are personal, caring, and respectful.[39]

And most salespeople find that it is much easier to sell a product if they truly believe in it. The "fundamental selling truths" are laid out by McCormack: "If you don't know your product, people will resent your efforts to sell it; if you don't believe in it, no amount of personality and technique will cover that fact; if you don't sell with enthusiasm, the lack of it will be infectious."[40]

It is likely, then, that, in general, the best way to *seem* honest and fair and civil and compassionate, is actually to *be* honest and fair and civil and compassionate. A visiting management consultant who was interviewing various employees of a firm found that they all very proudly told the same story when asked about the boss: "Elmer Smith? I'll tell you what kind of a guy Elmer Smith is." It seems that an employee had once borrowed Smith's new, expensive automobile and then managed to smash it up. When he called the boss with great and understandable trepidation to report the incident, Smith's immediate reaction was to wave off any concern about the car and urgently to inquire instead whether the employee had been hurt. It is possible, of course, that this was all an act: perhaps Smith really cared much more about his damaged vehicle than about his employee's health, but acted under the crafty realization that putting on a show of concern for the employee would be great coup for employee relations, causing him to be loved by his employees who would then be inspired to work happier and harder for the company and at lower wages, all of which would ultimately increase his profits. I suspect, however, that the interviewees had it right: the story really does tell you what kind of a guy Elmer Smith is. Moreover, if his employees came even to suspect that Smith's humane response had been calculated and manipulative, their reaction would be hugely negative—far worse than if Smith had expressed concern only about the car in the first place.

Therefore, successful capitalists will tend to be naturally honest and fair and civil and compassionate—like, it seems, Elmer Smith. Or perhaps they can acquire the virtues in the course of doing business.

Whether the virtue of honesty can be learned is questioned by Drucker: integrity, his one "absolute requirement" of a manager, "is not something a man can acquire; if he does not bring it to the job, he will never have it." Nonetheless, as will be discussed more fully in chapter 4, it does seem possible to learn to appreciate the economic value of honesty. P. T. Barnum did. He found that all the colorful "humbugs" of his early career "ended in disaster" and reduced him to the "pinching income of $4 per week." The fortune he acquired later "was accumulated almost wholly from enterprises which were undoubtedly legitimate."[41]

WHY NICE GUYS FINISH FIRST

All other things equal, deals among friends are both more secure and more likely to happen than deals among nonfriends. This is partly because the potential punishment for reneging on an agreement is higher than it is for a misfired deal among nonfriends. An injured friend has the usual array of weapons for inflicting punishment on an offending person—such as legal action or reputational retaliation like letting it be widely known that the reneger is a jerk. But an offending person who is a friend will obligingly undergo self-punishment in addition. That is, friends who let friends down punish themselves by feeling bad because, putting it in econospeak, the friend's welfare has entered their utility function (or, returning to English, they feel guilty). In fact, if they don't feel bad when they let the friend down, that condition suggests pretty conclusively that they actually weren't friends to begin with.[42] As McCormack puts it, "All things being equal, people will buy from a friend. All things being not quite so equal, people will *still* buy from a friend."[43]

Nice guys are quite a bit like friends. Again pretty much by definition, a nice guy will feel bad (punish himself) if he causes harm. Consequently, all other things equal, it is sensible to prefer to deal with someone you consider to be a nice guy because a nice guy will be hurt more than a non-nice guy if he lets you down—he will feel your pain. Thus, a deal with a nice guy is effectively more secured (less risky) and therefore more likely to happen.

In addition, cutting a deal with a nice guy will usually generate some pleasure and so one might be quite rationally willing to give in a bit more in a deal with a nice guy than in one with a non-nice guy. The casual business phrase, "It's a pleasure doing business with you," may not always be sincerely felt, but it does suggest an emotional element that can have real economic benefit to those who supply the pleasure.

In result, nice guys, on average, have a competitive advantage over non-nice guys, and accordingly they will tend to prosper. Sometimes, of course, it is darkly suspected that nice guys will, precisely because of their niceness, be incapable of making hard, but necessary, business decisions—cutting back the workforce in bad times, for example. In this case, however, niceness is a problem not for its own sake, but because it is correlated with incompetence or with an economically foolish sentimentality: it hampers a person's ability to do a job effectively. My argument is not that incompetent nice guys will do better than competent non-nice guys, but that nice guys will do better than non-nice guys who are comparably competent.

EXTRAPOLATING THE CAPITALIST VIRTUES

In principle, if a person is virtuous in business, those qualities need not necessarily affect other areas of that person's life because there is no necessary reason why one can't successfully be (or act) virtuous in business and still be a cad and liar in other aspects of life. In practice, however, a schizophrenic life style could be economically dangerous. If people come to see a person as dishonest, unfair, uncivil, and uncompassionate in private life, they may assume the person is a sleaze and cannot be trusted in business either, thus potentially exacting an economic cost. In general, then, it makes sense to carry business virtues over to private life.

McCormack discusses a man who had sold his house to someone who suddenly wanted to back out of the deal because of an unexpected death in the family. The seller agreed, and McCormack observes: "There was no long-term benefit for him, but it was the right thing to do."[44] However, the very fact that McCormack relates this story and undoubtedly has told it to many businesspeople over the years, suggests that there probably *was* long-term benefit. Or, put another way, if the seller had refused to bend under the circumstances, McCormack would still be telling the story, but now the man would be painted as a heartless sleaze, to his long-term detriment.

Moreover, given the difficulty most people find in putting on an act, people who are naturally virtuous will tend to do best in business as I have already argued, so there is likely to be a kind of reinforcement of virtuous behavior. There may also be a process of habituation or spillover. Wilson hopefully suggests, for example, that the civility forced upon a young McDonald's worker might just be carried over to other portions of that person's life. And Adam Smith suggests that merchants bring probity "into fashion," a proposition that will be examined in chapter 4.[45]

It seems to be remarkably easy, however, for different moral standards to prevail when one is dealing with the revenuers. Honesty may be central to ordinary business transactions where both parties gain and where each often has a long-term reputation to maintain, but the acquisitive have a strong incentive to minimize the confiscation of their wealth (e.g., taxes) by any means feasible. Even in societies where honesty is rampant, tax evasion is probably kept in check substantially by the effective threat of detection and coercion.

The tax collectors will, of course, be aided if the people in the society would be likely to distrust a known tax evader—that is, where a reputation of dishonesty toward the government could hurt one's private transactions. The publication of names of tax miscreants could then be a useful method of control. But it seems entirely possible for tax cheats to be lauded, or at least accepted, while still being trusted fully in business or private life. Adam Smith, probably the most important non-fan of tariffs in history, observed that the smuggler, although a patent breaker of laws Smith famously and influentially considered foolish, was often accepted as "an excellent citizen" and an "innocent" nonetheless. Indeed, "to pretend to have any scruple about buying smuggled goods . . . would in most countries be regarded as one of those pedantick pieces of hypocrisy" which would expose the pretender "to the suspicion of being a greater knave than most of his neighbours." Similarly, although, as Richard Tilly observes, business behavior in Britain and Germany became noticeably more honest during the course of the nineteenth century (a phenomenon to be assessed more fully in chapter 4), the "tax morality" of businessmen does not seem to have risen at the same time.[46]

I was once working on a project with a man from Denmark, the country with perhaps the highest marginal tax rates in the world.

He is one of the most decent and honest people I have ever met: if he found an unsealed envelope with five thousand dollars in cash in it and the owner's address on the outside, I fully expect he would deliver it to its owner immediately—in fact, he would probably stuff a few more bills into the envelope out of sympathy. However, when he was told he could be paid for his work on the project in cash, he seemed to be uncommonly delighted. It is possible, of course, that when he got back to Copenhagen he went directly to the revenuers' office to declare his take and to let them hack out their generous slice, but somehow I doubt it. My suspicions on that score, however, do not dampen my trust of him in the slightest.[47]

CAPITALIST CULTURE, CAPITALIST INEQUALITY AND UNFAIRNESS, CAPITALIST COMPETITION

I have mostly dealt here with capitalism at the individual level—considering the relations between deal-making businesspeople, between employers and employees, and between retailers and customers. But some criticisms of capitalism stress its unpleasant features more at the cultural level and at the level of relations between competitors.

In this regard, economic historian Stanley Engerman suggests that capitalism has had to contend with three central criticisms in seeking to gain acceptance. One critique points with dismay to the nature of the culture the system generates or seems to generate. Another bemoans the unfairness of the distribution of wealth and income that capitalism fosters. And the third voices alarm at the periodic and apparently uncontrollable economic catastrophes like the Great Depression of the 1930s that have often seemed to be an inevitable component of capitalism's workings. I will argue in chapter 5 that, because of the maturation of the science of economics, the last of these problems may now possibly be subject to some degree of control or at least of understanding.[48] However, there is no way the cultural and inequality problems can be fully finessed.

Culture

The cultural critique is inspired in part by the fact that capitalism is devoted to supplying people uncritically with what they happen to think they may want at the moment, no matter how banal or debased or even lethal, as long as the purchasers are willing and able to pay for it. In defending this result, capitalists can argue that they are simply supplying public tastes and therefore any blame for debased products and services should more properly be placed on the popular tastes themselves; otherwise, as George Stigler puts it, "It is like blaming the waiters in restaurants for obesity." And capitalists can also readily concede, with Stigler, that their system makes no provision for those "whose talents and interest are not oriented to profit-seeking economic activity." He observes, for example, that it does not supply an air force, alms for the poor, or even babies, and thus he simply concludes that "a society needs more than a marketplace."[49]

Critics of capitalism often contend, however, that, in R. H. Tawney's words, "A reasonable estimate of economic organization must allow for the fact that, unless industry is to be paralyzed by recurrent revolts on the part of outraged human nature, it must satisfy criteria which are not purely economic." Moreover, the critics sometimes argue that, rather than merely supplying needs (or wants), capitalists actively create them. That is, people don't actually *need,* for example, flush toilets: after all, Shakespeare, Mozart, Moses, and the rest of the human race survived quite well without them for millennia. Therefore the only reason people have come to consider that item desirable, nay, essential, is that they have been cleverly and insidiously brainwashed by agile and dissembling promoters from the megalopolistic plumbing industry.[50]

Capitalists certainly would dearly love to be able to fabricate demand for whatever they happen to be selling at the moment. But it is probably more accurate to say that, rather than confidently creating demand, capitalists put products and services on display in hopes that a demand for them will materialize, and that they mostly quest after unappreciated market niches that might profitably be serviced. And the results of such efforts are none too predictable: as noted, the vast majority, in fact, fail. The producers of the hula hoop were probably surprised (and elated) by the fact that people actually seemed, for a while at least, to need their nonsense item, just as the producers of the Edsel were surprised (and depressed) by the fact that few consumers seemed to need theirs. The promoters of compact discs found there was a large and ready market (or need) for their product out there, but the promoters of digital audio tape, a product that does everything a CD can do and records as well, did not.

In general, under a growing capitalist economy, desirable (or at any rate desired) goods and services tend to become cheaper, better, more abundant, and more widely dispersed.[51] Nonetheless, there will still be plenty of lamentable (and colorfully lamented) instances when, merely because that is what most people happen to want, the distasteful will drive out the refined, the machine-made the handcrafted, the schlock the subtle, the gross the quaint, the factory-made the artisan fashioned, the bland the distinguished, the fast the laid-back, the mediocre the splendid, the K-Mart the corner emporium, the engineered McDonald's the homey greasy spoon.

However, if some people—the Amish, for example—happen to want to pursue lifestyles of a different sort—more etherial and less materialistic, perhaps—the system will generally put no barrier in the way. In fact, it may well assist them in their endeavors if a profit can be made by so doing: capitalist Hollywood, for example, is quite happy to make movies that ingratiatingly, and profitably, service the prejudices of those hostile to capitalist culture, often making a pretty buck off movies that show capitalism to be debased, uncaring, deceitful, and brutal. And there are plenty of businesses selling equipment at attractive prices to provide basic comforts— even the occasional guilty luxury—for anyone who wishes to wander into the wilderness to commune with Nature or Whomever else is out there.

Capitalism also fosters, indeed depends on, competition, and this element of its culture is often deemed vulgar and grasping. As

Alfred Marshall observes, "the term 'competition' has gathered about it evil savour, and has come to imply a certain selfishness and indifference to the wellbeing of others."[52]

I have contended in this chapter that some of the criticism of the culture supposedly fostered by capitalism is based more on faulty, ideology-inspired, and cliché-ridden image-making than on reality. As capitalists have gradually discovered, capitalism tends to inspire (that is, systematically to reward) not the deceit and incivility and boorishness so commonly associated with it by detractors, but business behavior that is honest, fair, civil, and compassionate. However, capitalists can often be fiercely competitive, and the public crowing by some of the most self-obsessed and aggressive of them can often be arrogant and distasteful, a quality emphasized in the common disdain for the *nouveau riche*. Even Adam Smith was appalled at the tendency for high profits to "destroy that parsimony which in other circumstances is natural to the character of the merchant." People in business, particularly successful ones, can also become egotistic about their enterprises, not unreasonably seeing them as extensions of their personalities, and they can come to behave like despots in their self-generated and often rather petty domains. They can also become arrogant and superior about their success, attributing it entirely to their own skills and moral excellence: even the mild-mannered and genuinely pious John D. Rockefeller once disparagingly asserted that "the failures that a man makes in his life are due almost always to some defect in his personality, some weakness of body, mind or character, will or temperament."[53]

But there is something of a selection bias here. Those capitalists who remain quiet and unassuming and who fail to engage in such colorful and irritating behavior tend not to be noticed.

Moreover, my point in all this, of course, is not to argue that arrogant and boorish business behavior does not exist, but that such behavior is, on balance and in the long run, economically foolish. Certainly, it is easy to find instances where capitalists have allowed themselves to become entrapped by ego and end up paying the price. An excellent case in point is furnished by John Ringling. He became so outraged at the (sensible) business decision of Madison

Square Garden in 1930 to continue its highly profitable Friday prize fights during the run of the circus that he cascaded into bankruptcy in part because of his futile effort to show the Garden management up.[54]

Behavior like that does not come about because capitalism mandates it, but because, on the contrary, people in business have sometimes allowed themselves to give in to instincts and proclivities that cloud their judgment and that are not a sound expression of sensible, self-effacing acquisitive behavior. And capitalism often punishes them for it.

Inequality and Unfairness

Capitalism must plead guilty as well to the second criticism, that it necessarily leads to economic inequality and that it often is—or seems—fundamentally unfair in its results.

In principle, I suppose it could be argued that capitalism as a system does not necessarily *require* inequality. It is vital to the system that people be given an incentive and opportunity to enrich themselves for otherwise they will scarcely subject themselves to the system's rigors, uncertainties, and sacrifices. But a capitalist determinedly bent on self-enrichment doesn't mind if everyone else becomes equally rich at the same time—in fact, the richer other people are, the easier it will presumably be to sell one's product or service to them.

In practice, however, some people will do better than others at the self-enrichment process. And, in consequence, notable, even glaring, economic inequalities will emerge.[55]

Moreover, capitalism, like life and democracy, is inherently unfair in the sense that, while ambitiousness, hard work, resourcefulness, careful planning, virtuous business behavior, and frugal sobriety may increase one's chances of success, luck and timing (including the capricious whims of the consumer) also play an important role. Indeed, if it is true that the greatest profits (as well as the greatest failures) are accompanied by the greatest risks, people who have become very rich in business must usually have taken large risks and much of their success is very likely to have depended on luck.

Baseball's Branch Rickey famously and eloquently proposed that "luck is the residue of design." If so, Rockefeller was blessed with a huge residuum. He was a highly talented businessman but, as Ron Chernow observes, he also "benefited from a large dollop of luck in his life." In the beginning, Rockefeller poured all his money into petroleum, a speculation most judicious investors considered a "rope of sand" because of two "antithetic nightmares": the oil wells might dry up (as geologists routinely predicted) or vast quantities of oil might suddenly be discovered, creating a glut which would cause prices to fall below overhead costs.[56] Another of what Chernow characterizes as Rockefeller's "colossal gambles" was his heavy investment in some new oil that was almost completely unusable because when burned it smelled repellently— "skunk oil," they called it. Rockefeller couldn't even get his own board at Standard Oil to buy this idea and persuaded them only when he proposed to use his own money on the venture, selling the investment to the company if a way was found to eliminate the smell and taking the loss if it wasn't (it was).[57] Later he aggressively invested in the Mesabi iron range even though experts like Andrew Carnegie considered the ore useless because it clogged furnaces when heated. Rockefeller gambled—correctly, as it turned out— that a way could be found to remedy that defect. And Rockefeller's truly colossal fortune was created only after he had retired, when someone else happened to invent the automobile, causing demand for petroleum to skyrocket.[58]

Someone in business might gain a crucial advantage simply because of information casually picked up at a cocktail party or because a brother-in-law just happens to know someone who knows someone who is in the right position to help. Or because a competitor happens to make an exceptionally foolish decision: at one key point Microsoft was greatly benefited because a competitor was out flying around in his small airplane when IBM came to call. That is, in the classic whimsy, 6-Up could easily fail while 7-Up triumphs. Moreover, as Robert Cringely notes, "In business, as in comedy, timing is everything." Thus a product introduced in March may fail while the same product introduced the next October might succeed. Barnum substantially overstates the case (and not for the first time) when he advises, "Fortune always favors the brave, and never helps a man who does not help himself."[59]

Therefore, although capitalism tends to reward fairness at the level of the individual transaction as discussed above, economic inequality at the systemic level is inevitable, a result that is often considered unfair, unjust, or at least highly undesirable. There is no way capitalism can avoid a dilemma on this score since in an important sense, the system routinely creates not only the deserving poor but some rich people who certainly do not seem to have done much to deserve their wealth.

This can engender resentment, as well as bitterness, often mixed with jealousy perhaps, toward the whole system. Nevins's conclusion that "the best businessmen" take the market's "ups and downs with equanimity"[60] is only true if it is tautological; many losers in the competitive process have been among the most resentful, preferring to blame the system for their fate rather than facing up to their own inadequacies or admitting simply to bad luck, a phenomenon to be discussed more fully in the next chapter.

Often such resentments are focused on "bigness." In almost any commercial competition the successful are likely to develop, almost by definition, larger—often vastly larger—enterprises than the less successful, a disparity that may be further enhanced by the economies of scale big companies often enjoy in the marketplace.

That bigness may not be a necessary or notable evil is suggested by some of the earlier discussion. Big companies must normally take a longer-term perspective and are more likely than the small operator to find value in honest, fair, civil, and compassionate business dealings—indeed, as will be discussed in chapter 4, that discovery may have been one of the reasons for their comparative success. But the conventional bias against bigness can aid the comparatively unsuccessful in their efforts to use public resources to rein in the big and to coddle the small, an effect which sometimes has considerable political appeal however little economic sense it may often make.[61]

The result of capitalistic competition is, on average, economic growth. And in the end the only way to prevent greater inequalities from emerging from this process is to hamper development itself. Thus, the surging disparities in world economic development that have taken place over the last two centuries (see figure 4.1 on p. 74) could only have been curtailed by keeping the developed world from developing. Since most people win in a growing economy, if capitalism generates more growth than other systems, it also creates more winners. But there are always plenty of losers as well, and this inevitable result can seem heartless and unfair.

Mellowing the Equality and Cultural Effects

Nonetheless, government can be used to reduce both the equality and the cultural effects somewhat without destroying the system.

Frequently, the political establishment may seek to supply those commodities and services it believes are insufficiently supplied by the market. Cultural agitators, for example, have often been able to shame politicians into deciding that the sometimes inadequate market for the fine arts should be supported and embellished with public largess.

On the other hand, throughout most of history the very considerable market for such desired commodities as pornography, drugs, prostitution, gambling, and liquor has been suppressed or restricted by the government. More recently there has been a growing consensus that the market for cigarettes should be stamped out or at least severely inconvenienced, no matter how much pleasure smokers derive from their carcinogenic addiction. At the same time, however, the notion of banning one of the most destructive devices ever invented, the private passenger automobile, has never taken hold—or even been substantially advanced.[62]

In dealing with the fairness and equality issues, there is opportunity in the fact that capitalism tends to generate greater wealth than other economic arrangements. Once quite a bit of money is made in this way, some of it can be taxed away from the rich without undue pain, and these revenues can be used to redistribute income or to soften the blows that capitalism inevitably inflicts on some people—cushioning the pain of unemployment or bankruptcy, for example. Governmental redistribution policies have been generally accepted even by some of capitalism's most fervent advocates.

In addition, the wealthy can be goaded, or encouraged by judicious tax policies, into giving some—even lots—of their money away, thereby further easing inequality. Barnum may again overstate the case when he declares, "as a general thing, money getters are the benefactors of our race," but he is not completely off target.[63]

Sometimes those policies may be purchased at a cost in overall growth and efficiency that can make them unwise or even counterproductive, however. In many cases it may be sensible to leave the money in the hands of successful capitalists because it will be used for further development, engendering more jobs and wealth for the society. Although he was justifiably proud of his many philanthropic achievements, Rockefeller may well have been correct when he repeatedly insisted that these were far less important than the good he had accomplished in his business by creating jobs and by furnishing affordable oil products.[64]

Some concerns about capitalism's fairness focus on the fact that prices and supplies are determined by impersonal market forces rather than by specific and perceptible flesh-and-blood human beings. Thus in a 1998 visit to, appropriately enough, communist Cuba, Pope John Paul II may have gained a bit of favor with his superannuated host by denouncing capitalism because "it subordinates the human person to blind market forces."[65] This view is a common one, and it is unlikely ever to go away, as suggested by the outcries that erupt in advanced capitalist countries like the United States whenever cable television companies try to abandon prices that others deem "just" in favor of ones that merely reflect what the traffic will bear. At the extreme, this perspective has led to wage and price controls, a popular, if economically damaging, policy that, as discussed in chapter 5, is only now being overcome.

In spite of their quest to eliminate economic inequality, socialist and communist systems still contained a great deal of it—often even more than under capitalism, according to some studies.[66] Moreover, in the process they generally generated much less wealth and therefore effectively perpetrated more poverty. However, when a new, substantially merit-free aristocracy—the nomenklatura—arose under Communism, those less well off could console themselves in the belief that their humble position in society derived not from any inherent lack of worth, but from their noble refusal to subordinate themselves to the party nonsense—rather like a poor peasant who could blame his condition on the inevitabilities of the class system rather than on his own inadequacies.[67] Under capitalism such excuses are no longer available, and resentments, accordingly, can be given free play.

Although government policy may be able to mellow capitalism's cultural and equality effects somewhat, in the end the problems of culture and of economic inequality simply have to be lived with under capitalism. Therefore to get the system accepted its proponents must convince people to embrace a version of the Ralph's Grocery philosophy in order to cope. The culture, the inequality, and the apparent unfairness of result may seem distasteful and undesirable at times, but they are inevitable: you can't have capitalism without them. If you do not allow the economy to supply people with what they happen to think they want at the moment, if you do not allow people to profit from successful enterprise, and if you want prices to be settled by "justice" rather than by the market, you will not have capitalism. And if you want all people to be rewarded equally for their labors and if you want a system in which everyone all the time will feel that they have been treated fairly, you cannot have capitalism.

THE PROFOUND IRRATIONALITY OF CAPITALISM: INVESTORS AS UNINTENDED ALTRUISTS

A final comment on capitalism and its image may be in order. When one examines the oft-neglected issue of risk, it appears that many capitalists effectively act as altruists—that is, they knowingly and systematically take a financial loss that, as it happens, betters the economic condition of their fellow human beings. And the capitalist system is profoundly irrational because it importantly depends on such economically bizarre behavior.

Two facts are central to this conclusion. First, people who actively speculate on the stock market, even the most seasoned and highly skilled, do worse on average than those who simply and almost randomly buy the market across the board. Some individual investors, of course, may do better than random just as some coin flippers may come up with ten heads in a row. But there is abundant and widely appreciated evidence that those who do better than the stock-market average are actually less numerous than one would expect by chance, and that those who do well in one period are not notably likely to do so in the next one.[68]

Second, for its fundamental workings capitalism requires that speculative investment money be generally transferred from bad enterprises to good ones. That is, investors regularly evaluate their holdings and express their confidence and concerns by moving their money in such a way that, in general and on balance and over the long run, they reward well-managed, productive companies and penalize poorly run, underproductive ones. Indeed, a central argument for reducing the capital gains tax is to encourage such beneficial, even benevolent, economic behavior.

Economic growth would be substantially less coherent and capitalism would develop far less effectively if this vital evaluative behavior were not taking place. On the other hand, those who do speculate in this manner are, on average and on balance and in the long run, making less money than they would if they simply bought the market and stood pat. Consequently, stock-market speculators are effectively unconscious altruists: their activities are an important aid to productive economic growth, but on average they are taking a financial loss in performing their highly useful function. If no one engaged in such activity, the rest of us would be less rich, and therefore we owe a debt of thanks to the speculators who are, indeed, less well off than they would be if they stopped speculating.

Thus at base, capitalism depends on the self-lacerating thrill of the gamble. Speculators, of course, are not principally trying to aid the general economy, but to become rich themselves, prefer-ably quickly. However, in the end and on average, their collec-tive gambles aid the general economy, and the gains they derive from their curious behavior are less than optimal. While this result may not be intentional, its ultimate effect is benevolent and self-sacrificing—and therefore effectively altruistic.

Sources of Capitalism's
Negative Image

THE PREVIOUS CHAPTER developed the suggestion that acquisitive capitalists are well advised, in the punchy, bulleted official philosophy of the highly successful head of Harley-Davidson, to tell the truth, keep your promises, be fair, respect the individual, and encourage curiosity.[1] The standard and well-aged image of capitalism, however, is of course quite the reverse. This negative image has been propagated over history by a wide variety of dectractors: socialists, communists, fiction writers, intellectuals, religious thinkers, and aristocrats. But the advancement of capitalism's negative image has also sometimes been aided by inept capitalist propaganda, by disenchanted capitalists, and by economically foolish behavior by capitalists themselves.

SOCIALISTS AND COMMUNISTS

Some of capitalism's critics, like socialists and communists, champion an alterative economic system—one, they propose, that is more humane and fair and productive than capitalism. Their goal has had a considerable utopian appeal, and over the last couple of centuries, often armed with ingenious and appealing folk songs and stirring promises, they have proved to be extremely adept propagandists—well organized and colorful.

As part of their promotional activities, they have naturally criticized and caricatured the competition and have done so with great, and often highly effective, élan. They have also ably used capitalism's apparent lapses, like the Great Depression, to make their point.

STORYTELLERS

Another impressive source of negativism is storytellers who, quite apart from any leftist leanings, generally have found foolish capitalism to be more dramatic and interesting than its actual, boring sensible self.

Thus, gambling mobsters always seem inexplicably to rub out their debtors rather than cutting deals that might at least give them partial recompense. Employers who unwisely create dissension by brutalizing their charges are more engrossing than ones who maximize profits by cleverly maintaining a contented workforce. Landlords who mindlessly harass their tenants supply more dramatic punch than ones who realize they can charge higher rents if the tenants find the building to be especially desirable and its management especially pleasant. Labor negotiations that break down and lead to pitched battles between strikers and company goons are far more colorful than ones that lead to mutually satisfactory agreements. Wall Street entrepreneurs who cheat are found to be much more fascinating than ones who profit from integrity. Swindling adds grist to a tale even if it requires positing an improbable gullibility to the swindled.

And the factory system has rarely been portrayed by storytellers as the escape it often was from an unbearably grim, starvation-threatened, and highly exploitative rural existence, an escape which advanced the status of a class that "had never owned its own tools—or much of anything else, for that matter," as Rosenberg and Birdzell put it. Rather the factory system is almost invariably portrayed as something that cruelly reduced the status of independent artisans.[2]

Building a business can be an excitingly creative and dramatic experience. It requires quick thinking and improvisation in the face of enormous uncertainty; it is filled with risks and close calls; it frequently comes accompanied with personal, psychological, and family tensions; and it often ends in disaster. A great many people—from corner store owners to Wall Street wheelers and dealers—have been fascinated and excited by such risky, creative, and adventurous activity over the ages, and they have found enormous satisfaction in success and devastating misery in failure. It is impressive, therefore, how very few works of art have been devoted to exploring this process. We have uncountable tales of cops pursuing robbers, cowboys pursuing Indians, private eyes pursuing criminals, scientists pursuing space aliens, soldiers pursuing glory, men pursuing women, women pursuing men, athletes pursuing victory, artists pursuing expression, and courtroom lawyers pursuing what they hope will turn out to be the truth, but virtually none about entrepreneurs pursuing financial success.[3]

Perhaps capitalist risk-taking has been found to be difficult to portray because no one usually gets shot or involved in a car chase and because the costs of failure, the occasional suicide aside, show up in such unphotogenic and comparatively mild conditions as ulcers, insomnia, quiet despair, and reduced life expectancy. Indeed, in most fictional accounts, risk is rarely shown. For example, John D. Rockefeller worked assiduously and zealously to build his business, undergoing in the process emotional stress, nervous strain, physical fatigue, anxiety, indigestion, depression, and broken health, conditions that cumulated to force him into retirement at the age of fifty-two.[4] Then, even as he was retiring, electric and gas light began to destroy the demand for lamp oil which was, at the time, the main source of profit in petroleum. This was followed by fortuitous and nearly simultaneous invention of the internal combustion engine that caused demand for Rockefeller's product to soar.[5] A good story about such factors of risk and luck might be told, but mostly that capitalist is simply represented as effortlessly and ruthlessly successful.

Contrary to myth, in fact, capitalism is not treated sympathetically or realistically even in the Horatio Alger stories where the typical boy hero displays integrity, propriety, and industriousness, but is rewarded not through success in business, but because he stumbles upon an inheritance or because his virtues inspire the charity of an already wealthy patron. "'Money is the root of all evil,' my young friend. It is an old proverb, and, unfortunately, a true one," one of these patrons philosophizes in typically stilted manner in one of Alger's novels.[6]

Moreover, insofar as business activities are dealt with at all, there is a tendency to idolize and idealize lone inventors slaving self-lessly away in musty labs and dusky garrets and to neglect—in fact usually to caricature—deal-making marketers whose creative energies are often at least as important to an invention's eventual acceptance and success. In *Marketing Myths That Are Killing Business* (they come up with 172 of them), Kevin Clancy and Robert Shulman, point out, in fact, that when a product or service fails to sell it is usually the fault of marketing, not of inadequacies in the product or service itself. Similarly, it is the hired director who is generally held up as the central guiding force in the success of a motion picture, when in reality the producer's creative contribution in garnering funding, choosing scripts, and casting the major roles (as well as in marketing the final product) is often at least as important.[7]

It turns out, then, that if you build a better mousetrap, the world is entirely likely to be able to contain its enthusiasm for beating a path to your door, at least until someone, often at great cost and risk, is able to make it conveniently available at an attractive price—and the world may not come visiting even then. Rosenberg and Birdzell note that "innovation is a product of the organized enterprise, not just of the individual with an idea." In other words, as virtually any entrepreneur can attest—but scarcely any story-teller has ever noticed—an idea by itself is simply not enough. As Robert Cringely stresses, "There is an enormous difference between starting a company and running one. Thinking up great ideas, which requires mainly intelligence and knowledge, is much easier than building an organization, which also requires measures of tenacity, discipline, and understanding. Part of the reason that nineteen out of twenty high-tech start-ups end in failure must be the difficulty of making this critical transition from a bunch of guys in a rented office to a larger bunch of guys in a rented office with customers to serve." Apple Computer, he finds, tends to have good products, but poor "follow-through," while Microsoft has had a "terrific implementation of mediocre products." In this contest, Microsoft wins.[8]

As Irving Kristol has rhetorically observed of capitalism, "what poet has ever sung its praises? what novelist was ever truly inspired by the career of a businessman?"[9] Instead, over the centuries writers have persistently disparaged capitalism in broadside and in banner, in polemic and in poem, in tract and in novel, in movie and in folk song, for its supposed heartlessness, cruelty, vulgarity, and casual exaltation of debased human values.

INTELLECTUALS

More generally, there has also been something of a natural, historic antipathy toward capitalists on the part of intellectuals. In George Stigler's understatement, "The intellectual has been contemptuous of commercial activity for several thousand years"—Plato pointedly consigned the trader to the lowest level in his ideal society—and this perspective, Donald McCloskey argues, has escalated to a "sustained sneer" during the last century and a half. Or, as César Graña puts it, the "tradition of intellectual contempt for the bourgeoisie" has become "not only an attitude of dismissal, but a habit of implacable accusation."[10]

Intellectuals, almost by definition, tend to prize flights of fancy, grand generalizing, and cosmic conceptualizing: to Václav Havel, for example, "an intellectual is a person who has devoted his or her life to thinking in general terms about the affairs of this world and the broader context of things."[11] On the other hand, people who are successful in business must be comparatively practical, mundane, materialistic, banal, unreflective, methodical, pedestrian, plodding, unideological, routine, unromantic, patient, tidy, and, ultimately, boring to those who exalt evanescent and often vaporous flights of fancy.

Many intellectuals, like prophets of religion, have an alternative vision of what people ought to want, a vision insufficiently serviced, in their eyes, by rapacious capitalism. Consequently, they are often distressed, even offended, at the drive of capitalists uncritically to service whatever tastes the consumer might happen to have at the moment.[12] Thus, Havel exalts those intellectuals who care "whether

61

a global dictatorship of advertisement, consumerism, and blood-and-thunder stories on TV will ultimately lead the human race to a state of complete idiocy."[13] Reflecting a perspective like this, intellectuals in Europe controlled radio and television for decades and made sure the media only presented programs that people *should* want to experience as opposed to the ones misguiding capitalism was likely to determine they might actually prefer.

Such thinkers as Alexis de Tocqueville, Thomas Jefferson, and Montesquieu professed great concern that rampant commercialism would lead to a timid and indifferent citizenry, leaving a country ripe for despotism. And the scholar-bureaucrats who guided traditional China through most of its history (and, in the process, kept it comparatively poor) emphasized classical learning and cultivated a contempt for material goals and acquisitiveness, though, of course, these value preferences do not appear to have implied that they, themselves, need necessarily pursue an ascetic lifestyle.[14]

In addition, the overly gregarious, glad-handing, hail-fellow-well-met demeanor of many people in business also can seem offensive, vulgar, and phony to many garret-loving, library-haunting, muse-awaiting intellectuals. Much of the uninformed association of capitalism with the novels of Horatio Alger may stem from the satisfaction of being able to ally business with works of fiction that are simplistic, banal, manipulative, and formulaic.

Intellectuals may also be understandably turned off by the often embarrassingly ingenuous and simple-minded prose of business books, most of which have all the wryness and subtlety of cheerleading as they exuberantly assemble lists of business principles that often seem banal, flip, corny, self-contradictory, and perhaps hypocritical, and as they rail on and on about loving the customer and assembling a "winning team."[15] For example, the ultimate "Key No. 9" in Lester R. Bittel's typically exuberant *Nine Master Keys of Management* (if there had been ten of these, the "keys" would no doubt have been labeled "commandments") turns out to be "Know Your True Self" for which the author conveniently supplies a "Self-Knowledge Tree."[16]

Businesspeople have also often been prone to high-minded

rhetoric that could appear disingenuous at best and hypocritical at worst to skeptical intellectuals. For example, a book on the rise of the Better Business Bureau is subtitled, rather too nobly, "A Story of What Business Has Done and Is Doing to Establish and Maintain Accuracy and Fair Play in Advertising and Selling for the Public's Protection." And in the book's introduction, Joseph Appel intones with off-putting self-righteousness: "When advertising . . . becomes . . . untruthful, insincere, fraudulent, and thus misleading and unfair to the consumer, it merely reflects the evils that exist in our social, political, and economic circumstances, all of which are inherent in the nature of man himself. The basic cause of these evils is *selfishness*. Commercial selfishness arises from human selfishness. And human selfishness is the root of all our problems."[17]

From the perspective of the intellectual, then, people in business may appear small-minded, crass, menial, and even stupid—though typically they will understand their business in greater depth and finer nuance than the average intellectual will ever understand anything. That the successful capitalist (intellectuals routinely ignore the many unsuccessful ones) makes far more money than the average intellectual can often inspire a special resentment among intellectuals. And they may be further offended of late by the prominence of successful businesspeople and by the fact that the economic function, as Graña observes eloquently, is "no longer a backstage chore relegated to classes which, since Plato, had been regarded as morally tainted by virtue of their very usefulness and efficiency."[18]

Robert Nozick stresses the role education may play in all this. Schools recognize and routinely reward intellectual achievement, not such business skills as "social grace, strong motivation to please, friendliness, winning ways, and an ability to play by (and to seem to be following) the rules." Thus, he argues, intellectuals, particularly "wordsmith" intellectuals, very often experience a sort of "relative downward mobility" of esteem when they enter real society after graduation, and they tend to focus their resentment at this perceived injustice on the capitalist system itself which, "by its nature, is neutral toward intellectual merit."[19] (However, intellectuals often do seem to pick up their anticapitalist views even while they are still in school and before they have discovered any personal devaluation in the larger society.)

Interestingly, the intellectual's antibusiness mentality often infects the views even of economists and of putative defenders of capitalism. When James Wilson announced that he would teach a course called "The Morality of Capitalism" at the UCLA School of Management, he reports that some of his business school colleagues "looked at me as if I were teaching one on 'Squaring the Circle' or 'Building a Perpetual Motion Machine'." Adam Smith gloomily maintained that the "commercial spirit . . . confines the views of men" with the result that their minds "are contracted, and rendered incapable of elevation." And his theory of the "invisible hand," whereby "natural selfishness and rapacity" and "vain and insatiable desires" have the effect, "without intending it, without knowing it" of advancing the interests of society, does have a rather patronizing tone and, as George Gilder suggests, rather "leaves the entrepreneur as a blind tool of appetite." John Maynard Keynes declared the capitalists' "money-motive" to be "a somewhat disgusting morbidity, one of those semi-criminal, semi-pathological propensities which one hands over with a shudder to the specialists in mental disease." Joseph Schumpeter, somewhat along the lines of Smith, argued (erroneously it seems) that capitalism would, or had, become stiflingly bureaucratized so that "human energy would turn away from business" and "other than economic pursuits would attract the brains and provide the adventure." And Francis Fukuyama, even while recently celebrating the triumph of capitalism, predicts that this success will lead to a "very sad time" notable chiefly for an all-consuming boredom: "The struggle for recognition, the willingness to risk one's life for a purely abstract goal, the worldwide ideological struggle that called forth daring, courage, imagination, and idealism, will be replaced by economic calculation, the endless solving of technical problems, environmental concerns, and the satisfaction of sophisticated consumer demands."[20]

What perspectives like these seem to demonstrate is the intellectual's inability to appreciate, even snobbish contempt for, the endlessly continuing drama, excitement, creativity, and even fun of the capitalist entrepreneurial endeavor.

RELIGION

Another traditional enemy of capitalism and an effective source of anticapitalist propaganda has been the church. St. Augustine denounced money lust as one of the three principle sins (right up there with power lust and sex lust), and Stigler identifies "a dislike for profit seeking" as "one of the few specific attitudes shared by the major religions."[21]

Capitalists can only prosper if they are able to come up with a product or service people genuinely value and (therefore) are willing to pay for. Accordingly, as noted in the preceding chapter, they routinely pander to the capricious whimsy, frivolous self-indulgence, crass materialism, all-consuming selfishness, and flighty narcissism of their customers. Religion, on the other hand, attained prominence in human life in part because it supplies relief from material woes and fates, and because it seeks to give higher meaning to a dreary and difficult life.

Therefore, it is not surprising to see the pope railing in a 1991 encyclical against capitalistic practices he finds distasteful, labeling them "consumerism," which he defines as a condition in which "people are ensnared in a web of false and superficial gratifications rather than being helped to experience their personhood in an authentic and concrete way."[22] Similar rejections of economic well-being and growth in favor of concrete personhood have routinely been advanced by such religious or semireligious leaders as Khomeini and Gandhi.

In the process, the church often seems to display what might be called a contempt for the consumer. For example, joining forces with like-minded socialists and with competition-fearing small businesses, it has often pushed to restrict shop hours in order to inconvenience trade and the general enjoyment of the mere material things in life.

ARISTOCRATS AND THE HONORABLE

The hostility of those who exalt the aristocratic and martial virtues—chivalry, honor, nobility, glory, valor, martial heroism—has also been a problem for capitalism. For these critics, observes McCloskey, "Don Quixote's idiocies in aid of chivalry are uncalculated, but noble," and an "impatience with calculation is the mark of romance."[23]

After quoting Benjamin Franklin on the economic value of hard work, honesty, punctuality, and frugality, Max Weber notes that such sentiments "would both in ancient times and in the Middle Ages have been proscribed as the lowest sort of avarice and as an attitude entirely lacking in self-respect," though, as Graña observes, this belief—or pose—has managed to retain much of its appeal in the nineteenth and twentieth centuries as well.[24]

Appropriately acquisitive capitalists will indeed routinely grovel. They will have no apparent sense of honor or self-respect or dignity as they seek to satisfy the whims of the consumer who, they feign to believe, is "always right" even when patently wrong. As long as they profit financially, they should be quite happy to let others walk all over them. Put positively, Mark McCormack praises an executive whose "greatest virtue is her ability to stifle her ego for the sake of others." Put negatively, novelist Richard Wright disgustedly tells of a man who allowed people to kick him for money, a service which could be considered entirely sensible from a strictly capitalistic standpoint.[25]

From such behavior, Adam Smith concluded that capitalism could render a man "incapable of defending his country in war. The uniformity of his stationary life naturally corrupts the courage of his mind, and makes him regard with abhorrence the irregular, uncertain, and adventurous life of a soldier." Smith did appreciate the bold, risk-taking behavior of merchants. But he put that kind of courage in an entirely different category, and then concluded, just like some of capitalism's most ardent opponents, that commerce "sinks the courage of mankind" with the result that "the heroic spirit is almost utterly extinguished," and the "bulk of the people" grow "effeminate and dastardly" by "having their minds constantly employed on the arts of luxury." By contrast, he held the "art of war" to be "certainly the noblest of all arts."[26]

Tocqueville was so alarmed at the prospect of the decadence of plenty that he advocated the occasional war to wrench people from their lethargy. And Immanuel Kant once argued that "a prolonged peace favors the predominance of a mere commercial spirit, and with it a debasing self-interest, cowardice, and effeminacy, and tends to degrade the character of the nation."[27]

Extollers of the martial virtues like Smith, Tocqueville, and Kant have been joined—or trumped—by such exultant war-glorifiers as the German historian Heinrich von Treitschke who fairly glowed at the turn of the century over the thought that war "brings out the full magnificence of the sacrifice of fellow-countrymen for one another . . . the love, the friendliness, and the strength of that mutual sentiment." By contrast with commerce, Treitschke held, something as sublime as a war should never be waged for mere "material advantage": "modern wars," he urged, "are not fought for the sake of booty." Similarly, German general Friedrich Bernhardi was of the opinion that "all petty and personal interests force their way to the front during a long period of peace. Selfishness and intrigue run riot, and luxury obliterates idealism. Money acquires an excessive and unjustifiable power, and character does not obtain due respect."[28]

Herbert Spencer concluded at about the same time that the destructive militancy of war should now be given over to the constructive competition of commerce, but war proponents like Homer Lea, an American military analyst of the time, while conceding that commercialism is "a form of strife," argued that it is a "debased one—a combat that is without honor or heroism."[29] Similarly, in Japan the code of Bushido held the pursuit of (material) gain to be dishonorable and accordingly held the economic pursuit of profit in contempt.[30]

Chivalry may, as they say, be dead, but chivalric contempt for the "bourgeois values" and for "trade" continues to this day in many quarters.

INEFFECTIVE CAPITALIST PROPAGANDA

Greed has never been an easy sell, and capitalism is, in economist Paul Samuelson's words, an "efficient but unlovable system with no mystique to protect it." Mario Vargas Llosa agrees: "unlike socialism, capitalism has never generated a mystique; capitalism was never preceded by a utopian vision."[31]

But even taking that into account, capitalists, many of whom have been spectacularly effective at selling their own products and services, have not been terribly good—or often, it seems, even very interested—in selling the system as a whole. Perhaps they have simply been too busy making money.

For example, promoters of capitalism sometimes try to pretend, utterly unconvincingly, that acquisitiveness is somehow secondary to its functioning. Or, as Peter Drucker laments, they go to the opposite extreme, and "make it impossible for the public to understand economic reality" as they crow, sometimes boorishly, over profit maximization, leaving risk and the cost of capital unmentioned and failing to explain why "profitability is a crucial *need* of economy and society."[32]

In addition, they generally stress capitalism's efficiency and economic productivity, leaving uncountered those who argue that capitalism is characterized by deceit, dishonesty, and uncaring cruelty. For example, Milton and Rose Friedman's 1980 book, *Free to Choose,* an agile and spirited defense of capitalism, tirelessly stresses the economic value of freedom, but nowhere suggests that capitalism inspires, encourages, or rewards honesty, integrity, compassion, or civility—indeed, those words do not even appear in the index. Meanwhile, Friedman's famous attack on corporate philanthropy may have a certain logic to it, but it plays magnificently into the hands of anticapitalists. And Friedrich Hayek's important and best-selling book, *The Road from Serfdom,* could be taken to assert uncaringly and absurdly that any government efforts to control business excesses or provide welfare for ordinary people will lead inexorably to totalitarianism.[33]

Thus, although the capitalist virtues are continually advocated in modern business books that are meant to be read by fellow acquisitive capitalists, the same virtues are rarely stressed by propagandists for the system as a whole. Rather, when they deal with such issues at all, they tend to emphasize the rather more modest qualities Montesquieu identified over two centuries ago as springing from "the spirit of commerce": frugality, economy, moderation, work, wisdom, tranquility, order, regularity.[34]

Notable politicians who have promoted capitalism have also sometimes been less than fully effective as propagandists. Ronald Reagan could be lovable, but he could also seem unaware and simple-minded, and Margaret Thatcher often came off as a strident, even threatening, schoolmarm. And both sometimes gave the impression that they simply didn't *care* about the poor and the unfortunate, a damaging inference that can also result from the many insufficiently nuanced attacks by braying conservatives on big government and welfare and handouts and high taxes and regulation and pointy-headed bureaucrats. There are welfare cheats, of course, but that doesn't mean no welfare check ever helped anybody in need or that the system is a complete failure. And, while environmental regulation may sometimes be foolish, it nonetheless deserves much of the credit for the enormous improvement in air quality that has taken place in the last decades.[35] At the same time, a remarkably small amount of procapitalist rhetoric has been devoted to showing how capitalism has actually been the greatest—indeed, the only significant—alleviator of poverty in history.

Ironically, two politicians from opposition parties, Bill Clinton and Tony Blair, have presided over what appears to be the final triumph of Reaganomics and Thatcherism in the 1990s (a phenomenon discussed more fully in chapter 5). These adept campaigners have substantially adopted their rivals' economic policies, but they have been able to convince people that they will nonetheless apply them with "compassion" and "inclusiveness" (Blair) because they "feel your pain" (Clinton).[36]

CAPITALISTS

In fact, many capitalists essentially seem to believe much of the anticapitalist caricature. Just as retail customers tend to recall most vividly the occasional instance in which they have been treated rudely or have been short-changed, businesspeople who may live daily in a business environment that is overwhelmingly honest, reliable, civil, and fair, often tend most graphically to remember and to recount the rare instances when they have been cheated, dealt with unfairly, or given painfully unkind treatment. That is, the many fair and honest deals or the general tone of easy and productive geniality do not live in the memory so much as the occasional fraud and the infrequent, if vivid, acts of boorishness and outrageous incivility—like the story McCormack relates of the (economically foolish) boss who berates and then summarily dismisses a worker in the presence of his co-workers.[37]

Moreover, many people in business are not really all that comfortable with competition. "Markets are," as George Shultz stresses, "relentless," and the change competition and development produce, notes David Landes, "is demonic; it creates, but it also destroys."[38] Losers in the process, who tend to have more time on their hands than winners, may, as noted in the previous chapter, spend much of it crying foul. As Alfred Marshall observes, traders or producers who are undersold by a rival often "are angered at his intrusion, and complain of being wronged; even though . . . the energy and resourcefulness of their rival is a social gain." (He also points out that this perspective can lead many to spend less time actually competing than seeking to reduce the risks of competition by guild or government regulation or through collusion and price-fixing.)[39] The alternative, of course, is to admit one's own failings or at least one's own bad luck. Blaming the winner, and positing nefarious motives and tactics, are often much more satisfying.

For example, after losing a dramatic, high-stakes, but essentially honest and straightforward buyout battle of the late 1980s, F. Ross Johnson was inspired loudly to proclaim his crisp and memorable, if newly discovered, "Three Rules of Wall Street": "Never play by the rules. Never pay in cash. And never tell the truth." Similarly, partisans of Apple Computer like to stress that the winning arch-demon, Bill Gates of Microsoft, lifted—or was mightily inspired by—some Apple ideas, rather than admit that Apple made a series of foolish marketing decisions. And although, as Alan Nevins stresses, Rockefeller generally paid a fair price for his rivals' property when he bought them out, he was routinely accused of underpaying, particularly by people who distrusted the future of the petroleum industry even though they had been part of it, and blundered by taking payment in cash rather than in Standard Oil Company stock which was later to appreciate massively in value.[40]

Partly in consequence of all this, the anticapitalist stereotype may historically have inspired capitalists detrimentally to behave, or to think they should behave, in a manner consistent with the negative image of capitalism. And such behavior in turn would, of course, reinforce the stereotype.

Moreover, the notion that it is to one's long-term economic benefit to carry on one's business with honesty, fairness, civility, and compassion may not be all that readily apparent even to the people who stand to profit from such behavior. For virtuous business behavior to take hold, someone must go against the age-old image and conventional wisdom to demonstrate the profitability of such behavior. Business virtue, it appears, comes about not necessarily naturally, but rather as an innovation. This phenomenon, an important one for economic development, is considered in the next chapter.

The Consequences of Capitalism's Image
for Economic Development

I HAVE ARGUED that business behavior that is honest, fair, civil, and compassionate is, on average, wealth-enhancing. It follows that, all other things equal, places where these business virtues flourish will be more prosperous than places where they don't.

And, indeed, that seems to be substantially the case. As Max Weber once pointed out: "The universal reign of absolute unscrupulousness in the pursuit of selfish interests by the making of money has been a specific characteristic of precisely those countries whose bourgeois-capitalistic development . . . has remained backward."[1]

As this suggests, one of the most important causes of economic development seems to have been the gradual acceptance of the business virtues. Policies like price controls or high taxes will cramp free economic activity and hinder economic growth as economists point out all the time. But so will business behavior that is routinely deceitful, unfair, uncivil, and uncaring. Because the cost of doing business in that sort of environment is effectively higher, people will engage in less economic activity, and economic growth, accordingly, will be lower.

This chapter advances five connected propositions. First, for countries to prosper, it is important that they develop the appropriate business virtues. Second, popular acceptance of capitalism's negative image—particularly by capitalists themselves—can hamper this process, often severely. Third, since the business virtues are economically advantageous, they can arise and flourish through normal competitive pressures and for the most part do not need to be superimposed from above by governmental, quasi-governmental, or religious authorities. Fourth, for this to happen, however, a sort of business innovation is required: because the value of virtuous business behavior has not typically been intuitively obvious, someone must actually come to realize that virtuous business behavior is economically beneficial in the long run and act accordingly. And, fifth, it is likely that the rise of business morality has been, and continues to be, a major, not an incidental, contributor to economic development.

THE UNEQUAL RATE OF ECONOMIC DEVELOPMENT

Perhaps the most important single fact about economics, economic history, and economic development—and, indeed, about human material well-being—is tidily conveyed in figure 4.1. In 1750, as can best be determined, all areas of the world were fairly equal economically—actually, equally poor by present-day standards since the vast majority of people everywhere, and at all times up until then, lived in substantial misery, even wretchedness.[2] Economic historian Paul Bairoch, whose data are displayed in the figure, estimates that the ratio of per capita wealth between the richest and poorest countries was no more than 1.6 to 1 in 1750. But, beginning in the nineteenth century, and accelerating over the next two centuries, an enormous gap opened between what we now call the developed world—North America, Europe, and, eventually, Japan—and the rest. By 1977 this disparity had become 7.7 to 1 when all the developed countries are compared to all the underdeveloped ones, or 29.1 to 1 when the most developed countries are compared to the least developed ones.[3]

This remarkable, even astounding, historic change has been dubbed "the European miracle" by Ernest Jones. It has also sometimes referred to as the industrial or the technological revolution, but it might more properly be called the capitalist revolution, for, as David Landes notes, "those economies grew fastest that were freest."[4]

One of the most comprehensive efforts to explain the West's economic growth is *How the West Grew Rich* by Nathan Rosenberg and L. E. Birdzell. Their assessment stresses technological innovation and development, an expansion of knowledge, science,

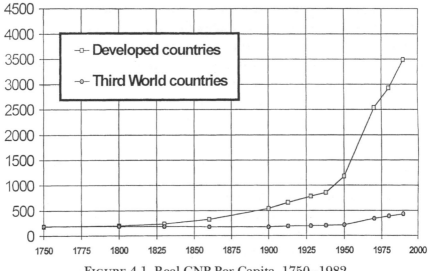

FIGURE 4.1. Real GNP Per Capita, 1750–1982
(1960 U.S. dollars and prices).

and education, and the fact that, government and religion came, advertently or inadvertently, to allow people the freedom to exploit and pursue economic opportunities as they arose or were created. Or, as Donald McCloskey puts it succinctly, growth was caused by "originality backed by commercial courage." As part of their explanation, Rosenberg and Birdzell stress the importance of organizational innovation including a notable rise in business morality.[5]

Of course, virtuous business behavior is not *sufficient* for economic development. Inept government policies, religious prescriptions (like a bias against usury), or detrimental social attitudes (like laziness or endemic distrust or the conventional acceptance of the notion that prices should be set by custom or tradition) will discourage business and entrepreneurship and hamper growth no matter how honest or fair or civil or compassionate the business norms. But norms are important to economic development because when people generally expect to be treated dishonestly, unfairly, or discourteously in business they will tend to avoid making transactions, and hence there will be less wealth and growth because there will be less economic activity.

74

SUPERIMPOSING THE CAPITALIST VIRTUES

If the capitalist virtues are important for economic development, it becomes equally important for these virtues to become accepted by people doing business. One possible route is for them to be superimposed from above.

Thus, in his important attempt to account for the rise of the business norms appropriate for economic development, Douglass North stresses the role of formal institutions which regulate, police, and enforce contracts and agreements. As a prime example of a place where such institutions do not exist, he points to markets of exchange in the Middle East and North Africa in which there is "a multiplicity of small-scale enterprises," where nearly half the labor force is engaged in the exchange process, where skill in exchange "is the primary determinant of who prospers in the bazaar and who does not," and where haggling "is pervasive, strenuous, and unremitting." He argues that "The key is men seeking gains at the expense of others. In essence, the name of the game is to raise the costs of transacting to the other party to exchange. One makes money by having better information than one's adversary."[6]

But high transaction costs in this system seem not so much to be the "name of the game" as the unintended, detrimental result. And, most importantly, given the sheer difficulty of dealing, and the attendant substantial danger of being treated dishonestly or unfairly, people—particularly insecure and underinformed ones—will tend to avoid engaging in economic exchange when they can. Thus, just about everyone will be poorer.

North finds it difficult to "understand why these inefficient forms of bargaining" should persist. One would expect, he suggests, that "voluntary organizations would evolve to ensure against the hazards and uncertainties of such information asymmetries." But that has not happened, he suggests, because "the fundamental underpinnings of legal institutions and judicial enforcement that would make such voluntary organizations viable and profitable" are missing. "In their absence," he concludes, "there is no incentive to alter the system."[7]

In their discussion of economic development, Rosenberg and Birdzell consider essentially the same puzzle, and they also mostly stress the importance of institutions. "Somehow," they note, "appreciable numbers of people with money . . . must have come to believe that others . . . were honest, diligent, and could be trusted." How this "business morality" came about "we cannot know for sure," but they suggest that it may have emerged from merchant associations, perhaps reinforced by the "appeal of the Reformation and its concomitant morality" or by religion more generally (though presumably not directly from the anticapitalist teachings of the Catholic Church).[8] Similarly, Alexander Gerschenkron, while noting that "a sociology of business honesty still remains to be written," speculates that "over large areas of Europe the historical experience of the craft guilds, with their attempts to increase and to maintain standards of quality and reliability, was of considerable importance in forming the business ethics of the community."[9]

But such reasoning may have gotten the causal flow backward. A mechanical imposition of appropriate legal, moral, social, religious, or judicial mechanisms is not adequate. Religions everywhere routinely prescribe moral behavior, yet the extension of this value to the business sphere is by no means obvious. And as North himself stresses, poor countries often remain that way even when they adopt the laws and formal institutions of developed countries: "Although the rules are the same, the enforcement mechanisms, the way enforcement occurs, the norms of behavior, and the subjective models of the actors are not." Similarly, Gerschenkron observes that the attempt by the Russian government to create guilds by fiat "could not yield the same positive results as did their spontaneous evolution in Western Europe."[10] Furthermore, it is difficult to see how such business-enhancing virtues as civility and compassion and, to a degree, fairness, could be formally enforced by courts, guilds, or regulatory agencies in any case.

In addition, it does not seem that government policy is hampering the development of sensible voluntary organizations at least in the markets North is assessing: as he observes, "governmental controls over marketplace activity are marginal, decentralized, and mostly rhetorical"[11] That is, the economy, perhaps mostly by default, is essentially free—but relatively poor.

VIRTUE AS A BUSINESS INNOVATION

What seems to be required is not so much formal institutions of control or enforced morality, but rather the realization by people doing business that honest, fair, civil, and compassionate dealing will be profitable. What the bazaar mainly needs are innovators with the enlightened business mentality of a Barnum or a Wanamaker. Neither they nor the Quakers needed "the fundamental underpinnings of legal institutions and judicial enforcement" to discover that honest, fair, civil, and compassionate dealing was a smart, profitable way to do business.

The mechanism of economic development, then, would run something like the following. Someone comes to the (apparently non-obvious and difficult) realization that honest, fair, civil, and compassionate dealing will lead to greater profits. Shattering tradition, that person innovates and puts together a business with those qualities. The business enjoys a competitive advantage and accordingly prospers (that is, there is no collective action problem: the innovating business will not place itself at a competitive disadvantage by its virtuous behavior). Other businesses, noticing the success of the innovator, follow suit, and eventually a substantial number of businesses become characterized by such behavior. This process reduces the sheer pain of doing business—effectively it reduces the costs of obtaining products and services by reducing the costs of the transaction itself. As a result, people more and more overcome their traditional, well-founded aversion, and cheerfully do business with such enterprises. Economic activity therefore increases overall and the general economy grows.

After honest, fair, civil, and compassionate businesses come to dominate an area of economic activity, they may become concerned that they are being given a bad name by the relatively few members who still engage in (economically foolish) dishonest, unfair, uncivil, and uncompassionate business practices. Accordingly the dominating honest, fair, civil, compassionate businesses form associations and work with the government to force the dishonest, unfair, uncivil, and uncompassionate businesses to shape up or to leave the industry.[12] People become more and more pleased with the ease and pleasure of doing business, and confidence soars. Growth happens.

When dishonest business practices are common, courts or regulatory systems would be swamped if they tried to eliminate these practices. But when honesty is the norm, the courts and regulators would be capable (strongly encouraged by the many honest businesses) of enforcing the comparatively rare breaches of contract and other infractions, thus keeping business transactions even more honest, and consequently further encouraging economic growth (though at no time will institutions become very important in enforcing norms of civility, compassion, and perhaps fairness). It seems likely, then, that effective institutions are more nearly the result of virtuous norms than the cause of them.

North notes that "we are not yet able to explain precisely the forces that shape cultural evolution," but "the most common explanations lean heavily upon evolutionary theory, although with the additional feature that acquired characteristics are culturally transmitted."[13] And he stresses the importance of "path dependence," the notion that current developments are the result of forces set in motion long ago in the society.

By contrast, the explanation for economic development I am suggesting stresses only the development of a key innovation: the grasping of the idea that honesty, fairness, civility, and compassion furnish a competitive advantage. Economies prosper when that idea is seized and then imitated.

The idea may seem very simple, but that doesn't mean it is obvious. Many ideas which seem in retrospect to be both simple and obvious took centuries, indeed millennia, to become accepted. As Landes points out, "just because something is obvious does not mean that people will see it, or that they will sacrifice belief to reality." For example, Rosenberg and Birdzell note that the factory system, an innovation of major historical significance, was only dreamed up around 1750 even though it could clearly have been invented and developed centuries earlier since it did not depend on the development of machinery and could have been profitably applied to ancient crafts like ceramics.[14] Something similar could be said for such notable innovations as Arabic numerals and the idea of zero, the wheel, the alphabet, separate left-turn lanes on city streets, just-in-time management techniques, and home delivery of pizza. Indeed, a major reason professional magicians protect their secrets so assiduously is that their successful illusions often exploit devices that are very simple but yet, clearly, are not obvious. When the tricks are explained, most of the previously mystified would probably react not with awe at the magicians' cleverness, but with amazement at their own naivete.

Evolution and "path dependence," it seems, are not necessary for economic growth to take place. All that is required is that people be acquisitive and that they understand that virtuous business behavior is profitable. Acquisitiveness seems to be built in: as Rosenberg and Birdzell put it, "it is not so much the urge to advance one's own interests which has varied conspicuously through human experience, as the possibilities of gratification and the way these possibilities have been pursued."[15] And the idea that virtuous behavior in business is profitable appears to be easy to grasp and imitate once its value is demonstrated by an innovator. Accordingly, whatever their historical path, economies can turn around quickly—something that seems to have happened in the last years in Spain and in a number of Latin American countries despite the rather gloomy implication North drew when he applied his path dependency approach to them in 1990.[16]

Wanamaker's Saga

The economic development process I have in mind can be illustrated by the experience of American retailing entrepreneur John Wanamaker. Judging from his recollections, American business practices in the 1860s were quite similar to those discussed by North for the Middle East and North Africa: "The law of trading was then the law of the jungle, take care of number one. The rules of the game were: don't pay the first price asked; look out for your-

self in bargaining; haggle and beat the seller as hard as you can. . . .
And when a thing was once sold—no returns. . . . Schools in stores
for training employees were unknown."

Shattering this ill-tempered tradition with its high transaction
costs—a tradition that probably goes back to the origins of commerce—Wanamaker consciously set out to provide "a service exactly
opposite to the ancient custom that 'the customer must look out for
himself.'" He applied set prices—called "one-price" since the same
price was paid by all buyers—and importantly combined this with a
money-back offer which essentially guaranteed a low price. Moreover, he carefully trained his employees. They were told to "place
yourself in the customer's place and give such service as you would
like to have given you were you buying instead of selling," to "give
information and show new goods just arriving without allowing an
unspoken grumble to appear on your face," and, when customers
come back with goods to return, to "be, if possible, more agreeable
than if they had come to make other purchases."[17]

The approach proved, in the words of business historian Joseph
Appel, "sound not only in morals, but in economics as well."[18]
Wanamaker became rich, his success was imitated by his competitors, a retailing revolution took place, customers became much
happier to part with their money, and the economy prospered. But
the revolution took an innovator—someone had to realize that
"ancient custom" was dictating a foolish way to do business, then
devise an effective alternative, and finally show that it would work
in practice.

Barnum's Fable

The same mechanism can be seen in microcosm in a story related
by my favorite capitalist, P. T. Barnum:

> One of the ushers in my Museum once told me he intended to
> whip a man who was in the lecture room as soon as he came out.
> "What for?" I inquired.
> "Because he said I was no gentleman," replied the usher.
> "Never mind," I replied, "he pays for that, and you will not con-

vince him you are a gentleman by whipping him. I cannot afford to lose a customer. If you whip him, he will never visit the Museum again, and he will induce friends to go with him to other places of amusement instead of this, and thus, you see, I should be a serious loser."

"But he insulted me," muttered the usher.

"Exactly," I replied, "and if he owned the Museum, and you had paid him for the privilege of visiting it, and he had then insulted you, there might be some reason in your resenting it, but in this instance he is the man who pays, while we receive, and you must, therefore, put up with his bad manners."

My usher laughingly remarked, that this was undoubtedly the true policy, but he added that he should not object to an increase of salary if he was expected to be abused in order to promote my interests.[19]

This story neatly illustrates several points. First, it shows the capitalist's acquisitive interest in subordinating classic, and apparently natural, notions of "honor" to ones of profit as discussed in the previous chapter. Second, it demonstrates that the business virtues are not necessarily self-evident: the usher had to have the company's interests explained to him. (It also illustrates what economists call the principal-agent problem or the problem of agency cost or risk: the personal interests of the business owner, the principal, are not identical to those of the employee, the agent, and a wise manager must make special effort to instill in the employees an awareness of, an appreciation for, and, at best, a personal identification with, the interests of the business at large.) And third, it shows that these interests are quickly grasped once they are explained and that they may soon be extrapolated to further logical and self-interestedly useful conclusions.

The Tale of the Saturn

A more contemporary illustration of the development process may come from a recent innovation in the automobile industry, which is just about the only American retail business after the Wanamaker revolution that still haggles with consumers.[20] It seems no coincidence that car salesmen consistently receive the lowest ratings for "honesty and ethical standards" in polls.[21]

Venerable traditions, however, are now being challenged by the Saturn automobile which has a policy of charging set prices. It happens that not only have Saturn sales been brisk, but in *Consumer Reports* questionnaires returned by 120,000 new car buyers in 1995, Saturn placed solidly first in satisfaction with the car-buying experience. Most interestingly, Saturn was most closely followed on the satisfaction list not by other inexpensive cars, but by expensive ones like Infiniti, Saab, Lexus, and Mercedes, whose high ratings are not surprising because, as the magazine notes, "The potential profit in an expensive car is a powerful incentive for such dealers to stroke their customers." Obviously, Saturn is exceptional, and it is clear that "the no-haggle policy followed by Saturn dealers contributes greatly to that make's high standing."

The magazine interestingly compares the process of buying a Saturn with that of buying a Toyota. The staff member who did the comparison actually got a better deal on the Toyota, which is, in addition, a better car. However, his attitude toward the buying experience is expressed this way: "In all, it took me nearly two hours to escape from the showroom" at Toyota while, at Saturn, he found things to be "relaxed" with "no haggling—just a civilized take-it-or-leave-it price." As a result, he paid more money for a worse car and was much more satisfied with the transaction. The magazine concludes, "for many people, the happy experience may be worth a little extra money."[22] Or, put another way, the Saturn effectively costs less because the cost (pain) of transacting business is lower.

There are signs other automobile dealers are beginning to follow Saturn's successful one-price or no-haggle or no-dicker policy. If so, the industry might well enjoy greater overall sales since more people will buy more cars more often—essentially because the transaction costs have been substantially reduced. But the value of this approach, which may come to seem obvious, has clearly not been so until now. It will have taken an effort by one company to show the approach's value, after which other acquisitive retailers will follow suit to the benefit of just about everyone.[23]

Confiscating Autocrats

Martin McGuire and Mancur Olson have argued that autocrats with long-range perspectives ought, out of simple self-interest, to be benevolent to the societies they control since they will do better themselves if these societies are productive. Consequently, to maximize their extractions from the society in the long term, autocrats are best advised to limit their short-term extractions. Or, as Bradford De Long and Andrei Shleifer put it in a related study, governments which set lower and less destructive tax rates allow for faster growth and therefore benefit in the long run.[24]

However, when one looks at the behavior of autocrats in the dynastic systems of preindustrial Europe, short-sighted confiscation rather than enlightened benevolence was clearly the norm. And as a result, growth was generally quite low. In an effort to explain this curious phenomenon, scholars argue that the autocrats must have had short-term planning horizons.[25]

But while the princes and kings in Europe often led challenged regimes, many of them reigned for decades and almost all, probably, wanted very much to believe that they were establishing dynasties which would last for ages. Consequently, it seems more plausible that these autocrats engaged in self-interestedly foolish behavior not because they thought only in short run terms, but because it never occurred to them that benevolence was to their long-term benefit, and accordingly they applied confiscatory and arbitrary taxation policies that were substantially self-destructive. What they lacked was not a long-term perspective, but an enlightened and ingenious innovator like Wanamaker who could show them the advantage of abandoning established custom. This wisdom, so clear to twentieth-century economists, was not so to ancient autocrats—any more than the wheel was to American Indians.

THE RISE OF BUSINESS VIRTUE

It seems to me, then, that Montesquieu is quite correct when he proclaims, "it is almost a general rule that wherever manners are gentle, there is commerce," but that he exaggerates when he adds, "and wherever there is commerce, manners are gentle." Similarly, Adam Smith seems in error to argue that "Whenever commerce is introduced into any country probity and punctuality always accompany it. These virtues in a rude and barbarous country are almost unknown"; or to insist that "when the greater part of people are merchants they always bring probity and punctuality into fashion, and these, therefore, are the principal virtues of a commercial nation." The same problem exists when James Q. Wilson suggests that capitalism fosters "a reasonable concern for the opinions of others," or when Daniel Klein concludes that "commerce elevates manners and probity," or when an eighteenth-century Scottish historian, William Robertson, contends that commerce "softens and polishes the manners of men."[26]

There is clearly plenty of commerce in the bazaar North discusses or in the American business "jungle" Wanamaker grew up with and helped revolutionize, but apparently little in the way of probity, gentleness, or soft and polished manners. These virtues, then, do not follow automatically from commerce; it is quite possible to have commerce that is also rude and barbarous. North's bazaar and Wanamaker's jungle are not "barbarous" or "backward" because they lack commerce or trade. Rather, they are "barbarous" or "backward"—that is, relatively poor—because commerce and trade are being carried out without the capitalist virtues.

An interesting discussion in Adam Smith may help to illustrate this process further. Smith makes three connected observations. First, "mercantile manners" in Spain and Portugal are worse than those in London, and these in turn are worse than in Amsterdam. Second, the merchants of Spain and Portugal are a good deal less rich than those of London who, in turn, are less rich than those of Amsterdam. And third, the rate of profit is highest in Spain and Portugal, lower in London, and lowest in Amsterdam. From this set of observations, Smith concludes that high rates of profit cause one to have bad mercantile matters.[27]

But there is another interpretation. The merchants of Amsterdam are relatively rich *because* they have good mercantile manners. Moreover, the relatively high rates of honesty and fairness among the merchants of Amsterdam mean they can safely invest even when the rate of return is low, while those in unmannerly, unreliable Spain and Portugal only make deals with high rates of return because they need to compensate for the higher risks that prevails in their uncertain and unreliable (and unmannerly) commercial atmosphere.

It appears, then, that capitalists are not necessarily gentle or honest simply by nature. For them to become so, it must occur to them that honest, fair, civil, and compassionate business behavior will increase their long-range profits. And it may well have taken quite a long time for them to grasp the economic benefits of such behavior. Indeed, one of the reasons for capitalism's negative image may be that for millennia capitalists—like those in Wanamaker's jungle and in North's bazaar—often *were* dishonest, unfair, and uncivil at various levels because, like Europe's autocrats of old, they were foolishly unaware of their own long-range economic interests. Lacking was *enlightened* self-interest.

Business Virtue Before the Nineteenth Century

It is difficult, but not impossible, to find a clear appreciation for the economic value of the business virtues before the nineteenth century. The Quakers did bring virtue to business early on, and they prospered because of that behavior, but they were virtuous for religious reasons, and their wealth perhaps therefore could be seen in a sense to have been accidental or incidental. As early as 1748 Benjamin Franklin stressed the economic value of honesty in enhancing one's ability to obtain loans,[28] and there have long been informal reputational mechanisms like guilds and systems of merchant law for policing honesty among businesspeople.[29] Like Franklin, Daniel Defoe appreciated the value of business honesty. He was a businessman for decades before he became a novelist— indeed, invented the novel—with *Robinson Crusoe* in 1719 at the age of fifty-nine. In an insightful discussion of business practices of the time, he does chance to observe that "An honest tradesman is a jewel indeed, and . . . is valued wherever he is found."[30] And even if the capitalists of his era were not systematically writing about the capitalist virtues, Adam Smith did, as noted above, detect probity and a gentleness of manner as common characteristics at least of the commerce in his neighborhood.[31]

Undoubtedly some capitalists have long understood the value of virtuous behavior and did not bother to articulate the practice into an explicit business principle because it was second nature. Thus, a modern businessman, Mark McCormack, contends that keeping your word is part of the "unwritten code of business" and that believing in your product is one of the "self-evident truths of salesmanship."[32] At once, then, he declares such notions to be so obvious that they hardly need to be explicated, and then does exactly that by writing his book. (However, neither notion, it seems safe to suggest, has ever been self-evident to any Hollywood scriptwriter.)

The Rise of Business Virtue in the Nineteenth and Twentieth Centuries

However, as an elaborated, self-conscious principle, the notion that honesty and especially fair dealing, civility, and compassion bring wealth—a notion commonly found in contemporary books on business like McCormack's—seems to have been generally discovered, or to have been made clearly explicit, only in the nineteenth century or so. In fact, P. T. Barnum's mid-century tract, *The Art of Money-Getting*, is the earliest publication I have been able to find in which the profitability of virtuous business behavior is specifically and extensively laid out.

This rather remarkable silence suggests that the explicit discovery of the capitalist virtues and their conscious application to actual business behavior may be fairly recent. In fact, the rise of these virtues seems very much to have coincided with the remarkable economic rise of the West documented in figure 4.1, and probably importantly helped cause it.

I was once struck in this regard by a passage in a recent guidebook to Italy. Travel guides tend to be very upbeat, but when the author got to Naples he became unhinged: a beautiful spot, he pointed out, but avoid dealing with Neapolitan merchants because they are unrelievedly vicious and, given half an opportunity, will rob you blind. This sort of reputation, one suspects, was none too good for the local tourist industry or for the area's economic development more generally.[33] Similarly, Edward Banfield tells of the labor situation in a southern Italian town he visited in the 1950s: "An employer who can get away with it is almost sure to cheat his employees," and relations with employees are accordingly poisoned by "anxiety, suspicion, and hate." The result of this condition is not only that the employees work less hard and less reliably for their employers, thus reducing profits to the enterprise, but that the economic development of the whole area suffers. Banfield notes that "mutual distrust between landlords and tenants accounts in part for the number of tiny, owner-operated farms," because: "rather than work a larger unit on shares, an arrangement which would be more profitable but which would necessitate getting along with a landlord, the peasant prefers to go it alone on his uneconomic holding." Many peasants simply subsist on their private plots, and since these are too small to keep them occupied much of the time, the result is that a great deal of labor potential is lost to the economy. Banfield notes that in some towns in the area the upper class, out of tradition, "has always been brutal toward the peasants," a phenomenon that would similarly hamper economic development.[34]

This business behavior seems to be a contemporary holdover from the kind that was once quite standard in Europe. For example, a prominent business writer in 1771, declaring what Rosenberg characterizes as the "conventional wisdom" of the time, argued, "Every one but an idiot knows that the lower classes must be kept poor or they will never be industrious. . . . they must (like all mankind) be in poverty or they will not work." Or Sir William Temple, in his severely mistitled *Vindication of Commerce and the Arts*, published in 1758, let it be known that the only way to make laborers "temperate and industrious" was "to lay them under the necessity of labouring all the time they can spare from meals and sleep." And Richard Tilly points to an "employer ideology" that was quite common in the nineteenth century: the belief among industrialists that "workers were naturally lax, undependable, opportunistic, and that only the threat of extreme poverty supplied adequate motivation to work." In partial response to such employer attitudes, the labor movement grew and demanded that these attitudes be changed: for example, there were a series of strikes in Poland in 1905 in which the workers explicitly demanded not only that certain particularly hated company officials and supervisors be fired but that company officials treat them with respect and dignity, in part by abandoning the use of familiar forms of address that implied they were children.[35]

To allow a condition to develop in which employee-employer relations are so filled with hate and suspicion that workers feel they have to *strike* to be treated with dignity and respect and trust is almost mind-bogglingly stupid by the standards of modern business management—or, more precisely, from the standpoint of the management it is economically foolish.[36]

Gradually, the notion, now accepted as elemental and even simple-mindedly obvious, that "a happy employee is a productive employee," has taken hold. For example, Tilly traces the dawning awareness during the nineteenth century by industrial entrepreneurs that "peaceful industrial relations and high labour productivity have generally gone together." This realization made them "increasingly willing to deal with their workers as economic partners who had the right to fair and honest treatment." By 1996, when strikes in the United States dropped to a fifty-year low, corporate officials suggested that the phenomenon stemmed from "increased employer-employee team-work and from management's treating workers with more respect."[37]

Before such now-conventional approaches were discovered, however, businesses must have frequently, even routinely, been run with a fair amount of what we would now consider arrant (and foolish) viciousness toward employees because management believed workers would only produce when threatened with poverty. Accordingly, employer-employee relations must have been filled with the rancor, distrust, and intense hostility Banfield found more recently in southern Italy. Small wonder unionism and revolutionary socialism began to grow.

The admonitions of famous and successful capitalists like P. T. Barnum probably helped businesspeople begin to grasp the business virtues. So, perhaps, did the striking revelations of the experiments at the Hawthorne Works of Western Electric in the 1920s which systematically suggested that higher employee morale led to greater and more efficient production.[38]

But the most effective approach in disseminating these essential insights was probably simple competition. Those business which have prominently gone against the once-conventional wisdom and have treated their employees as partners rather than as children and with respect rather than suspicion have benefited economically, and other businesses have either had to follow suit or, on average, to fall behind economically. Management consultants Thomas P. Peters and Robert Waterman supply a litany of modern instances.[39]

Similarly, the setting of prices for retail goods and the sense of fairness the practice induces, which began only in the nineteenth century thanks to such innovators as Wanamaker, is now accepted as standard operating procedure in developed countries. So, more generally, is the concentrated and dedicated effort to make the shopping experience a pleasant one rather than an encounter filled with inefficient—and, for many people, alienating—rancor and dispute as buyer and seller trade wary insults across a counter in a manner neatly caricatured in 1727 by Daniel Defoe:

> *Lady.* I like that colour and the figure well enough, but I don't like the silk, there's no substance in it.
>
> *Mercer.* Indeed, Madam, your Ladyship lies, 'tis a very substantial silk.
>
> *Lady.* No, no, you lie indeed, Sir, 'tis good for nothing, 'twill do no service.
>
> *Mercer.* Pray, Madam, feel how heavy 'tis; you will find 'tis a lie; the very weight of it may satisfy you that you lie, indeed, Madam.
>
> *Lady.* Come, come, show me a better; I am sure you have better.
>
> *Mercer.* Indeed, Madam, your Ladyship lies; I may show you more pieces, but I cannot show you a better; there is not a better piece of silk of that sort in London, Madam.
>
> *Lady.* Let me see that piece of crimson there.
>
> *Mercer.* Here it is, Madam.

Lady. No, that won't do neither; 'tis not a good colour.
Mercer. Indeed Madam, you lie; 'tis as fine a colour as can be died.
Lady. O fie! You lie, indeed, Sir; why it is not in grain.
Mercer. Your ladyship lies, upon my word, Madam; 'tis in grain, in-
dced, and as fine as can be died.[40]

Despite Defoe's witty mockery, it took the better part of two centuries before retailers came fully to the apparently non-obvious realization that this sort of activity was economically foolish. Those
who did so not only prospered (on average), but so did the
economies they flourished in. Robert Frank suggests that "the art
of bargaining" is "in large part the art of sending misleading messages" about how much one would be willing to buy or sell an item
for. The problem is that to the degree people don't like to receive
(or send) misleading messages, they will be disinclined to deal at
all.[41]

Although it is difficult to chart precisely or to quantify, Tilly argues that honesty in business affairs grew notably during the nineteenth century in Britain and Germany. Entrepreneurs, he finds,
increasingly came to view "individual transactions as links in a
larger chain of profitable business ventures, as building blocks in
a long-run process of capital accumulation" rather than as "one-
time opportunities to be exploited to the utmost." He notes, for
example, that, even though business activities were expanding
greatly, there was no rise in the number of complaints about
breaches of contract or fraud. Indeed, the business done by Prus-
sian banks expanded by 563 percent over a forty-year period, while
their bad debts accounts declined by 20 percent. At the same time,
"'honest' business practices such as the refund of cash or the exchange of bad merchandise to disappointed buyers, the introduction of fixed prices, brand labels and also longer-run credit agreements, would seem to have become more widespread."[42]

Writing in 1890, economist Alfred Marshall could see this happening. He noted that the quickly developing modern economy
"has undoubtedly given new openings for dishonesty in trade."
New ways "of making things appear other than they are" had been
discovered, and "the producer is now far removed from the ulti-

mate consumer" and thus "his wrong doings are not visited with the prompt and sharp punishment which falls on the head of a person who, being bound to live and die in his native village, plays a dishonest trick on one of his neighbours." However, although "the opportunities for knavery are certainly more numerous than they were . . . there is no reason for thinking that men avail themselves of a larger proportion of such opportunities than they used to do. On the contrary, modern methods of trade imply habits of trustfulness on the one side and power of resisting temptation to dishonesty on the other, which to do exist among a backward people."[43] But in my opinion, the modern economy was developing precisely *because* habits of trust had been developed, not, as Marshall suggests, the other way around.

Tilly finds that "established business leaders played a dominant role in the deliberations and negotiations that produced legal codification of business norms" but also that the legalization of behavioral norms took place precisely when the norms had already become widely accepted. For example, fraud and dishonest practices by the larger German merchant houses in wholesale trade had become quite rare because they were "'monitored' (or controlled) by competition, and the problem was to extend these practices to the smaller firms which were often "devoid of any solid mercantile tradition" and had "no reputation to lose." This process can also be seen in the history of the American circus. By 1910, circuses like Barnum and Bailey and Ringling Bros. had profited by clean business practices and had come to dominate the industry. They became concerned, however, that business on the road was being harmed by bad business practices that still persisted. Consequently, the successful circuses, at the instigation of Charles Ringling, met to create agreement that the generally profitable "Sunday School" approach should dominate.[44]

This is all quite recent, it seems. Concentrated efforts by businesses to establish agencies to police industry-embarrassing and therefore profit-harming fraud and misrepresentation began in the United States only about a hundred years ago: Underwriter's Laboratories, for example, was not founded until 1901, the Better Business Bureau not until 1912. But by the time modern economics was coming into its own in the twentieth century, its practitioners were so used to honest business behavior that their economic models, as Stigler observes, "almost invariably postulate transactions free of fraud or coercion," a regularity which suggests to him that the profession has implicitly concluded that fraud and coercion "are not empirically significant elements in the ordinary economic transactions of an enterprise economy."[45]

Spreading Virtue

Rather curiously, then, as the experience with the bazaar cited by North or the American business jungle observed by Wanamaker suggests, capitalism per se doesn't seem necessarily to generate a long-term perspective: although acquisitiveness may be natural, it has apparently often taken an effort for people—like Barnum's usher, many nineteenth-century business leaders, or princes in preindustrial Europe—to grasp the concept of enlightened, long-term economic self-interest. Indeed, in Poland workers were striking to get management to do something that, Peters and Waterman would insist, was overwhelmingly in the business interest of the people they were striking against, who, however, were too boneheaded—or too steeped in erroneous conventional business wisdom—to figure this out on their own.

But, as in the case of Barnum's usher, once the concept is clearly and profitably introduced by an innovator, its economic value can be easy to grasp. This may bode well for the economies of many postcommunist countries in Europe, despite "path dependence" problems arising both from the fact that their peoples lived for decades under a system that was devotedly anticapitalistic and from the fact that these countries were comparatively poor even before that—a condition Gerschenkron attributes in part to "disastrously low" standards of honesty in business.[46] For the most part, people in these countries now seek to achieve the wealth of the West, and many seem quite willing, even eager, to imitate Western business practices to do so. Moreover, they have local role models in the newly established branches of successful Western businesses which routinely and prominently apply established and tested procedures of honesty, fairness (including set prices accompanied by a return policy), civility, and compassion to their business practices.

Thus the invasion of institutions like McDonald's and K-Mart can have a very beneficial impact on the business climate in many places. The new Russkoye Bistros in Moscow provide "fresh ingredients and fast and pleasant service in a clean environment," and the marketing director of the Moscow McDonald's remarks, "I really see it not so much as competition as the acceptance of our way of doing business. They have seen what we can do and I hope they will learn from it." Indeed, local businesses that fail to follow suit, by, for example, continuing to treat their customers with the incivility so familiar in the Soviet era, are likely quickly to find themselves in financial trouble.[47]

THE RELATIVE IMPORTANCE OF BUSINESS VIRTUE IN ECONOMIC DEVELOPMENT

The rise of business virtue, then, seems to have been strongly associated with economic development: "business honesty and capital accumulation," observes Tilly, "go hand in hand." Although it would be extremely difficult to determine with precision the degree to which economic development can be attributed to the rise of capitalist virtue, it is quite possible that the rise of such virtue is massively and crucially important. Indeed, as Tilly suggests, "Honesty, in the sense of adherence to generally accepted rules of behavior, would seem to be a fundamental prerequisite for the development of market economies."[48] And so, in my view, would be the associated virtue of fairness, as well as those of civility and compassion, that are so important to effective management.

Per capita income in the United States quadrupled between 1869–78 and 1944–53, and an important study by Moses Abramovitz concludes that changes in capital and labor inputs as conventionally defined and measured can account for only a small fraction of this remarkable increase: in fact, about 90 percent of the economic growth remained to be explained, a portion economists, straining the language almost to the breaking point, came to label "the residual."[49]

In assessing this striking finding, Rosenberg, in an article pointedly entitled, "Neglected Dimensions in the Analysis of Economic Change," suggests that what may be mainly important in economic development are "important qualitative changes in the human agent as a factor of production . . . which typically escape the scrutiny of the economic theorist." As examples he lists "knowledge, technical skills, organizational and managerial abilities, levels of economic aspiration, responsiveness to economic incentives, capacity to undertake and to adapt to innovation, etc." And he concludes that "economic growth is, in many important respects, a learning process whereby the human factor acquires new skills, aptitudes, capabilities, and aspirations."[50]

In this, Rosenberg, an academic economist, comes perilously close to embracing the point of view of a huge number of how-to management books that embody the perspective expressed in the title of one of them: *What They Don't Teach You at the Harvard Business School.* Typical is the harangue by Peters and Waterman in their multiyear bestseller, *In Search of Excellence.* The approach to management typically taught in business schools, they argue, "doesn't tell us what the excellent companies have apparently learned." What they have learned, it seems, are essentially the business virtues: "to love the customers," to appreciate "the rock-bottom importance of making the average Joe a hero and a consistent winner," to "show how strongly workers can identify with the work they do if we give them a little say-so," to understand that "self-generated quality control is so much more effective than inspector-generated quality control," to "overspend on quality, overkill on customer service, and make products that last and work," and to know that "good managers make meanings for people, as well as money."[51]

Tilly observes that "In economically underdeveloped countries of the twentieth century one can observe low standards of business morality reminiscent of Europe's backward areas of the eighteenth and nineteenth centuries."[52] Similarly, Marshall noted in 1890 that among those peoples "who have none of the originating power of the modern business man, there will be found many who show an evil sagacity in driving a hard bargain in a market even with their neighbours."[53]

Although there are many reasons economies grow, developed countries are distinguished from underdeveloped ones, it seems, not so much by differences in natural resources or in native brainpower or in skill levels as by differences in business virtue. And the European experience strongly suggests that a deficit in business virtue is a problem that can be readily overcome.

THE RELEVANCE OF AN EFFECTIVE LEGAL SYSTEM
TO ECONOMIC DEVELOPMENT

"Little else," Adam Smith once said, "is requisite to carry a state to the highest degree of opulence from the lowest barbarism, but peace, easy taxes, and tolerable administration of justice."[54] Following Smith, many have argued that a viable judicial system is important for the development of capitalism, particularly as the ultimate arbiter of contracts and property rights and as final recourse against fraud.

However, an effective court and norm-regulating system, while certainly valuable, may be somewhat less vital to economic development than might first appear. A fair and reliable judicial system facilitates capitalism and may be useful as an accepted ultimate arbitrator, but it is a clumsy and costly expedient. (And, as observed above, it is unlikely to be able to do much to enforce such important business-enhancing qualities as civility, compassion, and often fairness.)

Daniel Klein observes that "the simple explanation for integrity would seem to be that agreements are enforced by court and constable." However, "everyday experience and numerous scholarly studies suggest that official contract enforcement is often costly and impractical, yet promises usually work out nonetheless." For example, in his study of actual business behavior, Stewart Macaulay found that only five of the twelve purchasing agents and only two of the ten sales managers he interviewed "had ever been involved in even a negotiation concerning a contract dispute where both sides were represented by lawyers," and *none* had ever "been involved in a case that went to trial." Instead, he found that "disputes are frequently settled without reference to the contract or potential or actual legal sanctions." Indeed, "there is a hesitancy to speak of legal rights or even to threaten to sue." As one respondent put it, "You don't read legalistic contract clauses at each other if you ever want to do business again. One doesn't run to lawyers if he wants to stay in business because one must behave decently." In this regard, "holding a customer to the letter of a contract is bad for 'customer relations.' Suing a customer who is not bankrupt and might reorder again is poor strategy."[55]

Principally, then, people in American business rely on trust and reputation to make deals happen. For example, the agreements between Standard Oil and the railroads in the nineteenth century, of enormous economic consequence to both parties, were mostly sealed simply with a handshake. Indeed, if there is even a small chance that the courts would be required to make a deal work, the deal will probably not be consummated in the first place. Macaulay, in fact, is able to find remarkably few reasons written contracts exist at all, and many of these are essentially extralegal. He points out that contracts are often mainly put together because they are required by the federal government, or by a lender of money, or for the convenience of outside lawyers who are obsessed with avoiding "any possible legal difficulty" and demand a formal contract because it makes their job easier in the (highly unlikely) event that a future dispute will have to be settled in court or by legal pressure.[56]

Actually, where trust has arduously, and profitably, been built up, efforts to further guarantee honesty by mechanical legalistic devices could actually be counterproductive, even in the consumer field. Suppose, for example, that the successful mail-order merchant, L. L. Bean, were to attempt to enhance its reputation for business integrity by establishing a policing organization in cooperation with a governmental agency guaranteeing that any customer cheated by the company would receive quick and full recompense. It seems likely that this innovation would generate, rather than lower, concern about the company's integrity, and it would almost certainly reduce sales. It is sounder business for Bean to rely simply on its reputation for honesty, even though this is secured by nothing grander than its appreciation for the fact that this reputation is money in the bank.[57]

It is surely desirable to have enforceable antifraud legislation, but it is worth noting that the buyer must still be wary of fraud even in the United States with its highly developed and substantially incorruptible court system. A consumer who has been cheated can report the fraud to the authorities, and the cheater may perhaps eventually be put in jail. But as a practical matter the swindled have very little chance of ever getting their money back, particularly since the courts are already jammed with criminal (especially drug) cases. Moreover, a huge portion of transactions do not involve enough money to make a civil suit a sensible recourse—and, of course, many agile swindlers will wisely keep their fraudulent profit per sucker low enough to make sure of that.[58]

In fact, it appears that an effective court system came relatively *late* in the economic development process. For the most part, European states mainly absorbed preexisting commercial and merchant law into their evolving legal systems. And, as Rosenberg and Birdzell suggest, this did not come about even in advanced England until late in the eighteenth century after a great deal of commercial expansion had already taken place: an effective court system did not *cause* commerce but rather was "a *response* to the expansion of commerce"; as such it (merely) "*added* to the ability to predict the behavior of others." Or, as Adam Smith observes, "commerce and manufactures gradually introduced order and good government," not the other way around.[59] Similarly, as noted above, the codification of economic norms into law and government-enforced regulations generally took place after the norms had already become fairly standardized forms of behavior.

Furthermore, as the experience of contemporary China demonstrates, if other conditions are appropriate, a great deal of economic development and investment is possible even when a commercial legal system can scarcely be said to exist. The process, however, does tend to put a premium on informal contacts with government, and there tends to be an emphasis on shorter-term investments and transactions.[60]

What is mainly needed for the emergence of an effective court system, it appears, is the development of such business norms as honesty, integrity, fairness, and reliability. At that point, the relatively few miscreants will stand out and can perhaps be dealt with by the courts; without the norms, the courts would be utterly overwhelmed. It is the central message of this chapter that, because those adhering to the norms have a competitive advantage in the long run, the norms tend to emerge naturally out of ordinary competition when an innovator grasps the economic benefit of such virtues and demonstrates their advantage by putting them into practice.

Development, Happiness, and the Rise of the Politically Incorrect One-Handed Economist

As NOTED in the previous chapter and as charted in figure 4.1, over the last two centuries or so an enormous and accelerating expansion of economic wealth and well-being has taken place in the developed world. This development has been utterly unprecedented in the history of the human race, and in my view it has been importantly enhanced by the gradual acceptance by people in business of the virtues of honesty, fairness, civility, and compassion as innovative capitalists discovered the economic value of these virtues.

The rather uniform anticipation among economic historians is that this remarkable economic expansion will continue, broaden, and even escalate in the future.[1] This cheery prediction may prove pessimistic, however, because it leaves out the enhancing benefits that will derive from the efforts of the economics profession itself.

The remarkable economic expansion of the past has taken place substantially by accident or default: it was not notably guided by government policy—indeed, it frequently took place *despite* government policy. This is because it occurred when economists often didn't know what they were talking about or fundamentally disagreed, or, when they could agree, were often ignored by decision makers who were pursuing divergent agendas, were mesmerized by faulty economic folk wisdom or ideology, or were paralyzed by political cowardice.

In this chapter I propose that there has been an important change in this condition by the end of the twentieth century. Economists, I suggest, now basically have reached a substantial and probably correct consensus about how economies work, and they are able to prescribe policies that have a good chance of enhancing an economy's ability to grow. And there is another change. In the past, the advice of economists was very often politically unattractive—politically incorrect—because policymakers gave noneconomic values higher priority, or because other advisers seemed to have more intuitively plausible palliatives, or because acceptance of the advice would cause short-term political pain. Now, however, the economists' advice is increasingly being accepted by decision makers.

This chapter explores the rise of economic science, its increasing acceptance, and the consequent prospects for vastly expanded economic growth worldwide. In the process, economists and like-minded idea entrepreneurs seem substantially to have managed to get across four highly consequential and enormously controversial ideas: the growth of economic well-being should be a dominant goal; wealth is best achieved through exchange rather than through conquest; international trade should be free; and economies do best when the government leaves them substantially free.

The chapter also muses over the curious fact that advances in economic well-being do not necessarily cause people to profess that they have become happier. Rather, each improvement seems quickly to be taken in stride, and standards are continually raised to compensate. However, this phenomenon seems to help stimulate further economic development, and it may have a kind of intellectually invigorating quality of its own.

ONE-HANDEDNESS

Lawrence Henderson of Harvard University once suggested that by 1912, for the first time in human history, "a random patient with a random disease consulting a doctor chosen at random stood better than a fifty-fifty chance of benefiting from the encounter." This vivid observation suggests how recent the rise of medical science has been and, further, it points to the fact that not so long ago, physicians, while perhaps generally dedicated and well meaning, often did more harm than good. After all, a doctor who doesn't understand germ theory may innocently carry a disease from one patient to the next, making matters far worse than if the patients had instead consulted a priest, a shaman, or a snake oil salesman, or if they had simply stayed quietly at home in bed. In a similar vein, Sir William Osler of Johns Hopkins observed in 1894 that "we may safely say (reversing the proportion of fifty years ago) that for one damaged by dosing, one hundred are saved."[2] Chanting a thousand "Hail Marys" may not do much good physically (though it might have a beneficial placebo effect), but misguided, if well-intentioned, bleeding or leeching or uninformed dosing could easily make the malady worse—and, by Osler's reckoning, did so almost all the time as late as the mid-nineteenth century.[3]

Economics, it seems to me, is now about where medicine was a century ago. Essentially, economics has probably reached the point where the random government official or business executive consulting the random economist is likely to benefit from the encounter. Fifty years ago, Harry Truman, frustrated with economic advisers who kept telling him on the one hand that a certain consequence could be expected from a particular action, while on the other hand the opposite consequence might come about, frequently expressed a yearning for what he called "a one-handed economist." Increasingly over the twentieth century, economists, through trial and error, experiment and experience, abstraction and empirical test, seem to have developed a substantial consensus about broad economic principles, if not always about nuance and detail. And thus we seem to be approaching the age Truman yearned for—the age of the one-handed economist.

I need to stress that I am applying a standard here that is significant, but not terribly exalted. By present standards, after all, medicine was woefully inadequate at the turn of the century, and physicians were still misguidedly killing a fair number of their patients. But, as figure 5.1 demonstrates, over the course of this century medicine has advanced from a base that has turned out to be essentially sound, and the result has been a spectacular and historically unprecedented increase in life expectancy, first in developed countries, and then more recently in the less-developed world.[4] In like manner, although economics is hardly an exact science, if economists have, at last, essentially gotten the basics correct, this

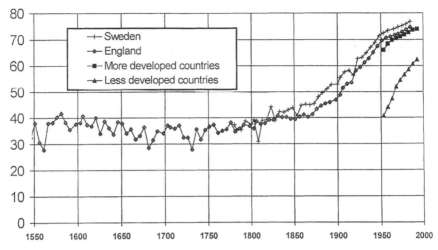

FIGURE 5.1. Life Expectancy at Birth, 1550–1990.

accomplishment is potentially of enormous importance to the advancement of economic well-being.

The "economists" I am referring to might perhaps be better designated "policy economists"—people whose business it is to derive coherent and practical policy prescriptions from what they take to be the central notions of economic science. Included in this group would be not only many academics in economics departments and business schools, but also policy and financial analysts working for or running think tanks, private businesses, and investment firms, as well as those hanging out at policy agencies like the Federal Reserve, the Congressional Budget Office, the International Monetary Fund, and the World Bank. It would also include those seeking to develop technical tools for analyzing and assessing the real world—as, of course, modern medicine has been dependent for much of its success on the development and proliferation of a raft of probing, measuring, and analyzing methods and tools.[5]

I do not propose that these economists now have an all-embracing theory of the economy: after all, physicians were correctly convinced that aspirin relieves pain and that smoking causes cancer before much of an explanation was developed for why these things were so.[6] Nor, certainly, do I mean to suggest that economists never disagree or err. The removal of tonsils has ceased to be routine. And for a very long time physicians ordered parents to warm formula milk before feeding it to their infants, presumably on the plausible assumption that bottled milk should be the same temperature as breast milk; eventually, however, someone determined that babies were generally quite capable of digesting cold milk, and the conventional advice was accordingly abandoned after causing great inconvenience to parents and occasional danger to their babies when sleepy parents inadvertently fed them scalding milk.

But I propose that, in general, economists now are substantially on top of their topic, that they are amassing knowledge in a manner that is generally progressive and cumulative, and that the advice they render is likely—or more likely than not—to be sound.

A impressive indication of this came in the early 1990s when economists were confronted with a new and quite astounding problem. For various reasons, some two dozen countries with highly controlled (and underproductive) economies, including some of the biggest in the world, were suddenly freed of economy-stifling ideological controls and wished to become rich. As Lawrence Summers observes, the death of communism caught the economics profession unprepared: although there had been quite a few studies at that point about the transition of market economies to controlled or command economies, "there was not a single book or article on the problem of transforming an economy from the communist to a market system." Indeed, the word "privatization" had only been recently developed in connection with Margaret Thatcher's relatively modest efforts to denationalize comparatively small portions of the British economy.[7]

Economists were called in to sort out this novel problem. Even though their ideas about how to encourage economic well-being and growth had been principally developed through the analysis of economies that were relatively free, it is impressive testimony to the fundamental soundness of these ideas that the advice so generated proved to be substantially (though not invariably) sound even when applied under these unprecedented and unstudied circumstances. In case after case, countries that generally followed the advice have been able to achieve considerable (though certainly not painless) success in transforming their economies and in achieving meaningful growth, often in an astoundingly short period of time. Similar success, following similar advice, seems to have recently been achieved in many places in southern, eastern, and southeastern Asia and in much of Latin America.[8]

Thus, it appears that George Stigler had it essentially right in his 1964 presidential address to the American Economic Association when he assessed the state of the art and decided to gloat for a minute: "For 200 years our analytical system has been growing in precision, clarity, and generality, although not always in lucidity," he argued, and during the preceding half-century there had been an "immense increase in the power, the care, and the courage of our quantitative researches."[9] Moveover, it seems to me that economics, like medicine, has importantly improved in those respects in the decades since he delivered that address.

POLITICAL INCORRECTNESS

Historically, however, there has been another problem to overcome. Economists may render sound advice, but, as the variable postcommunist experience shows, the politicians and administrators who are their advisees may reject it because they find it politically incorrect.

They may find it so, first, because they disagree with the value or the goal the economists advocate. For the most part, this has not been a problem for medicine: the physician's goal—better health for the patient—is readily accepted. By contrast, the economist's goal of economic growth and well-being has often been rejected— been found to be politically incorrect—because people hold other, often conflicting, values, like honor or class differentiation or traditional justice or piety to be more important. Accordingly, for economic science to triumph, it has been necessary for economic goals to become dominant.

Second, modern economists, like modern physicians, have had

to convince their advisees that they know what they are talking about and that their proposed remedies will function. This has not been an easy task because, as modern economics has advanced, it has developed a perspective that often runs counter to some competing notions about how economies ought to work. Many of these alternative notions are morally appealing and alluringly common-sensical—and hence politically correct—like the still popular views that the best way to protect domestic employment is to restrict competitive imports or that the best way to beat inflation is for the government to dictate prices.

Finally, the advice of economists, even when accepted as valid, may be rejected because politicians and administrators find it to be politically painful to carry out. In this case, the analogy with medicine works quite well. As it has burgeoned, the science of medicine unfortunately did not discover that maladies could be cured by such agreeable remedies as eating chocolate. Rather, it kept coming up with remedies that involved cutting patients open, encasing them with plaster, drilling into their aching teeth, consigning them to passive inactivity, giving them bad-tasting tonics, denying them the tasty foods they most want to eat, mandating boring exercises, and puncturing them with long needles. (Lately, however, beneficial health effects have happily been found in the moderate, but regular, ingestion of red wine, liquor, and pizza.[10] Maybe things are beginning to turn around.) People had to become convinced that physicians and dentists knew what they were doing before they would follow advice like that. And they also had to become willing to swallow the medicine—that is, to suffer short-range pain for the promise of long-term benefit—particularly when priests and palm readers regularly arrived at palliatives that were less painful and more convenient.

In like manner, many—perhaps most—of the remedies modern economics has advanced have turned out to be politically painful, particularly in the short run. As Michael Weinstein puts it, economists "compulsively remind people to eat their spinach."[11] For example, if economists could discover that subsidies to politically active dairy farmers would not only help the farmers but also importantly benefit the economy as a whole, politicians would be hanging on their every word—the advice would be pure political chocolate. Unfortunately, economists have generally prescribed political spinach: cutting the dairy farmers from the public dole— no matter how deserving they may be as people, no matter how bucolic their farms, no matter how well-groomed their cows—and letting them descend quietly into ignominious bankruptcy and then perhaps to seek other, unsubsidized, work. Moreover, there is very often a political dilemma in the fact that the people who will benefit in the long term from the economists' advice don't know who they are while those who will be disadvantaged in the short term know this only too well and are quick to scream.

FOUR ECONOMIC PROPOSITIONS THAT HAVE BECOME INCREASINGLY ACCEPTED

For the economists' politically incorrect perspectives and prescriptions to prevail, then, populations and policymakers have had to become convinced that economists know what they are talking about and also to accept their dominant goal—achieving a healthy, growing economy—as well as their often painful devices for achieving that goal. It has been a long, uphill struggle, but as the century closes, economists and their allies seem substantially to have been successful in this endeavor.

Four propositions seem central to this process, and each has been mightily contested over the last century or two. In my view, it has been essential for economists and like-minded idea entrepreneurs to get these propositions accepted in order to be effective— in order for economists to become, in Stigler's words, "the ornaments of democratic society whose opinions on economic policy shall prevail."[12]

Moreover, if these four elemental propositions have become substantially accepted, the ancillary consequences are enormous. Not only do they seem to hold the formula for a huge expansion of economic well-being, but in combination they suggest the demise of such central human institutions as empire and war.

1. The Growth of Economic Well-Being Should be a Dominant Goal

As central goals, economists often stress, or effectively stress, advances in economic well-being, a concept that usually includes considerations of economic growth as well as assessments of the way the wealth generated by that growth is distributed, particularly insofar as it brings people out of poverty. To develop this perspective, they frequently assume, model, and essentially favor people who are acquisitive: people who are centrally, indeed entirely, occupied with advancing their own long-term economic well-being.

As discussed in chapter 3, this perspective has traditionally rankled with people who treasure such values and goals as honor, heroism, empathy, altruism, sacrifice, selflessness, generosity, piety, patriotism, racism, self-respect, spirituality, nationalism, and compassion. They often condemn the economic motives as crass, materialistic, cowardly, vulgar, debased, hedonistic, uncaring, selfish, immoral, decadent, and self-indulgent.

Many economists are, or at any rate act like, economic determinists and, to be sure, when anything notable takes place there is almost always someone somewhere who is profiting financially. Agile economic determinists (working on the principle, "follow the money") can usually ferret out the profiters (or "profiteers") and triumphantly proclaim them to be the essential cause of the event. (The fact that there are also often many important and influential people *losing* money on the event rarely troubles them very much.)

However, noneconomic values have often been deemed more worthy than economic ones. For example, Simon Kuznets has pointed out that the quest for otherworldly eternity and the quest to maintain inborn differences as expressed in class structure have often been taken to be far superior to economic advancement. And, as Rosenberg and Birdzell observe, a number of business innovations that clearly have been successful economically—such as joint-stock companies, department stores, mail-order houses, chain stores, trusts, branch banks, and multinational corporations—have inspired great efforts to make them unlawful by those who prefer to maintain traditional, even folksy, ways of doing things even if this means slower economic development. At the same time, sentimental, economically dubious preference has often been shown for cooperatives, small farms, and mom-and-pop stores.[13]

An important area in which noneconomic values have usually dominated is war. Like murder, war rarely makes all that much economic sense even though it would be difficult to find a war from which no one has profited financially. For the most part, in fact, economic motivations often seem like a rationale for impulses that are actually more nearly moral, aesthetic, emotional, or psychological. As Quincy Wright observed after a lifetime of study of the matter: "Studies of both the direct and the indirect influence of economic factors on the causation of war indicate that they have been much less important than political ambitions, ideological convictions, technological change, legal claims, irrational psychological complexes, ignorance, and unwillingness to maintain conditions of peace in a changing world." Consider, in this respect, the conclusions of historian Hartmut Pogge von Strandmann about the process by which Germany began World War I:

> The drive to the east and to the west was underpinned by an imperialist culture which spread the virtues of Social Darwinism, the conquest of markets, the penetration of spheres of influence, competition between capitalist partners, the winning of living-space, and the rising power of the state. Buoyed up by an assumed military superiority, general economic strength and particular industrial vigor, widespread optimism and a mood of belligerence, the military and political leaders found, when they made the decision to push for war, that this was an acceptable option to many Germans, possibly even to the majority. . . . Confidence, determination, and the belief in victory were the ingredients of a willingness to fight an expansionist war.[14]

Economics—the "conquest of markets"—is in there, but buried among a fusillade of other, and probably far more important, motivating factors. Moreover, if businessmen had actually been running the combatant nations in World War I, they would likely have found it sound business to cut losses once the war devolved into the inconclusive, pointless, and hugely punishing trench warfare phase.

Similarly, Hitler's invasions a generation later were linked to a sort of crackpot economic theory about "living space," but to see his goals as primarily economic is to give short shrift to his egomania and to his much more motivating notions about race and the value of war in nation building.[15] Elsewhere and at the same time, Japan's catastrophic refusal to abandon its hugely—even absurdly—costly effort to conquer China when the United States so demanded made little economic sense. And, on the other side, the main reason the United States became involved in Asia in opposition to Japan in the late 1930s was an aesthetic, sentimental, or moral impulse to keep the heroic, persecuted Chinese from being dominated by a vicious foreign regime: as Bruce Russett notes, "by embargoing Japan in 1941 the United States was giving up an export trade at least four times that with China."[16]

The Cold War and its various damaging hot wars in places like Korea and Vietnam were mainly impelled by a communist expansionary ideology that stemmed not so much from economics as from an elaborate theory about social class warfare that was profoundly romantic and sentimental (and misguided). The Cold War abruptly evaporated not out of economic necessity, but because the communists abandoned their threatening theory.[17]

Likewise, although the Gulf War of 1991 is often considered to have been primarily about petroleum, if economic considerations of that sort had indeed been dominant, Saddam Hussein would have quickly retreated after his economy was destroyed and it became clear he would be unable actually to sell the oil he had just conquered in Kuwait. Moreover, George Bush (motivated, it appears, mainly by aesthetic or humanitarian repulsion and by personal pique) would never have invaded because any problem of oil supplies had already been solved by the quite cheerful willingness of Saudi Arabia and other countries to pump additional supplies— indeed, the only thing keeping oil prices high at the time was Bush's threat to start a war.[18]

It seems likely, then, that, if people with business motivations had actually been running the world, its history would have been quite a bit different (and generally better). Economists and their like-minded allies have made an important contribution by helping to teach the world to value economic well-being above passions that are often economically absurd.[19]

As Bush and Hussein demonstrated in 1990, the pursuit of wealth is hardly the only motivating factor today. The desires in China for reintegrating Taiwan or in South Korea for reunification with the impoverished north are essentially romantic and sentimental, and tempestuous and violent disagreement over the fate of Jerusalem scarcely makes much economic sense either. One can even find sober, deliberative Canadians who would rather be less wealthy than open up their trade with the United States because that, they fear, might besmirch the quest for a Canadian national identity. As one former Canadian diplomat, an opponent of expanded trade with the United States, put it, "Canada has never made economic sense, and Canadians have always had to pay an economic price for their political and cultural identity."[20]

However, the single-minded pursuit of wealth has come generally to be unashamedly accepted as behavior that is desirable, beneficial, and even honorable, and we seem now to be reaching the point where business motivations have become much more important than they have been in the past. Thus in formulating his policy toward China in the 1990s, American President Bill Clinton decided that economic considerations should substantially dominate ones about human rights—a conclusion that, however dismaying to some rights groups, generally went down well politically.

In this regard, it may be useful to review the association, noted in chapter 3, once proposed by Immanuel Kant between the "commercial spirit" and "self-interest, cowardice, and effeminacy." Maybe he had it right, and maybe that's not such a bad thing.

After all, under the free systems advocated by economists, people can service their long-term economic self-interest only if they are able to provide a good or a service other people freely find of value. And in the process of producing this good or service, acquisitive providers have generally discovered, as argued in previ-

ous chapters, that they can profit better when their business practices are honest, fair, civil, and compassionate.

Moreover, although it may be cowardly by the standards of those
who exalt the martial virtues to turn one's back when insulted, it
is possible, by other standards (the ones Barnum uses in his fable
on p. 80), to suggest that lethal battles fought over the cut of one's
coat or over the color of one's sneakers or over "spheres of influence" or over a chunk of land not big enough to bury the slain, are
not only economically foolish, but quite childish.[21] Perhaps a
world where a form of cowardice is rampant might be better than
one where people are routinely running around looking for fights
to prove, or test, their manhood—constantly seeking the bubble
reputation even in the cannon's mouth, as Shakespeare's Jaques
puts it.

And it may be effeminate to avoid unnecessary conflict, to temper anger, and to be guided by the not entirely unreasonable notion that other people do, in fact, sometimes have feelings. But, as
I have suggested, such gentle, accommodating behavior is, in general, economically beneficial—that is, it enhances the general
prosperity. And a world where that quality is in abundance may
not, after all, be all that undesirable even if it sometimes comes
laden with a degree of treacly sentimentality.

Thus, a society dominated by "self-interest, cowardice, and effeminacy" might, under some circumstances, prove to be entirely
bearable. And, in part through the insidious efforts of generations
of economists, societies in the most advanced portions of the world
have increasingly moved in that direction.

2. Wealth Is Best Achieved Through Exchange, Not Through Conquest: The Demise of Empire and War

The nineteenth-century British historian Henry Thomas Buckle
hailed Adam Smith's *Wealth of Nations* as "probably the most important book that has ever been written" because it convincingly
demonstrated that gold and silver are not wealth but are merely its
representatives, and because it shows that true wealth comes not

from diminishing the wealth of others, but rather that "the benefits of trade are of necessity reciprocal."[22] Smith's insights are elemental and profound, and, as Buckle suggests, they had once been counterintuitive—that is, Smith and others had to discover them and point them out. Thanks in part to the promotional efforts of legions of economists and other like-minded idea entrepreneurs, they have now substantially infused the world.

The gradual acceptance over the course of the twentieth century of propositions 1 and 2 has helped lead to one of the most remarkable changes in world history: the virtual eradication of the ancient and once vital notion of empire. Putting it another way, "the conquest of markets," a notion identified by Pogge von Strandmann in the German thinking of 1914, has declined markedly as even a partial reason, or excuse, for military action.

For millennia, the size of a country's empire was accepted as one of the chief indicators of its greatness. Although the quest for empire was often impelled by noneconomic factors such as the appeal of adventure or the need to "civilize" or convert the unenlightened, it was often partly based—or rationalized—as well on economic or pseudo-economic reasoning. Over the last century, economists and allied idea entrepreneurs like the best-selling English journalist and economic writer, Norman Angell, have successfully undercut the appeal of empire by convincing people more and more that economic well-being, not the vague sense of "owning" distant lands, should be the dominant goal and that trade, not conquest, is the best way to accumulate wealth.[23]

Another combined effect—not necessarily intended—of agreement with propositions 1 and 2 is that war becomes unacceptable.

In 1795, reflecting a view of Montesquieu and others, Immanuel Kant argued that the "spirit of commerce" is "incompatible with war" and that, as commerce inevitably gains the "upper hand," states would seek "to promote honorable peace and by mediation to prevent war." However, this notion is incomplete because, as Buckle pointed out, "the commercial spirit" has often been "warlike."[24] Thus, commerce truly becomes "incompatible with war" only when *both* the second proposition—that wealth is best achieved through exchange rather than conquest—*and* the first one—that wealth-enhancement should be a dominant goal—are accepted.

This was also understood by Angell. His critics, such as the prominent American naval historian Admiral Alfred Thayer Mahan, argued that even if it were true that war is economically unprofitable, nations mainly fight for motives other than economic ones such as "ambition, self-respect, resentment of injustice, sympathy with the oppressed." Angell replied by continuing to stress, reflecting proposition 2, that the inescapable economic chaos of war "makes economic benefit from victory impossible." But he also argued, in line with proposition 1, that nations should come to realize that "bread and a decent livelihood" are of paramount concern, not such vague and elastic goals as honor, power, and influence.[25]

Angell helped to crystallize a line of reasoning that has been gaining in acceptability ever since. It is the central contention of Richard Rosecrance's important book, *The Rise of the Trading State,* for example, that over the course of the last few centuries more and more countries have come to the conclusion that the path to wealth is through trade rather than through conquest, and he cites the striking and important examples of two recent converts: "Today West Germany and Japan use international trade to acquire the very raw materials and oil that they aimed to conquer by military force in the 1930s. They have prospered in peaceful consequence." Among trading states, Rosecrance observes, "the incentive to wage war is absent."[26] Put another way, free trade furnishes the economic advantages of conquest without the unpleasantness of invasion and the sticky responsibility of imperial control.

Thus war is unlikely if countries take prosperity as their chief goal *and* if they come to believe that trade is the best way to achieve that goal. Thanks in part to the success of economists, both propositions have now gained wide currency.

Furthermore, although war has hardly evaporated from the planet, it is worth noting that the advanced nations of the world have avoided war with each other for the longest period of time since the days of the Roman Empire, a remarkable development that is partly (though certainly not entirely) due to the increasing joint acceptance of propositions 1 and 2. Thomas Jefferson once referred to Europe as "an arena of gladiators," and countries like France and Germany once seemed to spend almost all their time either preparing for wars against each other or fighting them. But they have now lived—and prospered—side by side for over half a century without even a glimmer of war talk. Whether this will set the pattern for the rest of the world remains to be seen, but it is certainly of interest and may be of consequence that areas like Latin America and east and southeast Asia, where wars were endemic for decades after World War II, have now opted for peace and, not unrelatedly, for the banal pleasures of economic development.[27]

3. International Trade Should Be Free: From Adam Smith to Bill Clinton

One may accept economic development as a primary motivation and agree that exchange is a better way to prosper than conquest, but one could still conclude that prosperity is best achieved by restricting imports in order to favor and protect local enterprises—the once-dominant mercantilist view. Free trade, in fact, has been a hard sell, but at the end of the twentieth century it seems to have emerged triumphant, and the active proselytizing of the economics profession has probably been especially crucial in this important development.[28]

In 1993, the American president, Bill Clinton, committed one of the greatest acts of political heroism in the nation's history: energetic (and successful) support for approval of the North American Free Trade Agreement. He was well positioned politically to finesse and evade the issue and was urged to do so by many of his political advisers. Nevertheless, he decided to counter not only this recommendation but also the adamant desires of one of his party's most important supporters, organized labor, as well as those of many of his party's major figures including the majority leader in the House of Representatives.[29] (It is not true that "only Nixon could have gone to China"—Democratic presidents before him tried several times to improve relations with that country only to find the door closed—but it does seem likely that no Republican could have amassed the necessary (mainly Democratic) votes in Congress to pass NAFTA.)[30] As far as I can see, Clinton took up this painful and difficult task for only one reason: he had come to the conclusion that NAFTA—and, more generally, free trade—was good for the country in the long term.

From this remarkable achievement Clinton (predictably) gained no notable electoral advantage. Indeed, his advocacy chiefly inspired the (temporary) hostility of labor which seems to have been inclined to sit on its hands in the 1994 elections, something that may have helped bring about the losses Clinton's Democrats sustained in that contest. However, by his actions Clinton strongly put the Democratic imprimatur on the notion of free trade, got the world off its decades-long delay on advancing the General Agreement on Tariffs and Trade, and essentially put a consensual cap on a notion that economists had gradually come to accept over the two centuries since the publication in 1776 of Adam Smith's *Wealth of Nations*.[31]

Thus, by the end of the twentieth century the world has come substantially to embrace the idea, not only that wealth is enhanced by exchange rather than by conquest as in proposition 2, but that unfettered trade between countries is the best way for everyone to prosper. There will, of course, be countless bobbings and weavings, and even some notable setbacks, on this principle in specific application as countries jockey to obtain the best deal in a rapidly changing world. But what is important is that the basic idea seems substantially to have been accepted.

In many ways, the increasing acceptance of free trade is quite remarkable because political logic is notably on the side of protectionists and mercantilists. After all, domestic businesses (and labor organizations) have great clout in a country's politics while foreign businesses generally have little, and the locals should be able to use their advantageous position to keep foreign competition out.[32] In addition, the businesses and workers who will be hurt by cheaper or better foreign products are likely to know who they are, while those who will gain from exports are less likely to be aware of their advantage since the benefits are likely to materialize only in the long term. Moreover, even if a firm does find a market abroad and thus has an incentive to lobby for free trade, the firm is often likely to discover soon that entrepreneurs in the nation to which is it exporting espy its success, set up local competition, and then pressure their government to close out the hapless innovative foreigner. Finally, free traders are up against the sentimental, intuitive appeal of autarky or self-sufficiency, concepts that go back at least to Aristotle and have been dominant for millennia.[33]

Deeply awed by such obstacles, George Stigler suggested gloomily in 1975 that free trade was "unattainable without a fundamental restructuring of the political system." No such restructuring has taken place. Yet, although Clinton was surely well aware that free trade was a politically incorrect venture, he still went ahead with it. It seems to me that the chief reason he and other otherwise sensible politicians have been willing to bear that pain is that they have finally—and understandably, rather reluctantly—bought the free-trade line that has been consensually touted for decades now by economists. As a certifiable policy wonk, Clinton has undoubtedly heard and ingested the arguments economists make about why free trade is a good idea, but he is not an economist himself, has never made a systematic analysis of the idea on his own, and has probably never even read a technical study of the issue. Chiefly, I suspect, he favors free trade (even to the point of risking his political life on the issue) because, like the patient who dutifully swallows the distasteful medicine prescribed by the authoritative physician, he trusts the expert consensus.[34]

Economist Paul Krugman considers free trade to be "as close to a sacred tenet as any idea in economics," and Milton Friedman agrees: "no subject has so united economists since Adam Smith's *Wealth of Nations* was published in 1776 as belief in the virtues of free trade." Unfortunately, Friedman noted in 1984, "that professional consensus has not prevented one country after another from imposing trade barriers."[35] But now, in considerable part because of Clinton's (and Friedman's) efforts, a substantial international consensus by policymakers on this issue does seem finally to have been achieved. Whatever waffling and backsliding there may be on the details of implementation, the general thrust and trend seem clear.

The relation between peace and trade. Although Kant and many others have proposed that trade enhances the prospects for peace, history does not suggest that this notion has much validity: most wars, after all, are civil conflicts, waged between groups which know each other only too well and trade with each other only too much.[36]

But a good case could be made for the opposite causal proposition: peace often leads to, or at any rate facilitates, trade. That is, peace ought to be seen not as a dependent, but rather as an independent, variable in the relationship.

For example, the long and historically unprecedented absence of war among the nations of Western Europe since 1945 has not been caused by their increasing economic harmony. Rather, their economic harmony has been caused, or at least expedited, by the peace they have enjoyed. Similarly, the rise of the multinational corporation and the building of the long-envisioned Channel Tunnel between France and Britain are the consequences of peace, not its cause.

Put the other way, international tensions and the prospect of international war have a strong dampening effect on trade. Each threatened nation has an incentive to cut itself off from the rest of the world economically in order to ensure that it can survive if international exchange is stifled by military conflict, and policies of autarky, self-reliance, and self-sufficiency are likely to be very appealing. In the peaceful modern trading world, however, such once-seductive notions have become to seem quaint.[37]

Similarly, the Cold War could be seen in part, as Edward Yardeni has pointed out, as a huge trade barrier.[38] With the demise of that politically derived and economically foolish construct, trade will be liberated. But it is peace that will have facilitated trade, not the opposite.

4. Economies Do Best When Governments Leave Them Substantially Free

As Japan has shown, one can accept free trade between nations while still maintaining that the domestic economy should still be kept under major governmental control. But, as the notion that international trade should be free and open has become increasingly accepted, so has the proposition that the domestic economy should also be free.

This is a fairly recent development. It has not been that long since Joseph Schumpeter famously and repeatedly declared "centralist socialism" to be the "heir apparent" to capitalism. In 1976, Fred Hirsch published a book about why the twentieth century had "seen a universal predominant trend toward collective provision and state regulation in economic areas," and around the same time Milton Friedman presented a paper (a very depressing one from his point of view) seeking to explain why collectivist beliefs flourish in the world of ideas.[39]

However, things have changed markedly since then. As economist Robert Heilbroner, not usually known as an ardent free-marketeer, noted only a few years ago: "There is today widespread agreement, including among most socialist economists, that whatever form advanced societies may take in the twenty-first century, a market system of some kind will constitute their principal means of coordination. That is a remarkable turnabout from the situation only a generation ago, when the majority of economists believed that the future of economic coordination lay in a diminution of the scope of the market, and an increase in some form of centralized planning." Likewise, in the words of an economist who *has* been a consistent free-marketeer, R. M. Hartwell, "The intellectual agenda about the role of the government has changed from one determined by the desirability of intervention to one determined by the desirability of market economy." The big question, he observes happily, is no longer "Why not more government, more public ownership, and more control and regulation of the market," but rather "Why not less government, more privatization, and less interference with the market?"[40]

These are particularly interesting observations in light of Henderson's assessment of the state of medicine in 1912. Essentially, Heilbroner and Hartwell are saying that, by the present state of economic knowledge, the random politician or governmental official consulting the random economist only a generation ago was likely to get the wrong advice: it would perhaps have been better, on average, to consult a reader of tea leaves or an astrologer.

Much of the most widely accepted economic thinking of the time derived from the work of John Maynard Keynes, whose central theme, according to his biographer, was "the state is wise and the market is stupid." Working from that sort of perspective, India's top economists for a generation supported policies of regulation and central control that failed abysmally—leading one of them to lament recently, "India's misfortune was to have brilliant economists." And Latin American economies were misdirected for decades by antimarket *dependencia* theory as forcefully and confidently advocated by well-regarded economists in the United Nations Economic Commission on Latin America. "I well remember," says Tony Judt, "sitting in the graduate lounge of Cambridge University in 1969 while a tenured member of the economics faculty assured us that the Chinese Cultural Revolution, then at its paroxysmic height, was the last best hope for humankind."[41]

In many respects the economic consensus Heilbroner and Hartwell note has burgeoned only recently, particularly after the abject and pathetic collapse of command and heavily planned economies in the late 1980s and early 1990s. As a top Indian economist put it recently, "Between the fall of the Berlin Wall in 1989 and the collapse of the Soviet Union in 1991, I felt as though I were awakening from a thirty-five-year dream. Everything I had believed about economic systems and tried to implement was wrong."[42]

The economic advice decision makers around the world are hearing, and increasingly are accepting, is to rely on the market rather than forcing upon it externally derived and politically comfortable concepts of fairness and justice. And with this acceptance, a set of alternative propositions about the virtues of revolution and about the justice possible through a command or heavily manipulated economy have effectively been scrapped as romantic, unrealistic, unproductive, and, increasingly, irrelevant.[43] In practice, all capitalist, or market capitalist, states, may not end up looking a great deal like each other, any more than all democracies do. In particular, the degree to which the government intervenes in the economy with tax and welfare policy, regulation, trade restrictions, price supports, and direct control over certain individual enterprises varies considerably. But the trend seems clear.

119

The new consensual approach can probably be summed up in one short phrase: "trust the market." Like the rise in international trade, this advice has been facilitated by a decline of war fears: as a prominent Italian economist has put it, "A state company has to do with war, national interest, and self-defense," whereas privatization "is driven by the absence of war, and by the opening of the international system that makes raw materials, money, and technology available to everyone."[44]

One of the principles that inform this advice, that international trade should be free, has already been discussed. Among the others seem to be the following:

Wages and prices should be allowed freely to find their own ranges and limits. It would be difficult to overestimate the economically pernicious effects of efforts to determine the "just wage" and the "just price" by nonmarket judgments. Yet for millennia prices were substantially set by custom, government, or the church, and the progressive abandonment of this intuitively appealing and hence politically correct approach has been one of the major achievements of modern economics—it is quite possibly the economic equivalent of the germ theory. And it has been a tough struggle. Rationing has enjoyed quite a bit of political appeal even in peacetime, and many politicians, like Harry Truman, have had a deep and abiding belief in wage and price controls; while a Republican president, Richard Nixon, suddenly reinstituted them as late as the 1970s.[45] The quest for the "just price" is still popular in some areas—over cable television rates, for example, and rent control lingers in a declining number of places—but, substantially, the battle has been won.

Government regulation is often unwise and can be counterproductive. For the most part, the quest for optimal regulation or for full-bore economic planning has been changed to a preference for reducing or even ending regulation and planning in many areas. Government may still sometimes play a helpful economic role by maintaining a viable justice system to enforce contracts and property rights and to police fraud and violent coercion, and it may also usefully seek to regulate matters of health and safety and to control socially undesirable side effects or externalities like air pollution—

though even here regulations designed to shape parameters to allow the market to do the hard work may well prove to be sounder than efforts to plan. But, as Yergin and Stanislaw put it, the idea would be to move the state away from being the "producer, controller, and intervenor" to being the "referee, setting the rules of the game to ensure, among other things, competition."[46]

The government should abandon enterprises that can be handled by the private sector. "Privatization" is a word that came into notable use only in the last decades of the twentieth century, intended to be used in pointed distinction to a much older word, "nationalization." The realization has taken hold that private enterprise simply does much better than the state at providing a whole series of goods and services—from communications to transportation to education to utilities to mail service to shipbuilding—that many once felt could be provided better, and more justly, by the state. Privatization has been a key development in the postcommunist states, and even the highly entrenched welfare states of Western Europe have sold off over a hundred billion dollars in state assets since 1985.[47]

High taxes, especially at the top, can be economically counterproductive, and capricious or discretionary ones almost always are. The campaign against confiscatory and discretionary expropriation, which was once a standard practice by rulers around the world, has been a long and arduous one even though, as noted in the previous chapter, tax restraint has almost always been to the long-term economic advantage of the confiscators.[48]

A considerable amount of economic inequality is inevitable and essentially desirable. Government may sometimes play a useful social or safety net role by cushioning pain through the judicious transfer of some degree of wealth from the economically successful to the unsuccessful.[49] But the communist experience suggests that efforts to induce true economic equality are likely to fail and, to the degree they are successful, to exact a cost—often a very considerable one—in economic growth.

Uncompetitive enterprises should not be subsidized and should be allowed to fail. This notion is, of course, extremely painful politically, but the disastrous experiences in the Soviet Union and elsewhere (in India a major state fertilizer company with twelve hundred employees, completed in 1979, had by 1991 yet to produce any fertilizer for sale) have helped economists to underscore its wisdom.[50]

Government spending should be kept reasonably low and government deficits should be kept under control. A form of the welfare state remains in place in all developed countries, but the belief that such spending can very detrimentally get out of hand seems increasingly to be accepted, and some of the most entrenched welfare states are judiciously trimming back.[51]

Principles like these centrally informed the successful advice given to the postcommunist states and to others seeking economic growth, and they have often been considered counterintuitive, immoral, or unjust. But these notions, however politically painful, seem increasingly to be accepted by policymakers and politicians around the world.[52]

Of course, the gathering—indeed, gathered—consensus among economists does not mean there is no room for debate. There may be controversy, for example, over the desirable trade-offs between growth and the distribution of wealth, or over whether it is better to go for maximum growth or to sacrifice some development in order to reduce the amplitude of the boom-and-bust cycles around an upward path, or over how high a government's deficit can rise without stifling the economy, or over the degree to which a regulation will hurt more than it will help, or over what rate of inflation is most desirable. But, substantially and increasingly, the debate is likely to be more nearly a matter of degree than of fundamental principles.

The Prospects for Massive Economic Growth

If it is true that economists now generally know what they are talking about and if it is true that policymakers are now substantially and increasingly willing, however reluctantly, to accept and act upon their often counterintuitive and politically painful advice, the prospects for major economic advances in all—or virtually all—corners of the globe are highly favorable. This expansion would go beyond even the optimistic predictions based essentially on projecting into the future the economic development much of the world has experienced over the last two centuries as seen in figure 4.1 (p. 74). As the state of medical knowledge at the turn of the current century portended major health improvements in the century to come, we may now be on the verge of similar advances in the area of economic growth as we enter the next one.

Of course, there is no way to be sure that economists really know what they are talking about, any more than one could have been certain a century ago that Henderson and Osler were correct about the state of contemporary medical science. It is, I suppose, possible that the economists' current affinity for markets will prove as faddish and unsound as the bias many of them once showed toward planning, regulation, and trade restrictions. If so, we are in big trouble to the extent that their advice is increasingly being accepted by decision makers. However, judging from the depth of the emerging consensus and in particular from the frequent successes of economic analysis and advice in recent years, I find it reasonable to propose that this time, at long last, the economists may very well have gotten it right, and that the consequent benefits to the well-being of the planet's population could be enormous.

ECONOMIC DEVELOPMENT, PROFESSED HAPPINESS,
AND THE CATASTROPHE QUOTA

A considerable expansion of economic well-being does not mean people will feel—or at any rate say they feel—happier, however.

Aristotle once argued that "The happy man is one whose activity accords with perfect virtue and who is adequately furnished with external goods." Or in the words of a Slovak filmmaker, "It is better to be rich and healthy than poor and sick." Or, as Pearl Bailey put it even more succinctly, "I've been rich, and I've been poor, and rich is better."[53]

If people will be furnished with external goods in the next century to a degree scarcely imaginable even by our present standards of affluence, it might seem to follow that, as long as virtue at least holds its own, people will become much happier. The evidence, however, suggests that this will not occur.

Three Conclusions about Happiness

Happiness, or a sense of well-being, is a rather elusive quality, but insofar as it can be specified and measured in public opinion surveys, there seem to be three reasonably clear conclusions.

1. People profess to hold economic considerations important when they assess the degree to which they are happy. When people in various countries are asked about happiness and their personal concerns, economic matters—including such issues as the standard of living and housing—tend to be the most often mentioned. Not surprisingly, health also scores highly as do family and personal relationships.[54]

2. Moreover, wealthier people are more likely to profess being happy than poorer ones in the same society. One survey of the happiness literature describes as "overwhelming" the amount of evidence showing that there is a positive—though sometimes not a very high—correlation between income on the one hand and happiness and other measures of subjective well-being on the other. This relationship holds even when other variables such as education are controlled.[55]

3. However, when a country grows economically, the professions of its people as to their state of happiness do not similarly grow. The very considerable economic growth the United States experienced in the postwar era was not associated with a corresponding increase in professions of happiness in public opinion surveys. Data from Western Europe from the 1970s and 1980s suggest much the same thing.[56]

One study, however, argues that these results are not surprising because they deal with economic improvement in areas that were already comparatively affluent. It contends that a notable rise in happiness in England, France, the Netherlands, and West Germany took place between the terrible immediate postwar years and the 1960s or 1970s. Thus, it is concluded, the wealth-happiness connection is subject "to the law of diminishing returns": once a person is adequately furnished with external goods, in Aristotle's phraseology, further increases in happiness do not take place.[57]

At best, of course, this suggests that happiness will increase only when a country moves from misery to some degree of economic security and that little additional gain is to be expected thereafter. But, as Richard Easterlin notes, even this conclusion is questionable when one looks at data from Japan. By 1958, that country had substantially recovered from the war, but it sported an income level lower than or equal to ones found in many developing countries today. During the next thirty years, Japan experienced a truly spectacular economic resurgence in which real per capita income multiplied fivefold and in which the benefits of economic growth were quite widely spread throughout the population. Yet there was little or no increase in Japanese happiness ratings.[58]

Four Explanations for the Remarkable Inability of Economic Growth to Inspire Professions of Happiness

If economic growth is what it is all about, then, the world is likely soon to experience massive improvement. But if happiness (or at any rate professions thereof) is what it is all about, it won't.

There seem to be several possible explanations for this curiously infelicitous state of affairs about felicity.

1. It is relative wealth, not absolute wealth, that matters. In exploring this explanation, Easterlin has ferreted out a crisp observation by Karl Marx: "A house may be large or small; as long as the surrounding houses are equally small it satisfies all social demands for a dwelling. But if a palace rises beside the little house, the little house shrinks to a hut." Thus, the argument runs, people may use a relative standard, not an absolute one, when assessing their well-being. If everybody's wealth increases at more or less the same rate, accordingly, relative incomes remain the same, and so does happiness. There exists a "consumption norm," suggests Easterlin, and one gauges one's happiness relative to this norm, not to the norm's absolute placement.[59]

But this cannot be the full explanation. After all, health is also an important component in happiness self-evaluations, and while people may think of wealth in relative terms, they are unlikely to think of health in the same way. That is, people simply do or do

125

not feel healthy, and the health of others is likely to be quite irrelevant to their judgment on this issue. Since health has been improving at least as impressively as income in places like the United States, happiness should be going up even if people adopt a relative standard with respect to the wealth component of the happiness calculation. But it isn't.

There is a difference, of course, between the two issues in that one can imagine a maximum, satiated condition of health but not necessarily of wealth (moreover, sick people are obviously less likely than poor ones to be interviewed in surveys). However, concerns about one's future must play a role in health considerations, just as they do in ones about wealth. Thus, healthy people in, say, the 1940s should have found their happiness tainted a bit by fears that they or their children could at any moment come down with polio. When medical science cured that problem, people should, to that degree, have become happier; but they didn't.

2. Nonmaterial concerns dominate perceptions of happiness. The observation that happiness does not increase when material well-being increases has logically led to the conclusion that material well-being is not very important to people's sense of happiness. Angus Campbell adopts such a point of view and concludes that happiness is positively related to status and marriage and to having family, friends, and a satisfying job.[60]

But economic and health considerations are clearly of very considerable importance in personal assessments of happiness and well-being, as noted above. And, since there have been enormous improvements in wealth and health in the United States and other surveyed countries, the failure of happiness to rise cannot be due to other factors unless it can be shown that these have greatly deteriorated over the same period of time—something Campbell does not find.[61]

3. Material accumulation leads not to satisfaction, but to boredom and discontent. Tibor Scitovsky argues that prosperity, particularly in the United States, is simply not very satisfying—that it has led not to contentment and pleasure, but to leisure-induced boredom and then to rebellion, drug-taking, violence, and environmental deterioration. People, he suggests, seek "satisfaction in the wrong things, or in the wrong way, and then are dissatisfied with the outcome."[62]

This perspective distrusts prosperity—a process in which people are bountifully and indiscriminately supplied at an attractive price with the things they happen to think they want. The concern is that, in a world that lacks danger and stimulating challenge, people will come to wallow in luxury and to give in to hedonism (some may even be tempted to slouch toward Gomorrah). In the process, not only do their minds rot, but they wallow in malaise, ennui, and Weltschmerz until they become dissatisfied and unhappy.

It is an old fear for successful capitalism, a fear voiced even by some of its champions. Adam Smith anticipated that as workers came to concentrate on repetitive tasks, they would "become as stupid and ignorant as it is possible for a human creature to become" and be rendered incapable of exercising "invention" or "of conceiving any generous, noble, or tender sentiment." Similarly, Alexis de Tocqueville was concerned that when "the love of property" becomes sufficiently "ardent," people will come to regard "every innovation as an irksome toil," "mankind will be stopped and circumscribed," the mind "will swing backwards and forwards forever without begetting fresh ideas," "man will waste his strength in bootless and solitary trifling," and, though in continual motion, "humanity will cease to advance." In this century Joseph Schumpeter opined that managers would lose vigor and initiative as they became embedded in huge bureaucracies.[63]

There may be something to such concerns, but they would lead one to anticipate that happiness should actually decline in affluent areas, something that hasn't happened.[64] In addition, they tend to square rather poorly with indications that the world's economy is becoming increasingly, not decreasingly, competitive and that human capital—drive, intelligence, innovation, and risk-taking initiative—is fast becoming the quality in greatest demand. Intellectuals who consider business to be boring, mindlessly repetitive, unsatisfying, or lacking in daring, courage, and imagination have never tried to run—much less start—one.

4. Improvements in well-being are effectively unappreciated: the catastrophe quota. I have yet to run into an American over the age of forty-seven who regularly observes, "You know, if I had been born in the nineteenth century, I'd very probably be dead by now." Nobody really thinks in such terms, yet the statement is completely true—and, of course, I don't mean in the sense that just about everybody who happened to be born in the last century is no longer with us, but that life expectancy in the United States as late as 1900 was forty-seven years.

It is often observed that people don't appreciate their health until they get sick, their freedom until they lose it, their wealth until it is threatened, their teeth until they ache. In other words, when things get better, we quickly come to take the improvements for granted after a brief period of assimilation: they become ingested and seem part of our due, our place in life.

Occasionally, people in affluent societies might pause to wonder how they, or anyone, ever got along without air conditioning, credit cards, faxes, EKGs, jet transportation, frozen pizza, VCRs, garbage disposals, cable television, automatic money machines, flu shots, Vanna White, laser surgery, thermal underwear, telephone answering machines, or quilted toilet paper, but on those rare occasions, the pause is brief, the observation is generally something of a joke, and few are willing seriously to concede that at least some of these eagerly accepted additions to their lives might somehow have made them happier. As Ludwig von Mises puts it philosophically: "Under capitalism the common man enjoys amenities which in ages past gone by were unknown and therefore inaccessible even to the richest people. But, of course, these motorcars, television sets and refrigerators do not make a man happy. In the instant in which he acquires them, he may feel happier than he did before. But as soon as some of his wishes are satisfied, new wishes spring up. Such is human nature."[65]

Lebergott proposes that if every economically significant good added since 1900 were to disappear, and if the remaining items—like salt pork, lard, and houses without running water—were marked down to 1900 prices, few would judge their economic welfare to have improved. Yet nostalgic images of, say, 1900 American life rarely remember rotten teeth, or note that each day at least three billion flies were created in cities by horse manure. Instead there is a tendency to look back at the past myopically, forgetting its complexities, horrors, and inconveniences, and often bathing it in a golden glow.[66] As part of this, we like to view the past as a simpler time, though the plays of Shakespeare and Aeschylus rather tend to suggest that people in olden times really did have some pretty complicated problems. Similarly, successful people in the postcommunist countries often complain that they now spend so much time accumulating wealth that they are no longer able to spend long evenings with friends drinking cheap vodka and talking and laughing.[67] Complaints like this arise even though economic development generally increases options; it does not close them off. As the Amish have shown, it would still be entirely possible to reject economic change and to wile away evenings unproductively with friends. Opportunities may increase, but that doesn't mean one has necessarily to reject the old ones.

A systematic, if quiet, process of standard raising also takes place. A label poised above an old carpet sweeper on display in an exhibit in the Strong Museum in Rochester, N.Y., observes, "Labor-saving devices like carpet sweepers helped middle-class people satisfy their desire for cleanliness within the home." Lest one conclude that this was an improvement however, the label writer quickly adds, "Unfortunately, each new development raised standards and expectations for cleanliness, making the ideal as hard as ever to achieve."[68]

The media may play something of a role in all this. Good news often doesn't sell well. For example, life expectancy at birth for Americans rose in 1993 to a record 75.5 years, a fact the *New York Times* found so boring that it simply reprinted an Associated Press dispatch on the issue and buried it on the thirteenth page of its September 1 issue. The *Atlantic*, seems addicted to articles like "The Crisis of Public Order," "The Drift Toward Disaster," "The Coming Anarchy," and "The Coming Plague," and the editors will only be truly happy, some suggest, when they come across an authoritative article entitled, "World Ends, Experts Say." Sensitive to such proclivities, a *New Yorker* wag once proposed as the first line of a poem: "Harm's bordello is the op-ed page."[69] In part because of such press proclivities, the remarkable long-term trends documented in Figures 4.1 and 5.1 often surprise people.

129

The political process is also essentially devoted to bringing out the bad news. Incumbents may often like to stress the positive, but challengers can't—they must work very hard to ferret out things that are wrong and that, at the same time, concern a fair number of voters. If they are successful in this, it would be impolitic for the incumbents simply to dismiss the voters' concern. They must agree, or appear to agree, that the problem is genuine and then propose a solution that seems superior to the one proposed by the challenger. The process leads to nice anomalies: air quality in the United States has improved markedly over the last decades—yet most people think (and many people seem to *want* to think) that the opposite is true.[70]

Moreover, although some advances, like the end of the Cold War, can come about with dazzling speed and drama, many improvements of the human condition are quite gradual and therefore difficult to notice. Rosenberg and Birdzell observe that the remarkable transformation of the West from a condition in which 90 percent lived in poverty to one in which the incidence of poverty was reduced to 20 or 30 percent of the population or less took a very long time: "Over a year, or even over a decade, the economic gains, after allowing for the rise in population, were so little noticeable that it was widely believed that the gains were experienced only by the rich, and not by the poor. Only as the West's compounded growth continued through the twentieth century did its breadth become clear."[71] Clearly, the same can be said for the massive improvements in life expectancy over the last century that have proved to be so easy to ignore.

In result of all this, the catastrophe quota always seems to remain comfortably full. When a major problem is resolved or eliminated or eased substantially or when a major improvement is made, there may be a brief period of reflective comment, but then problems previously considered small are quickly elevated in perceived importance.

Nowhere is this clearer than in international affairs where the Cold War and the threat of nuclear holocaust have evaporated in recent years to the distinct inconvenience of doomsayers everywhere. But with scarcely a pause for breath they have adroitly come up with a list of "new" problems to plague us in our "new world disorder"—for example, "the proliferation of weapons of mass destruction and the ballistic missiles to carry them; ethnic and national hatreds that can metastasize across large portions of the globe; the international narcotics trade; terrorism; the dangers inherent in the West's dependence on mideast oil; new economic and environmental challenges."[72] But wars deriving from ethnic and national hatreds are neither new nor increasing in frequency in the world, and nuclear proliferation is no more a new problem—in fact, may well be less of a problem—than it was in 1960 when John Kennedy repeatedly pointed out with alarm that there might be ten, fifteen, or twenty nations with a nuclear capacity by 1964.[73] And the international drug trade has obviously been around for quite some time, while the West's supposedly dangerous dependence on Mideast oil has been a matter of pointed concern at least since 1973. The impact of terrorism has often been more in the exaggerated hysteria it generates than in its actual physical effects—fewer Americans are killed by international terrorists than are killed by lightning.[74] Economic and environmental challenges are hardly new either, but new alarms can be raised.

And if these concerns don't seem alarming enough, we can always hark back to the time when we could ventilate about the government's budget deficit, a problem chiefly caused by the fact that people were living too long: improved medical care not only generated a wonderful new problem to complain about (for a while at least), but supplied the average American with nearly thirty additional years of lifetime in which to do so.[75]

As prosperity expands, we will also be nicely poised to become concerned that people will become overwhelmed, even paralyzed by the array of choices confronting them in the marketplace. One pundit asserts that "As social scientists, we know that with an increase in choices, people tend to become more anxious"; a sociologist points out that "If you have infinite choice, people are reduced to passivity"; and a futurist ominously worries about "overchoice—the point at which the advantage of diversity and individualization are canceled by the complexity of the buyer's decision-making process." Clearly, if Hamlet was faced by only two alternatives and found himself agonizing over it for five full acts, we must be far, far worse off today. This conundrum seems to be an updated version of the classic philosophic puzzle known as "Buridan's ass" in which the animal is placed at an equal distance from two bundles of hay and eventually starves to death in terminal indecision.[76] There seems to be no evidence any ass ever actually underwent this agony, but the information thus far is merely anecdotal, and this might well be one of those many issues crying out for well-funded systematic research. (Such research, however, might sometimes find that the problem solves itself: if customers in supermarkets become paralyzed with indecision in front of, for example, the corn flakes, they will block the aisles, threatening the profits of the store owner who will then logically be forced to increase the aisle space, reducing in turn the choice angst confronting the customers.)

DEVELOPMENT AND THE QUEST FOR HAPPINESS

In the end, however, there may be benefits to the endless, and endlessly successful, quest to raise standards and to fabricate new desires to satisfy and new issues to worry about. Not only does this quest keep the mind active, but it probably importantly drives, and has driven, economic development as well. Rosenberg and Birdzell find it unlikely that a "self-satisfied people could move from poverty to wealth in the first place," and David Hume observes that commerce "rouses men from their indolence" as it presents them with "objects of luxury, which they never before dreamed of," raising in them a desire for "a more splendid way of life than what their ancestors enjoyed."[77]

By contrast, Richard Easterlin puts a rather negative spin on all this when he applies the phrase, "hedonic treadmill," to the process and concludes that "each step upward on the ladder of economic development merely stimulates new economic desires that lead the chase ever onward." The word "treadmill" suggests an enveloping tedium as well as a lack of substantive progress. However, the "chase" not only enhances economic development, but often has invigorating appeals of its own. As Hume notes, when industry flourishes people "enjoy, as their reward, the occupation itself, as well as those pleasures which are the fruit of their labour." As part of this process, "the mind acquires more vigour" and "enlarges its power and faculties."[78]

Moreover, there is no evidence that economic development exhausts the treaders, lowers their happiness, or inspires many effective efforts to turn back the clock. Professions of happiness may not soar, but, despite the anguished protests of some intellectuals, people do not seem to have much difficulty enduring a condition of ever-increasing life expectancy and ever-expanding material prosperity.

DEMOCRACY

*

* CHAPTER 6 *

Images and Definitions

THERE IS a famous Norman Rockwell painting that purports to portray democracy in action. It depicts a New England town meeting in which a workingman has risen in a contentious situation to present his point of view. His rustic commonsense, it appears, has cut through the indecisiveness and bickering to provide a consensual solution to the problem at hand, and the others in the picture are looking up at him admiringly.

As it happens, that misty-eyed, idealized snapshot has almost nothing to do with democracy in actual practice. Democracy is not a process in which one shining idea conquers all as erstwhile contenders fall into blissful consensus. Rather, it is an extremely disorderly muddle in which clashing ideas and interests (all of them "special") do unkempt and unequal, if peaceful, battle and in which ideas are often reduced to slogans, data to distorted fragments, evidence to gestures, and arguments to poses. Speculation is rampant, caricature is routine, and posturing is de rigueur. If one idea wins out, it is likely to be severely compromised in the process, and no one goes away entirely reconciled or happy. And there is rarely a sense of completion or finality or permanence: in a democracy, as Tod Lindberg points out, "the fat lady never sings."[1] It's a mess, and the only saving grace is that other methods for reaching decisions are even worse.

In this chapter I develop an approach to democracy that contrasts substantially with the romantic Rockwell ideal. It stresses petition and lobbying—the chaotic and distinctly nonconsensual combat of "special interests"—as the dominant and central characteristic of democracy and it suggests that while elections are useful and often valuable in a democracy, they may not be absolutely necessary. I also argue that democracy in practice is not about equality, but rather about the freedom to become politically unequal, and that it functions not so much by rule by the majority as

137

by minority rule with majority acquiescence, qualities which have productively allowed it to coopt, rather than to alienate, the rich. In the process I explore the possible virtues of apathy.

I also contrast democracy with other governmental forms. Although the advantage is only comparative, democracy seems to do better at generating effective governments, choosing leaders, addressing minority concerns, creating a livable society, and functioning effectively with real, flawed human beings. The following two chapters then assess some of the consequences of the image mismatch between the ideal Rockwellian caricature and grim democratic reality.

DEFINING DEMOCRACY: RESPONSIVE GOVERNMENT

In defining democracy, it is particularly important, I think, to separate the essential institution itself from the operating devices that are commonly associated with it—mechanisms like written constitutions, the separation of powers or "checks and balances" (including an independent judiciary), and even elections. Any definition of democracy is inadequate, I think, if it can logically be taken to suggest that Britain (which has neither a written constitution nor separation of powers) is not a democracy or that Switzerland did not become one until 1971 (when women were finally given the vote).[2]

For example, Samuel Huntington defines "a twentieth-century political system as democratic to the extent that its most powerful collective decision-makers are selected through fair, honest, and periodic elections in which candidates freely compete for votes and in which virtually all the adult population is eligible to vote." This definition, with its entangling focus on elections and mass suffrage, would exclude everything known as a democracy before the twentieth century, as he suggests in his definition, as well as very many putative democracies during it including Switzerland.[3]

By contrast, it seems to me that what is essential to democracy is that the government be routinely and necessarily responsive. The crucial point of democracy is not to have constitutions or a separation of governmental powers or even to hold elections. Rather,

138

it is to create, in Abraham Lincoln's classic phrase, something that resembles "government of the people, by the people, for the people."

This perspective is central to several definitions and approaches. Among political scientists, Robert Dahl says, "I assume that a key characteristic of a democracy is the continued responsiveness of the government to the preferences of its citizens, considered as political equals," and William Riker concludes that "democracy is a form of government in which the rulers are fully responsible to the ruled in order to realize self-respect for everybody." Historian Robert Wiebe finds democracy's "core" in the notion that it "entails some version of popular self-government that assures citizens access to the political process, never bars losers from that process, and keeps officials responsive to their constituents." Or in H. L. Mencken's irreverent pronouncement, democracy is "the theory that the common people know what they want, and deserve to get it good and hard."[4]

In my view, democracy is characterized by government that is necessarily and routinely responsive—although this responsiveness is not always even, fair, or equal. It comes into effect when the people effectively agree not to use violence to replace the leadership, and the leadership effectively leaves them free to criticize, to pressure, to organize, and to try to dislodge it by any other means. This approach can be used to set up a sort of sliding scale of governmental forms. An *authoritarian* government may effectively and sometimes intentionally allow a degree of opposition—a limited amount of press disagreement, for example, or the freedom to complain privately, something sometimes known as the freedom of conversation. But it will not tolerate organized attempts to replace it, even if they are peaceful. A *totalitarian* government does not allow even those limited freedoms. On the other end of the scale is *anarchy:* a condition which holds when a government "allows" the use of violence to try to overthrow it—presumably mainly out of weakness or ineffectiveness.

Authoritarian and even totalitarian governments can sometimes be responsive as well, of course. But their responsiveness depends on the will and the mindset of the leadership. By contrast, democracy is *routinely, necessarily* responsive: because people are free to develop and use peaceful methods to criticize, pressure, and replace the leadership, the leaders must pay attention to their critics and petitioners.

It seems to me that the formal and informal institutional mechanisms variously applied in democracies to facilitate this core consideration are secondary—though this does not mean that all institutions are equally fair or efficient. One can embellish this central democratic relationship with concerns about ethos, way of life, social culture, shared goals, economic correlates, common purposes, customs, preferred policy outcomes, norms, patriotism, shared traditions, and the like. These issues are interesting, but, as will be discussed more fully later, they don't seem to be essential or necessary to the functioning of democracy.[5]

ELECTIONS: USEFUL, BUT NOT ESSENTIAL

Dahl and Riker emphasize elections as a device to make democratic responsiveness happen—indeed, Riker argues that "the essential democratic institution is the ballot box and all that goes with it."[6] But it really does seem that if citizens have the right to complain, to petition, to organize, to protest, to demonstrate, to strike, to threaten to emigrate or secede, to shout, to publish, to export their funds, to express a lack of confidence, and to wheedle in back corridors, government will tend to respond to the sounds of the shouters and the importunings of the wheedlers: that is, it will necessarily become responsive—pay attention—whether there are elections or not.

There are plenty of nonviolent methods for removing officeholders besides elections. Governments often topple or are effectively threatened by scandal, legal challenge, formal petition, letter writing, street protest, pointed behavior at public meetings, embarrassment, strikes, capital flight, mass demonstrations, economic boycott or slowdown, threats to emigrate or secede, stock-market collapse, or other expressions of loss of confidence by key sections of the population.

The addition of elections to this panoply of devices may some-times change policy outcomes, and it probably makes the enter-prise more efficient in some sense because elections furnish a spe-cific, clearly visible, and direct method for replacing officeholders. Elections—fair and free ones, at any rate—also may make the process more just, at least by some standards, because they extend participation to those who only care enough about what's going on to meander to the polls every few years to pull a few levers or make a few X's (though the weight of an individual's vote on pol-icymaking is so small that the act of voting might be considered to be scarcely a rational use of one's time), and because they give a bit of potential clout to those who don't vote but could do so if suf-ficiently riled or inspired. Gerald Pomper aptly observes that "the effect of elections is to require government to pay greater atten-tion to unorganized mass groups and comparatively less to elite groups of smaller numbers." But, as he suggests, the difference is simply comparative and, "like any political device, popular elec-tions will tend to protect some interests more than others."[7]

In the end, most of what democratic governments actually do on a day-by-day basis is the result of pressure and petition—lobbying, it's called—and of their own reactions and policy initiatives. As Stephen Bailey observes in a classic study, majority opinion as ex-pressed in elections "can be, and frequently is, almost hopelessly splintered by the power struggles of competing political, adminis-trative, and private interests, and is finally pieced together, if at all, only by the most laborious, complicated, and frequently covert coalition strategies."[8]

As this suggests, the policy message of elections is almost always ambiguous and often utterly undecipherable: "votes," observes one analysis, "communicate little information about the concerns and priorities of the voter." For example, after the 1994 elections in the United States the victorious Republicans claimed they had been given a mandate to carry out the promises outlined in their prominent campaign document, the "Contract with America." Yet a month after the election a national poll found that 72 percent of the public claimed never to have heard or read anything about the highly touted Contract. Four months later, after endless publicity over the varying fortunes of the Contract, that number had not changed at all.[9]

Petitioners can sometimes use the threat of elections, implied or otherwise, to influence officeholders. And in some democracies contributions toward campaign expenses can help petitioners to facilitate access or to affect policy (a phenomenon that many see as a perversion). But the essential interaction between government and citizenry can take place without elections if the right of petition is viable and if people have the right to organize and to devise peaceful methods to pressure and overthrow officials.

Suppose, for example, that a governmental system were formed in which all authority were vested in a single person or group whose tenure in office was at the mercy of a sort of supreme court or council of elders whose duty it was to listen to, and weigh, the complaints and concerns of the citizenry who would be completely free to speak, publish, organize, demonstrate, and complain as long as they did so nonviolently. Even though there would be no elections under that system, it seems to me it would be essentially democratic: the government would be routinely and necessarily responsive to the concerns of the public.

Indeed, people excluded from participation in elections often have nevertheless profoundly affected policy if they had the right to petition and protest. A prime instance is the feminist movement, which achieved many of its goals—including eventually votes for women—even though the vast majority of its members were excluded from the electorate. As this experience demonstrates, it is absurd to suggest that people who are barred from voting can have no impact on public policy.

Moreover, there exist cases of what might be called democracies without elections: Mexico and British Hong Kong. People go to the polls in Mexico, of course, but the ruling party counts the ballots and for decades, curiously enough, never lost an election (though in most cases the ruling party probably would have won even if the ballots had been counted fairly). In Hong Kong, the government was appointed from afar. Yet in both places people have been free to petition and protest and organize, and the governments can be said in a quite meaningful sense to have been responsive to the will and needs of the population. Elections might shade or reshape policy in one way or another, and some democrats would undoubtedly deem the result to be more just, but the essential responsiveness is already there.

Thus, although they are fully aware of Mexico's electoral defects and although they document the fact that Mexicans have been equally aware of these defects, Gabriel Almond and Sidney Verba have no difficulty accepting Mexico as a functioning democracy in a classic study. As one Mexican observer has put it, "we have democracy 364 days a year and lack it only on one day—election day." Not ideal perhaps, but not all that bad as averages go. Mexico's record toward opposition voices is hardly perfect, but for the most part, political leaders are responsive: they "find out what their potential constituents want and establish a reputation for taking care of problems," observes Martin Needler, and, because of "the ideological range embraced by the Mexican ruling class and its ideological inclusiveness," the able dissident is generally coopted, rather than ostracized or suppressed. Similarly, Robert Scott notes that "the extent of accommodation of interest provided by Mexico's political mechanisms is little short of amazing."[10] Although elections may often have been fixed, people have still been substantially free in other ways, and the ruling party has usually responded to notable nonviolent dissent not by (undemocratic) suppression, but by buying off or coopting potential opponents, and it has shown a considerable desire to give people a sense that it cares about their welfare.

In Hong Kong, rulers were traditionally sensitive to vigilant and entrenched business elites who, in turn, helped to keep the rest of the population docile, reasonably content, and politically apathetic. When the government signed a treaty in 1984 promising to hand the colony over to China in 1997, however, this traditional apathy was substantially overcome as treaty opponents screamed loudly, organized pressure groups, signed petitions, staged mass demonstrations, and pointedly threatened to emigrate. An authoritarian government would have responded by suppressing the protest and jailing its leaders, but in Hong Kong the rulers acted like democrats: they listened, and they tried to mollify and coopt the protest movement by giving in to some of its demands and by letting it compete for some previously appointed leadership positions. When the opponents did well in this competition, the government further responded by replacing some of its hardline appointees with apolitical professionals.[11]

Although the government in Hong Kong was responsive, in the end, of course, it did not deliver on the central demand that Hong Kong remain independent of China. Responsiveness means that the government will necessarily and routinely pay attention to notable pressure, not that pressuring groups will inevitably get their way. Like the appealing and enduring yearnings for governments to at once lower taxes and increase expenditures, the demand that Hong Kong should remain independent, while highly attractive politically, was essentially unfulfillable.

Elections are, of course, a standard device in democracy, and they certainly do assist its functioning. But the cases of Mexico and British Hong Kong suggest that democracy can effectively flourish if people are free even if open and competitive elections are not held. On the other hand, if the freedom to speak, publish, protest, and organize is restricted, a country ceases to be a democracy by any definition. Thus, severe restrictions on the rights of speech and petition (as well as the vote) of blacks in the American South for much of its history and in South Africa for almost all of its history, suggest that those areas could not be considered democracies by either standard.

It is vital in a democracy that the right peacefully to speak, petition, publish, and organize be preserved, and the courts obviously can be an important part of that process. However, "judicial independence"—which does not exist, essentially, in democratic Britain where Parliament dominates—is not necessarily required. It is the result that matters, not the institutional devices that are erected to guarantee it.

None of this is to argue that the policies of democratic governments are entirely determined by the efforts of outside pressure groups and other petitioners. Parties, individual politicians, and government officials often have their own agendas and, in addition, often search out, and sometimes even invent, issues which might exercise citizens and citizen groups.[12]

POLITICAL INEQUALITY

Throughout history most democrats have advanced equality as an essential part of their intellectual baggage, and this theme has routinely been burlesqued by antidemocrats. Plato mockingly called democracy "a pleasant condition" which distributes "its peculiar kind of equality to equals and unequals impartially" because democracy seems to require a ridiculous leveling.[13] Similarly, in the Gilbert and Sullivan opera *The Gondoliers,* a couple of democrats, having inherited a kingdom and unwilling to abandon their "Republican fallacies," determine that in their kingdom "all shall equal be," whether they be the Lord High Bishop orthodox, the Lord High Coachman on the box, or the Lord High Vagabond in the stocks. Accordingly they establish "a despotism strict combined with absolute equality," in which as monarchs they spend their day variously making proclamations, polishing the plate, receiving deputations, and running little errands for the ministers of state.

In modern practice, however, democracy has not looked anything like that. It came to be associated with a special, and perhaps rather minimal, form of political equality, the kind usually called equality of opportunity. In a democracy all people are free—that is, equally unfettered as far as the government is concerned—to develop their own potential, to speak their minds, and to organize to promote their interests peacefully. Riker asserts that "equality is simply insistence that liberty be democratic, not the privilege of a class." And when John Locke concludes that "all men by nature are equal," he defines equality as "that equal right that every man hath, to his natural freedom, without being subjected to the will or authority of any other man," and he goes out of his way to point out that such attributes as age, virtue, and merit might give some a "just precedency." Thus political equality is something that seems to evolve without much further ado when people are free—it is sub-

145

sumed by, dependent upon, and, appears in fact to be indistinguishable from, liberty.[14] If people are free, they are, as far as democracy is concerned, politically equal as well.[15]

Initially, this freedom (and hence equality) of opportunity stood in opposition to class distinction, and it makes democracy subversive of hereditary class as it relates to politics: the pool from which leaders are chosen is widened to include everybody, and all are free to participate if they choose to do so. As the chief author of the American Declaration of Independence, Thomas Jefferson is generally held responsible for the most famous promulgation of the notion that "all men are created equal." But in other writings he made it clear that far from supplanting distinction, democracy merely replaces one form of distinction with another. Rather than having "an artificial aristocracy, founded on wealth and birth," he pointed out, a democracy would be ruled by "a natural aristocracy" based on "virtue and talents." Or as Pericles put it in ancient Athens, in a democracy "advancement in public life falls to reputation for capacity, class considerations not being allowed to interfere with merit."[16]

It is true that each member of the electorate in modern democracies has more or less the same voting strength at the ballot box. (Actually, this is often only approximately true: in the United States, for example, a resident of Wyoming has a substantially greater voting weight in national elections than a resident of a much more populous state like Ohio.)[17] However, the political importance of an individual is not very significantly determined by this circumstance, and therefore political inequality effectively prospers: some people are, in fact, more equal than others. A store clerk may count for as much in an election as does the head of a big corporation or a columnist for the *New York Times*, but, as I will discuss more fully in the next chapter, it would be absurd to suggest that the clerk is, or could readily become, remotely equal to the other two in ability to affect and influence government policy.

Unlike in authoritarian systems, therefore, the political weight of individuals in a democracy is not rigidly predetermined by class, personal loyalties, or ideological tests. One is free to try to increase one's political importance by working in politics or by supplying money in appropriate places, or one can reduce it by succumbing to apathy and neglecting even to vote. In practice, then, *democracy is a form of government in which individuals are left free to become politically unequal.*[18] That is, the actual working out of the process encourages people to explore, develop, and express their differences, not to suppress them. Democratic individualism, in fact, is in many respects the antithesis of the kind of equality that Plato and W. S. Gilbert ridiculed.[19]

The result of all this is that democracy, like life and capitalism, may often be notably unfair. Some people, because of their manipulative skills, social position, or sheer luck will do much better under the system than others. Unlike other systems, however, democracy gives to everyone the opportunity without regard to social status or ideological conviction to seek to manipulate the system in their favor. However, those who make little effort to do so may well be ignored, or maybe even persecuted, by it.

DEMOCRACY IN PRACTICE: COOPTING THE WEALTHY

Opponents have traditionally anticipated that in a democracy demagogues would mesmerize and bribe the masses and then rule as bloody tyrants. For example, Plato surmised that in a democracy all a politician need do is assert "his zeal for the multitude" and they would be "ready to honor him." Therefore, assuming that numbers were all that mattered in a democracy, he expected such demagogues to "plunder the propertied classes, divide the spoil among the people, and yet keep the biggest share for themselves."[20] That this grim scenario was not entirely fanciful was demonstrated in the years after the French revolution of 1789 where democracy soon degenerated disastrously into the sort of tyrannical, murderous mobocracy that Plato had envisioned two millennia earlier. Moreover, it eventually became associated with an expansionary ideology, with war, and, under Napoleon, with aggressive, continent-wide military conquest.

Generally, however, once democracy was put into practice (market-tested, it might be said), it turned out, quite amazingly, that

147

Plato's persuasively dire prediction did not come about. The result has been that in order *really* to plunder the propertied it has been necessary to abandon democracy—as in China, the Soviet Union, Cuba, Nicaragua, Burma, Iran, Vietnam, revolutionary France, Cambodia. Where the would-be plunderers have remained democratic—as in Sweden—the propertied have generally been able to hang on to many of their assets and have not felt it necessary to flee. A most extreme test of this will be in South Africa where a massive expansion of political freedom has put those who once ran the system very much into the minority. If the system remains democratic, experience suggests they should be able to maintain much of their privilege.

There seem to be at least three reasons for this substantially unanticipated development: political inequality, commonsense, and apathy.

Inequality

While it is true that the rich form a minority of the electorate, their money and status can be parlayed into substantial political influence on issues that they really care about such as confiscation of their property. As I have argued, the simple arithmetic of the ballot box is only a portion of the democratic effect, and perhaps not even a necessary one. Elsewhere, a sort of weighted voting takes place, and the rich, left free to become politically unequal, enjoy influence far out of proportion to their numbers on issues that really matter to thcm—something, as will be discussed more fully later, that other minorities have also discovered.

Commonsense

In addition, it turns out that in practice, the poor have not shown the shortsighted stupidity that Plato posited. Resentment of the wealthy may have some immediate demagogic appeal, but ordinary people have often shown a resistance to demagogues and a rough appreciation for the fact that a systematic dismemberment of the propertied class is not all that good for the poor either.[21]

148

Plato anticipated that bloody tyranny would emerge in a democracy because "he who is the president of the people finds a mob more than ready to obey him." In *Coriolanus,* set in at least semidemocratic Rome, Shakespeare vividly depicts such a process. A military leader is at first honored by the great unwashed, but he is unable to bring himself hypocritically to grovel before them, and soon the people, manipulated by wily demagogues, turn and crush him. For Mencken, too, "The most popular man under a democracy is not the most democratic man, but the most despotic man. The common folk delight in the exactions of such a man. They like him to boss them. Their natural gait is the goose-step."[22]

It is noteworthy, however, that once in authority, the tyrants who emerged in revolutionary France, as well as later ones who came into authority more or less democratically, like Hitler and Mussolini, felt it necessary to abandon democracy in order to maintain control. Wiser than Plato, Mencken, and even Shakespeare about mobs, they knew that if they left the field free to rivals, the people might well come to follow a competitor. That is, the notion that masses of people are readily, predictably, and consistently manipulable proved to be naive. Moreover, as will be discussed more fully in the next chapter, a cynicism toward politics and politicians, endemic in democracies it seems, may sometimes enhance popular resistance to the appeals of shallow demagogues and extremists. As such would-be manipulators as advertisers, public relations specialists, and political candidates could assure Plato, Mencken, or Shakespeare, putting out an idea a free public will buy is uncertain at best.

The agile demagogue and would-be tyrant is aware of the essential validity of a famous, and, at base, rather cynical, observation about democracy—perhaps the most profound thing ever said about the institution and a key to why, despite its patent defects, democracy more or less works. The observation concludes first that Plato, Mencken, and Shakespeare were right: people in general can *all* sometimes be faked out: "you can fool all of the people some of the time." Moreover, some people will *never* get it right: you can fool "some of the people all of the time." What makes anything work, however, is that people, in fact, are *not* equal: some-

149

where there are a few people at least who will eventually figure it out: "you can't fool all of the people all of the time."[23]

Additionally, it turns out that voters have often been inclined, rather surprisingly perhaps, to support rich people for office—something that has routinely driven Marxists crazy. This could be seen in the earliest competitive elections in the American colonies, a hundred years before the Declaration of Independence. As Edmund Morgan observes, the people elected "were generally those whose birth and wealth placed them a little or even a lot above their neighbors." Moreover, even "where most seats were filled by comparatively ordinary men, those who stood highest socially and economically seem to have been deferred to by the other representatives and appointed to the committees that directed legislative action."[24]

Accordingly, while democracy may open up the competition for leadership to people who would have been barred under an authoritarian system for genetic or ideological reasons, changes in leadership have not usually been terribly revolutionary: by and large, the same people, or sorts of people, remain in office. Thus democracy generally did not prove destructive of aristocratic dominance because voters tended to support many (though not all) of the same patricians who would have been in office if unalloyed monarchy had still been the order of the day. Democracies, like monarchies, have largely been run by the well connected and the well born, although democratic myth-builders, particularly in America, have usually chosen to emphasize the occasional political success of upstarts raised in log cabins.[25]

More recently, a similar phenomenon may be taking place in postcommunist countries as the (presumably more capable) members of the formerly ruling nomenklatura remain in place, often prosper, and frequently win free elections.[26] And the experience with democracy suggests that Adam Przeworski should not find it so "astonishing" that in Spain "the political system has been transformed without affecting economic relations in any discernable manner" and that "those who were satisfied with the Franco regime are also likely to be satisfied with the new democratic government."[27]

Apathy

Finally, apathy has also played a central role in making democracy function and in helping the rich to retain much of their privilege. Plato, Shakespeare, and Mencken not only exaggerate the ease with which people can be manipulated, but they also ignore the difficulty of gaining their attention in the first place.

In fact, one of the great, neglected aspects of free speech is the freedom not to listen. As Hubert Humphrey reportedly put it, "The right to be heard doesn't automatically include the right to be taken seriously." It is no easy task to persuade free people to agree with one's point of view, but as any experienced demagogue is likely to point out with some exasperation, what is most difficult of all is to get them to pay attention at all. People, particularly those in a free, open society, are regularly barraged by shysters and schemers, by people with new angles and neglected remedies, with purveyors of panaceas and palliatives. Very few are successful—and even those who do succeed, including Adolf Hitler, owe their success as much to luck as to skill.

As will be discussed later, apathy helps importantly with the problem that is usually called the tyranny of the majority. It is not difficult to find a place where the majority harbors a considerable hatred for a minority—indeed, it may be difficult to find one where this is not the case. Polls in the United States regularly have found plenty of people who would cheerfully restrict not only the undeserving rich, but also homosexuals, atheists, accused Communists, Nazi paraders, flag burners, and people who like to shout unpleasant words and perpetrate unconventional messages. But it is not easy to get this majority to do anything about it—after all, that would require a certain amount of work.

Because of apathy, therefore, people, sometimes despite their political predispositions, are effectively tolerant.[28] For democracies the danger is not so much that agile demagogues will play on hatreds and weaknesses to fabricate a vindictive mob-like tyranny of the majority: the perversions of the French Revolution have proved unusual. More to be feared, it seems, is the tyranny of a few who obtain bland acquiescence from the uninterested, and essentially unaffected, many.

MINORITY RULE AND MAJORITY ACQUIESCENCE

Essentially, then, democracy is characterized by minority rule and majority acquiescence. Surely, the history of the oldest large democracy supplies much evidence for this: often against the interests and the desires of the majority, beekeepers gain price supports for honey, selected industries are insulated from competition, gun enthusiasts secure protection from seizure, artists are granted medals and subsidies, and the credit union industry routinely enjoys special tax privileges even though it represents only a few percent of the market and even though its privileges are ardently opposed by the huge banking industry. Similarly, the tiny sugar industry continues to inspire benevolent governmental policies which artificially boost the price of sugar, a policy strongly contested by the huge soft drink industry and one that is clearly opposed to the interests of legions of soft drink guzzlers, many of whom vote quite regularly.[29] (On the other hand, as dieticians and dentists unpleasantly remind us with every health bulletin, sugar is a really terrible food. Therefore making it more expensive may contribute a bit to the public health—perhaps even to that vaporous commodity, the "common good," which so many supple philosophers have so often mused about at great and eloquent length.)

People routinely rail against such developments as the workings of "special interests," a phenomenon assessed in the next chapter. But pressure and petition are crucial and central to democracy, not a distortion of it. James Madison was alarmed at the prospect of what he called "faction," defined as a group of citizens "who are united and actuated by some common impulse of passion, or of interest, adverse to the rights of other citizens, or to the permanent and aggregate interests of the community."[30] But, to a substantial degree, democracy is a system of freely contending factions. That people with common interests should be allowed freely to attempt to sway government policy is, in fact, democracy's whole point.

DEMOCRACY IN COMPARISON

When asked, "How's your wife?" comedian Henny Youngman was given to responding: "Compared to what?" In an essay first published in 1939, E. M. Forster adopted just such an appropriate comparative approach when he observed that democracy "is less hateful than other contemporary forms of government." Or, as it is usually put: democracy is the worst form of government except for all the rest.[31] The ultimate appeal of democracy is, I think, not that it is, or could become, a perfect or ideal form of government, but that, however imperfect, it has distinct advantages when compared to other forms.

Governmental Effectiveness

Some of the competitors to democracy have seemed to offer admirable—even sublime—qualities that are not attainable in a democratic system. They cater to such natural desires as the need for order, security, certainty, and community, and they seductively proclaim the existence of a general will supplied by God, by temporal authority, or by a cosmic populist sense, thus relieving individuals of the burden of determining their own self-interest in matters of governance. They often offer to manage individual idiosyncrasies for the greater good and to give security to all by arranging to have the collective or an overseer protect the individual against the traumas of risk and failure. And they sometimes claim to be able to supply authoritative truth through comforting revelation, freeing people from the uncertainties of individual error. One classic if extreme, expression of this perspective is the Grand Inquisitor in Dostoyevsky's *The Brothers Karamazov*. As he sees it, people are terrified of the freedom and individualism of democracy, and they are willing, indeed anxious, to surrender it for bread, security, mira-

153

cle, mystery, authority, and the warmth of communal unity. "All that man seeks on earth," he explains, is "some one to worship, some one to keep his conscience, and some means of uniting all in one unanimous and harmonious ant-heap."[32]

It would seem that, if the Grand Inquisitor were right, prisons and slavery would be more popular. But it must be acknowledged that democracy is, and will always be, distressingly messy, clumsy, and disorderly, and that in it people are permitted loudly and irritatingly to voice opinions that are clearly erroneous and even dangerous. Moreover, decision making in democracies is often muddled, incoherent, and slow, and the results are sometimes exasperatingly foolish, shortsighted, irrational, and incoherent. As Tocqueville argued in the 1830s with respect to foreign policy, democracy "can only with great difficulty regulate the details of an important undertaking, persevere in a fixed design, and work out its execution in spite of serious obstacles. It cannot combine its measures with secrecy or await their consequences with patience."[33] And some, including James Bryce, have lamented that democracies do not often promote the best people in the society to political leadership (assuming, presumably, that the society would be better off with the best in those positions rather than in science, business, or medicine).[34] But the key question in all this remains Youngman's: "Compared to what?"

Dictatorships aspire to devise a method for governing that cuts through all the messiness and gets on with it. They have sought to come up with a system that sports a strong, wise, and effective leader—a guardian, a philosopher king, a superman—who can provide authoritative direction without all the compromise, contention, obstruction, and waffling. But how does one get people like that into leadership positions?

It is useful in this regard to look at the quality of the people democracies have generally selected and to compare them to leaders who have emerged in nondemocratic societies. In such a comparison, it seems, democracies do rather well.

The overall record for nondemocracies, after all, is fairly abysmal. Rebecca West may exaggerate somewhat when she observes that in 645 years of rule the Hapsburg family produced "no genius, only two rulers of ability . . . , countless dullards, and not a few imbeciles and lunatics," but she is not that far off the mark. Although not an entirely unbiased observer, Thomas Jefferson once had the opportunity to visit the monarchs of Europe and found them to be fools, idiots, hogs, and just plain crazy—except perhaps for Catherine of Russia who stood out only because she "had been too lately picked to have lost her common sense." A more sympathetic observer, Louis XIV of France, the longest-reigning monarch in European history and one of the most ardent exemplars of the monarchical system, was however also fully aware of the system's defects: "I have often wondered how it could be that love for work being a quality so necessary to sovereigns should yet be one that is so rarely found in them."[35]

In general, democracy looks pretty good, then, when one compares the leadership and decision-making qualities of the tsars of Russia or the kaisers of Germany or the kings of Saudi Arabia or the dictators of just about any place with those of the prime ministers of Britain or Canada or the presidents of the United States. As Jefferson plausibly concluded, "there is not a crowned head of Europe, whose talents or merits would entitle him to be elected a vestryman by the people of any parish in America."[36] While democratic governments have made their share of blunders, these, it might well be argued, pale in comparison to the disasters nondemocratic countries have experienced under such leaders as Hitler, Mussolini, Kim Il-Sung, Khomeini, Mao, Stalin, and Saddam Hussein.

Some of the democratic advantage in this comes about because any system of governance will tend to do better if the top leadership is regularly reevaluated whether through elections or some other mechanism. Leaders may be quite capable and effective at the start, but there is no guarantee they will remain so after years or decades in office, and occasional reexamination guards against such decline. If there is competition to replace the leaders, and if the current leaders, with all their advantages, can enter the competition, it seems unlikely that almost any set of judges will do worse than a system where such periodic reevaluations are not held. Even if the reviewers resolve merely to end the tenure of

155

rulers who have patently become monsters or utter incompetents things would be better.[37]

A case in point is the Soviet Union, an authoritarian system which did have provisions on the books for regular review of its leaders as well as for orderly succession. Nonetheless, Josef Stalin gained control and held it without effective challenge or further review for twenty-five years during which time he launched a massive tyranny. Later, leadership devolved into the hands of Leonid Brezhnev whose experience is in its way an even more devastating commentary on the Soviet review process than the Stalin case. Stalin terrorized and murdered his potential reviewers, but Brezhnev's reviewers did not have that to worry about. Nonetheless Brezhnev held on to authority even as his effectiveness dwindled because of illness and even as evidence mounted that his policies were leading the country into economic, political, and social stagnation and ruin.

This problem might be reduced somewhat if dictators responsibly groomed their successors. But the danger is that a designated successor of capacity who is truly able might be inclined to come into office early by overthrowing the reigning tyrant. Therefore it often makes sense to select sycophants, weaklings, and mediocrities for the role.

Only democracies generally have been able to establish effective review and succession arrangements and thereby solve an elemental problem of governance.[38]

In addition, in a democracy those who yearn to become leaders have a peaceful and legal device for fulfilling their ambitions. If they don't like the way the present incumbents are performing, they can work to try to replace them. Thus, democracy furnishes a safety valve for discontent: those with complaints may or may not ever see relief of their grievances, but rather than wallowing in frustration, they are supplied with the opportunity to express themselves and potentially to change things in a direction they prefer.

And it seems that the rigors of the democratic leadership-selection campaign process is a fairly good selector by itself, though some of these qualities can also be required in leadership struggles within an authoritarian government. To succeed, a candidate must be able to work hard, to avoid public blunders, to improvise under adverse conditions, to size up and placate disparate personalities, to communicate well, to exude a sense of purpose and direction, to be able to differentiate the tactical from the strategic, to seize opportunity, to inspire confidence, to make prudent and timely decisions, and to be able to deal with people both individually and in groups. All of these qualities are valuable for leaders as well.

Critics of democracy have argued that the campaign process puts a premium on image, on the toothy grin, on the slick facade. But too many nonmesmerizers—Lyndon Johnson, for example— have handily attained high office to conclude that a seductive television image is a necessary or vital component of success in democracies. And the public's resistance to shallow demagogues has been discussed earlier. There is of course no surefire way to predict how a candidate will perform in office, and to rely on the commonsense of the masses—including those among them who can't be fooled all the time—seems, rather remarkably, to work comparatively well. Interestingly, in an important sense, voters in democracies often do not have a great deal of choice. Parties generally put forward candidates who are ambitious, hardworking, and dedicated—thus, on those dimensions at least, voters can't make a mistake. On the other hand, candidates with those qualities are put forth in the belief that they have what the electorate is looking for.

In the end, William Riker's perspective on all this seems sound: a liberal democracy is characterized not by "popular rule" but by various devices providing for "an intermittent, sometimes random, even perverse, popular veto" which "has at least the potential of preventing tyranny and rendering officials responsive." Riker agrees that this is "a minimal sort of democracy," but he contends that it "is the only kind of democracy actually attainable." If people remain free to use whatever common sense they choose to muster at the moment, and if they are free to generate competing ideas, there's a reasonable chance they'll get it more or less right eventually.[39]

There have been mistakes and exasperations and sometimes

even disasters. But it can be plausibly argued that democracies on the whole have done comparatively rather well at managing their affairs, at correcting their inevitable mistakes, and at choosing and evaluating leaders, and that governments so instituted have been responsive to the will, if any, of the people—or at any rate to the apparent will of those who choose to organize and to complain.

The Persecution of Minorities

Carole Pateman, following arguments by Joseph Schumpeter and Peter Bachrach, argues that a country that persecutes groups like Jews, witches, and Christians cannot be considered democratic even if the persecution measures were established by democratic methods.[40] Experience suggests, however, that democracies do frequently persecute minorities. Unlike nondemocracies, however, they allow persecuted groups the freedom to petition and organize to alter or revoke offending laws, regulations, and policies. And, in fact, offended minorities are often able to gain redress even when the majority remains essentially hostile to them.

For generations (actually, for millennia) homosexuals have been persecuted both in democracies and nondemocracies, and their defining sexual activity has been routinely outlawed. This tiny minority is still held in open contempt, even disgust, by many members—probably most—of society.[41] Nevertheless, it has gradually been able to undo a great deal of official persecution in democracies in the space of only a couple of decades.

It is significant that this change took place only after homosexuals came out of the closet and openly organized to advance their interests. Democracy is not very good at inflicting pain on some people in order to supply benefits to other people who don't seem to want them. But once a minority organizes responsibly to put forward its demands, democratic governments are often remarkably responsive. And it is quite possible to imagine that other contemptuously dismissed groups whose principal activity has been outlawed—like drug addicts and prostitutes and, increasingly it seems, cigarette smokers—could obtain similar redress if they organized and worked on it.

Similarly, although all problems between blacks and whites in the United States have hardly been resolved, black people there, although they constitute little more than 10 percent of the population, have been able to get an enormous amount of legislation passed to lift discriminatory laws and practices and to guarantee their rights and position in society—including even some laws which give them preferential treatment. Notably, the vast bulk of this legislation came about only in the last forty years, after blacks themselves began to organize on a really substantial basis. Indeed, a central point of the massive and historic March on Washington, led by Martin Luther King in 1963, was to demonstrate that, contrary to the arguments of many hostile politicians, blacks generally—not just a troublemaking elite—actually wanted reform.[42] Important legislation was passed only a year later.

Often groups can get their way in a democracy even when they are denied the vote. As noted earlier, the American feminist movement achieved many of its goals even though the vast majority of its members were excluded from the electorate. Fairly quickly, and long before women gained the vote, feminists were able to secure passage of important legislation to protect women's rights on marriage, property, employment, and education issues. Gaining the vote was more difficult in large part because the movement was unable to demonstrate that women in general actually wanted it: an advisory referendum in Massachusetts in 1895, for example, went disastrously awry when, inspired by an antisuffrage movement comprised mainly of women, hardly any women even showed up to vote. A truly mass movement for suffrage in the United States was only achieved by 1916, or by 1913 at the earliest, and Congress passed the suffrage amendment in 1919.

Or there is the case of the disabled, a group that historically has not been so much persecuted as simply neglected. A considerable amount of legislation benefiting this minority was passed once the disabled were able to get their act coherently together even though the legislation caused notable inconvenience and expense to the majority.

Like the interests of the wealthy in earlier days, minority interests can be maintained in a democracy, but this comes about not particularly because the majority will embrace the minority with fraternal good will, but because democracy leaves the minority free to organize to pursue its interests—and effectively vastly to increase its political weight—on issues that matter most to it.[43] The majority may not come to have all that much sympathy with members of a minority group, but as long as the minority is reasonably subtle, circumspect, and unthreatening (and persistent) about pursuing its interests, it can expect a fair amount of benign neglect—effectively, tolerance—from the generally distracted and uninterested majority.

Often there are additional benefits to a pressuring group when it organizes for democratic combat: it may gain status and self-respect ("gay pride" activities have been central to the homosexual political movement), and there is a tendency for responsible and effective leaders to arise within the group itself. It will be of great interest to see if the people in central and eastern Europe at the bottom of the status ladder—the gypsies or Romanies—will organize to protect and advance their interests and coherently to chart their destiny.[44] Democracy affords the opportunity.

A Livable Society

Beyond these considerations, democracy also rather automatically comes encumbered with certain values and perspectives that many find congenial in themselves, quite apart from how they may or may not affect the political order. The act of voting or of participating in public discussion carries with it a sense of belonging that some people find quite satisfying psychologically. And among those who believe in the democratic myth, the voting act is taken to bestow a certain sense of legitimacy upon the government so chosen (those who believe that only God can choose leaders, on the other hand, will remain unimpressed).

Riker suggests that democracy gives people a sense of dignity and self-respect, while Robert Dahl plausibly finds that the democratic process "promotes human development, not least in the capacity for exercising self-determination, moral autonomy, and responsibility for one's choices."[45]

In general, democracy also comes accompanied with a permissiveness and effectively a tolerance, an openness, and a comparative absence of cant and mendacity, that are quite appealing to many—and are also qualities that may be very helpful for economic growth, as will be discussed in the concluding chapter. E. M. Forster, for example, likes democracy because it "admits variety" and because it "permits criticism." Those are his "two cheers" for democracy.[46] The folks at Ralph's Grocery would probably deem two cheers to be quite sufficient—pretty good, in fact.

DEMOCRACY AND REAL PEOPLE

It seems, then, that democracy, like God, works in mysterious ways its wonders (such as they are) to perform—ways that call into question many theories, hypotheses, expectations, and images generated both by supporters and by opponents about how the institution really ought to work. Democracy, it seems to me, is built not on political equality, but on political inequality; not on majority rule, but on minority rule and majority acquiescence; not on enlightened consensus, but on apathy and distraction; and not nearly so much on elections as on the frantic and chaotic interweavings and contestings of isolated, self-serving, and often tiny special interest groups and their political and bureaucratic allies.

Democracy is an admirable form of government, in my view, not because it furnishes a guide and goal for people to become ever better in a quixotic quest for atmospheric and unreachable Rockwellian ideals, but because it is a governmental form, generally compatible with a vigorous and productive society, that functions rather well when people manage, on average, to be no better than they actually are or are ever likely to be: flawed, grasping, self-centered, prejudiced, and easily distracted. In fact, democracy does not require a great deal from people: they do not need to be particularly good or noble, but merely to calculate their own best interests or, if they wish, interests they take to reflect those of the collectivity, and, if so moved, to express them.

In 1823, eight years after the end of the Napoleonic Wars, the

161

British writer and essayist Sydney Smith penned a letter railing exhaustedly against war in all its vigor, absurdity, and "eloquence," and in the process he expressed a yearning for four qualities of a more basic, even mundane, nature: "apathy, selfishness, common sense, arithmetic."[47] In this view, human beings are not incapable of such admirable qualities as eloquence, nobility, grandeur, altruism, self-sacrifice, and unblinkered obedience. But they are a flawed bunch, and it seems wiser, and certainly less tiring, to work with human imperfections rather than to seek zealously to reform the race into impossible perfection.[48]

To begin with, people have in them a strong streak of apathy and are not readily roused to action. In other words, they will tend to pursue concerns that matter to them rather than ones that other people think should matter to them. As it happens, some people will be quite content to spend their time taking naps, watching television, hanging out on street corners, boozing away the evening, or reading trashy novels rather than pursuing high culture, changing the world, or saving souls. (Sir John Falstaff, who might be seen as a sort of quintessential caricature of the Smith liberal, mutters at one point, "I were better to be eaten to death with a rust than to be scour'd to nothing with perpetual motion.") Relatedly, they will be selfish—guided more reliably by their own interests than by perceptions of the general good.

At the same time, however, people do not act randomly but rather apply commonsense and arithmetic. That is, they have a canny, if perhaps not terribly sophisticated, ability to assess reality and their own interests and to relate things in a fairly logical way. If left free, therefore, there's a good chance that a number of them will eventually see through even the most effusive flatteries and the most exquisite fabrications of the most dazzling illusionists.[49] At any rate, cagey illusionists seem to have been aware of the danger: once in political control they have quickly moved to destroy democracy before it destroys them.

An institution is likely to prove particularly effective if it can be fabricated so that it will function properly even when people need exhibit virtues no more exalted than those which emerge in the Smith—or the Ralph's Pretty Good Grocery—perspective.

Democracy has proved to be fundamentally sound—in harmony with human nature—in the sense that it does not routinely require much more from the human spirit than apathy, selfishness, common sense, and arithmetic. Indeed, in some respects it exalts and revels in these qualities.

Consequences of the Democratic Image

In the previous chapter, I developed a perspective about democracy based not on ideal images but rather on how the form actually seems to work, stressing that it is characterized by a chaotic interplay of special interests in a political environment distinguished by inequality, by minority rule, and by a sort of majority acquiescence that substantially derives from inattentiveness and apathy. The chapter concluded with something of a paean to democracy, albeit one that some democratic idealists might well consider a bit perverse.

While many of those exalting the democratic ideal might grudgingly agree that democracy does more or less work the way I have described it, they hold that things would be much better if democracy in practice were more nearly to approach its attractive theoretical ideal. They urge, therefore, that there should be continual efforts to make people more equal politically and to refashion democratic decision making so that it is more nearly a process of deliberative consensus carried out, or watched over, by a citizenry that is active and enlightened—or at least knowledgeable.

Often these reforms seem to be advocated for their own sake. That is, it is held to be important for democracies to more closely approximate the democratic ideal because it is important for democracies to more closely approximate the democratic ideal. Sydney Verba and Norman Nie, for example, declare that "if democracy is interpreted as rule by the people then . . . the more participation there is in decisions, the more democracy there is."[1] They do not maintain that decisions or policies will somehow be objectively better—that is, they do not suggest that there is something wrong, even rotten, in, say, the state of Switzerland, and then argue that higher voter turnout there will likely fix it. Rather, reformers often essentially conclude that participation—or equality or deliberation or knowledge—are important for their own sake.

I do not necessarily oppose the reformers' efforts, but I think it unlikely, realistically, that much progress can be made. And in this chapter I suggest there may actually be some negative consequences to the quest to close the very considerable mismatch between the democratic ideal—its impossible dream—and what I take to be its grim, grimy, and unavoidable reality.

To begin with, it seems to me that constantly stressing the clash between democracy's shining ideal image and its decidedly unlovely reality often induces, or at any rate reinforces, a cynicism about the democratic process that is uncomprehending and mostly (though not entirely) undesirable. Sometimes it becomes common, even fashionable, opaquely to dismiss the whole system as "corrupt." The cynicism about the form so commonly found in democracies, and so often lamented by democratic idealists, in fact, is partly—maybe even substantially—caused by them.

Second, I suggest that the continual overselling of equality by democratic idealists has encouraged the rise of a destructive and profoundly antidemocratic form—I call it hyperdemocracy—when this ideal is transferred to the economic realm. At various times, important activists, like Vladimir Lenin, have come to the (correct) conclusion that democracy allows the rich minority to protect its advantages and thus that democracy cannot deliver anything like strict economic equality. Therefore, they have sensibly, if murderously, concluded that the only way to achieve true economic equality is to crush democracy itself.

I argue, third, that adherence to the democratic image can logically lead some minorities to fear that, if the form is actually about equality, majority rule, and active participation, they stand to be persecuted in a democracy. In fact, as argued in the previous chapter, it happens that democracy has a rather good, if far from perfect, record of dealing with minorities, in large part because selective minority agitation is facilitated by majority apathy or inattentiveness. But minorities can be led to rebel in misguided desperation if they take the democratic ideal too seriously.

Finally, I append a few cautionary comments about the burgeoning field of transitology which sometimes tends to advance a perspective that can inspire a damaging short-term perspective in new democracies, and I also question the usefulness of the concept of "democratic consolidation."

In the following chapter I consider some of the consequences of the image mismatch on democratic development.

CYNICISM ABOUT THE DEMOCRATIC PROCESS

Democratic reformers, theorists, and image-makers often express alarm at the almost palpable cynicism routinely expressed by the public in democracies, both ones which have been around for a while and ones which have only recently emerged. Indeed, cynicism about the form seems to be the quality people most quickly pick up when their country turns democratic.[2]

A number of studies argue that things have gotten worse on this score lately, at least in the United States, where it is held that cynicism, discontent, frustration, and a sense of disempowerment and helplessness have markedly increased since the 1960s. For example, in a provocative recent book Michael Sandel points to polls showing that more people in the 1990s than in the 1960s say they distrust government to do what is right, think it wastes a lot of money, and feel it is run by a few big interests rather than for the benefit of all. He blames this increase on Vietnam, the assassinations of Robert Kennedy and Martin Luther King (but not on the inconveniently early one of John Kennedy), Watergate, the inflation of the 1970s, oil shocks, the Iran hostage crisis, the stagnation of middle-class incomes, the escalating deficit, crime, drugs, urban decay, and various other problems. Others, like Robert Putnam, add that there has also been an alarming decline in interpersonal trust over that period and attribute this to congenital press negativism or to that perennial receiver of brickbats, television.[3]

Interestingly, Sandel and Putnam do not notably allege so much that government has actually *become* less competent or trustworthy or more wasteful or interest-dominated, but only that people have come to *feel* that this is so. Thus, Sandel argues that people feel a "loss of mastery" or a "sense of disempowerment," not that they actually *have* less "mastery" or "empowerment" than in days of old.[4] The problem, therefore, apparently is not so much with reality as with perception.

The implication of these studies is that trust and confidence in the United States have traditionally—that is, until the middle or late 1960s—been high. But quite a bit of data suggest that although expressions of cynicism may have been relatively low in the early 1960s, the seeming increase in cynicism and distrust since that time is more nearly a return to normal levels. Consider, for example, the responses of Americans to two questions asked at various points over the last half century, shown in the accompanying tables.

If you had a son, would you like to see
him go into politics as a life's work?

	Yes	No
1945	21	68
1953	20	70
1955	26	60
1962	23	69
1965	36	54
1973	23	64
1991	24	72
1993	22	70
1994	25	71
1995	32	63

Do you think most people can be trusted?

	Yes	No	Don't Know
Mar 1942	66	25	9
Mar 1948	66	30	4
Aug 1952	68	30	2
Nov 1953	57	39	4
Jan 1954	62	34	4
Nov 1954	66	32	2
Apr 1957	75	22	3
Nov 1963	77	21	2
Mar 1983	56	41	3

Similarly, turnout rates reached a sort of peak in the early 1960s and afterwards returned to more normal levels, and confidence in the United States Congress peaked in the mid-1960s before declining again. More broadly, there is good reason to believe that political participation even in the "golden years" of American politics before the Civil War were, contrary to the usual supposition, marked mainly by apathy and political cynicism.[5]

In addition, if one examines the 1945–60 period—when, according to Sandel, a "sense of mastery prevailed"—it is quite easy to generate a list of calamities that rivals the one he delineates for the later one: food and housing shortages, continuous labor unrest, the rise of the Cold War, the fall of China, McCarthyism, Communist victory in Indochina, racial tensions over school integration, the continual humiliations due to Sputnik and the space race, the rise of Castro, various scandals over corruption in the government, incompetence at Suez, U.S. impotence when Soviet tanks crushed Hungarian independence, the arms race, continuing crises over Berlin, the looming threat of thermonuclear war, and, above all, the Korean War.[6]

In fact, during Sandel's age of mastery a huge sociological or pop-sociological literature was spawned about "alienation," "lonely crowds," the sameness of ticky-tacky suburban developments, and conformity and grey-flannel suits, as well as about how terrible it was that American soldiers allowed themselves to be brainwashed in Korea, that the clean-cut Charles Van Doren lied on a prime time television quiz show, and that CIA spy Francis Gary Powers neglected to kill himself when his U-2 spy plane was downed over the Soviet Union.

For example, in 1960 Murray Levin declared that "voters find voting to be meaningless . . . the electoral process to be a sham . . . the average voter feels that politicians are selfish and irresponsible. . . . they indicate a widespread disgust and disillusionment with the political process and politicians in general." And in the same year, Harvard's Kenneth Keniston, while acknowledging that there remained "pockets of enthusiasm," managed to miss any sense of mastery in the age, arguing instead that "there has seldom been as great confusion about what is valid and good as there is now," and found the age characterized by "alienation, estrangement, separation, withdrawal, indifference, disaffection, apathy, noninvolvement, neutralism." Similarly concerned that the country had lost its sense of national purpose (while the surging Communists supposedly knew exactly where they were going), President Eisenhower went so far as to appoint a national commission to find out what the country's goals, after all, were.[7]

Thus, even granting that political cynicism may have risen in recent decades, the quality itself seems more nearly to be a constant than a variable quality in American politics. And while this rise of cynicism may be mostly undesirable, it is hardly terminal: long and extensive experience with democracy suggests that E. J. Dionne is patently wrong when he argues that "a nation that hates politics will not long survive as a democracy" as is Michael Nelson when he asserts that the form "cannot long endure on a foundation of cynicism and indifference."[8]

To counter such lamentable, or at any rate widely lamented, qualities, democratic thinkers have resolved to reform the democracies and the peoples who make them up more nearly to approximate their ideal images of what it, and they, should be like.

Thus, Sandel suggests that democracy "depends" on a "civic life" which we must "restore" (thereby implying that it once really existed). This apparently means we must share in self-rule, which in turn requires "the capacity to deliberate well about the common good," which further implies that "citizens must possess certain excellences—of character, judgment, and concern for the whole." A tall agenda, clearly, but he sees hope for "our impoverished civic life" in campaigns like those in New England against Wal-Mart stores where "civic values" triumph over "consumer values" and people (that is, groups of dedicated, self-interested agitators) array themselves around such uplifting slogans as "I'd rather have a viable community than a cheap pair of underwear."[9]

Putnam also tends to idolize Rockwellian town-meeting decision making—very unlike James Madison, incidentally, who found societies in which a small number of citizens assemble and administer government to be susceptible to mischievous passions and interests, to be "spectacles of turbulence and contention," to be "incompatible with personal security or the rights of property," and in general to be "as short in their lives as they have been violent in their deaths." Putnam urgently calls for the reversal of what he views as "a broad and continuing erosion of civic engagement" and consequently of "social capital."[10] Like Sandel, however, he writes at a time in which the American economy is soaring (in part, as suggested in chapter 4, because of high levels of business trust and honesty). And he fails to indicate that the trend he laments has actually had any tangible negative policy consequences.

In contrast to these perspectives, it seems to me that democratic cynicism stems not as much from the inadequacies of people or of democracy as from the ministrations of the image-makers: people contrast democratic reality with its ideal image, note a huge discrepancy, and logically become cynical about the process. If cynicism about the form is a problem, what may need to be reformed is not so much the system as the theory—and perhaps the theorists.

I should stress again that I do not hold efforts to increase political equality, deliberative consensus, participation, and citizen knowledge necessarily to be undesirable. However, I do think that long experience with democracy suggests that it is hopeless to imagine that things can be changed a great deal. Inequality, disagreement, apathy, and ignorance seem to be normal, not abnormal, in a democracy, and to a considerable degree the beauty of the form is that it works despite these qualities—or, in some important respects, because of them.[11]

The Quest for Political Equality

As noted in the previous chapter, the notion that all men are created equal suggests that people are *born* equal—that is, that none should necessarily be denied political opportunity merely because of their hereditary entrance into the wrong social or economic class or because they do not adhere to the visions or dictates of a particular ideological group. The notion does not, however, suggest that people must necessarily be equal in their impact on the political system, but this damaging extrapolation is often made by reformers, at least as a goal to be quested after.[12]

An extensive study on the issue of equality by a team of political scientists finds, none too surprisingly, that people in a real democracy like the United States differ in the degree to which they affect the political system. Political effectiveness, the study concludes, depends on three varying factors: resources, especially time, money, and skills; psychological engagement with politics; and "access to networks through which individuals can be recruited to political life." The variance of effectiveness, the authors then conclude, poses a "threat to the democratic principle of equal protection of interests." Another analyst, reviewing their findings, makes a similar observation: "liberal democracies fail to live up to the norm of equal responsiveness to the interests of each citizen."[13]

But instead of seeking to reform the system or the people who make it up, we may want instead to abandon, or at least substantially to modify, the principle and the norm. They clearly express a romantic perspective about democracy, a perspective which has now been fully and repeatedly disconfirmed in practice. Democracies are responsive and attentive to the interests of the citizenry—at least when compared to other forms of government—

171

but they are nowhere near equally responsive to the interests of each citizen.

Related is the perennial clamor against "special interests." As the futile struggle for campaign finance reform in the United States suggests, people who want or need to influence public policy are very likely to find ways to do so no matter how clever the laws that seek to restrict them. As Gil Troy observes, "for all the pious hopes, the goal of the Watergate-era reforms—to remove the influence of money from presidential elections—was, in hard and inescapable fact, ridiculous." (He also notes that the entire cost of the 1996 election campaigns was about 25 percent of what Procter & Gamble routinely spends every year to market its products.) A rare voice of realism amid all the sanctimonious, politically correct bluster from politicians about campaign finance reform in the United States in the 1990s was that of Senator Robert Bennett of Utah: "rich people will always have influence in politics, and the solution is not to create barriers that cause the rich people to spend even more money to hire lawyers and consultants to find ways around the law to get the same results."[14]

In the end, "special interests" can be effectively reined in only by abandoning democracy itself, because their activities are absolutely vital to the form. Indeed, it is quite incredible that two prominent Washington reporters merely deem it "simplistic" to argue that "people with common interests should not attempt to sway government policy." In a democracy the free, competitive play of "special interests" is fundamental. To reform this out of existence would be uncomprehending and profoundly antidemocratic.[15]

Most of the agitation against political inequality is focused on the special privileges business is presumed to enjoy. For example, concern is voiced that the attention of public officials can be differently arrested: "a phone call from the CEO of a major employer in the district may carry considerably more weight than one from an unknown constituent."[16] It is possible, of course, that the unweighty and unknown constituent has just come up with a plan which will achieve permanent worldwide bliss in the course of the next six months, but, since there are only twenty-four hours in a day, public officials (like the rest of us) are forced to ration their time, and they are probably correct to assume, as a first approximation at least, that the concerns of a major employer are likely to be of wider relevance to more people than are those of the hapless lone constituent.

But if the CEO's access advantage to a time-pressured politician is somehow reprehensible and must be reformed, what about other inequalities—that is, why focus only on economic ones? A telephone call from a big-time political columnist like David Broder of the *Washington Post* is likely to get the politician's attention even faster than that of the CEO. Should the influential David Broder hold off on his next column until the rest of us deserving unknowns have had a chance to put in our two cents in the same forum? Inequalities like these are simply and unavoidably endemic to the whole political system as, indeed, they are to life itself. It may be possible to reduce this inequality, but it is difficult to imagine a reform that could possibly raise the political impact of the average factory worker—or even of the average business executive—remotely to equal that enjoyed by Broder.

Robert Dahl aptly notes that "significant inequalities in power have been a universal feature of human relationships throughout recorded history; they exist today in all democratic systems." This, he concludes, "falls short of the criteria of the democratic process" and the result is a "serious problem for democratic theory and practice."[17] But it seems to me that the "serious problem" may lie not so much with the universal fact of inequality, but rather with the theory and with the "criteria of the democratic process" which, as Dahl essentially suggests, have clearly, repeatedly, consistently, and overwhelmingly been demonstrated to be fanciful.

Dahl, on the other hand, seeks a method by which citizens can "possess the political resources they would require in order to participate in political life pretty much as equals." He doesn't suggest that pretty much all of us should have something like a equal crack at the op-ed page of the *Washington Post,* but he does place quite a bit of hope in "telecommunications." These, he suggests, could be used to provide "virtually every citizen" with "information about public issues" and to establish "interactive systems" to "participate in discussions with experts, policymakers, and fellow citizens."[18]

Perhaps because newspapers, magazines, television, libraries, public meetings, telephones, and talk radio already supply much of this, and perhaps because most people freely choose to ignore this mass of readily available information, Dahl then essentially seems to abandon the equality theme by suggesting that what we really need is simply "a critical mass of well-informed citizens large enough and active enough to anchor the process, an 'attentive public,' as Gabriel Almond put it many years ago," favorably citing a book written forty years earlier that concluded that such a helpful elite group already substantially exists.[19]

Finally, Dahl resolves to save elective democracy for the future almost—it seems—by proposing to abandon it. To guarantee that at least part of the attentive public be "representative," he suggests that a group of some thousand citizens be selected by random methods (rather than by elective ones) and that it then be forced or hired to deliberate issues of the day (by telecommunications) and from time to time to "announce its choices." These choices would complement those made by elected bodies that already happen to exist, and would "derive their authority from the legitimacy of democracy." Using methods like this, "citizens in an advanced democratic country would discover others" and "the democratic process could be adapted once again to a world that little resembles the world in which democratic ideas and practices first came to life." Such romantic devices are necessary, Dahl concludes thunderingly, because "the democracy of our successors will not and cannot be the democracy of our predecessors."[20] In my opinion, it clearly will and it just as clearly can.

The Quest for Deliberative Consensus

Rather than accepting democracy for what centuries of experience have shown it to be, many democrats—both in old democracies like the United States and in new ones like those in postcommunist Europe—get angry when democracy allows them to watch the process in all its chaotic, unkempt finery. Instead of accepting Bismarck's wisdom comparing the making of laws to the making of sausages, many people continue to quest for an illusive, and, I think, illusory, ideal, one which suggests that lawmaking under democracy, in contrast to all other sorts, should be characterized by careful deliberation and consensual resolution in which the views of honest and naive little people, like moviemaker Frank Capra's mythical Mr. Smith, should eventually prevail.[21]

Thus Dionne lauds "the belief that self-government is not a drab necessity but a joy to be treasured," in which "politics is not simply a grubby confrontation of competing interests but an area in which citizens can learn from each other and discover an 'enlightened self-interest'."[22] However, in real world decision making grubbiness almost always prevails over joy for the simple, elemental reason that people happen to disagree, often profoundly, about many key issues. (In addition, because of the existence of cyclic preferences in the collective—shifting majorities may prefer A to B and B to C, but also C to A—it is often logically impossible to discover a true majority preference.)[23]

People seem to have an aversion to haggling and in result, as discussed in chapter 2, the practice has been virtually eliminated at the retail level in advanced capitalist countries. A comparable aversion to political contention, however, cannot be serviced because contention is both inevitable and necessary. Nonetheless, people contrast Bismarkian grubbiness with the Rockwellian image projected by Dionne and others, and they often come to dismiss it all as unseemly bickering—"politics as usual"—and become cynical.

Thus, in the United States, Congress and the president often slump in popularity whenever they are caught in the act of trying to solve or resolve a difficult and contentious problem. In October 1990, for example, President George Bush and the Democrats went at each other over the budget: there was a difficult deficit to confront, and this required such painful remedies as spending cuts or tax increases or (as it turned out) both. In due course they worked out a sensible compromise, but people, incensed over all the furor, started screaming—as the cover of the 22 October 1990 issue of *U.S. News and World Report* headlined—to "throw the bums out." The popularity of both Congress and the president reached conspicuous lows.[24]

A bit more recently, it could be argued that the health care debate in the United States in 1993 and 1994 showed democracy at its finest. A problem the voters had sensibly determined to be important was addressed and debated. President Bill Clinton had a solution, others in Congress had theirs, affected interested groups appropriately weighed in with theirs, and months of thoughtful and nuanced (if sometimes confusing and boring) discussion of this difficult topic took place. Admittedly, a solution (apparent or real) to this complicated concern was not smoothly worked out in two years of effort, but the problem did not have to be solved immediately, and there was plenty of time in the next years to come up with judicious remedies with this groundwork laid—something, indeed, that substantially happened. Yet voters, few of whom paid much attention to the substance of the often tedious debate, dismissed it all as "bickering," cried "gridlock," and often became angry and cynical.[25]

Two of Washington's top reporters, David Broder and Haynes Johnson, have written a book on this episode. In tone and substance the book continually suggests that the system failed in the health care debate—indeed, that the public was "duped." Despite the abundant evidence arrayed in their book of the wide-ranging discussion that took place on the issue, they somehow manage to conclude that a "great public debate" about health care never occurred. Yet the authors acknowledge that "Where no strong consensus exists, major change should wait"—which is exactly what happened.[26]

As they note, the experience may have heightened popular cynicism about the process. However, some of that came from books like theirs which suggest that democracy really ought somehow to be different from what history has regularly and consistently shown it to be: a disorderly, manipulative, but often remarkably productive, muddle.

At any rate, after this experience, the popularity both of the president and of Congress predictably plummeted. Exacting revenge in the 1994 elections for the unpleasant untidiness, the voters threw out many of the leading bums, particularly the ones who had started the contentious debate in response to the voters' earlier concerns. Thus, an analysis of exit polls in the election finds "no unifying theme" among the voters except for "an overall distaste for government." It suggests Clinton got the election's message, such as it was, when he concluded that the voters were saying "Look, we just don't like what we see when we watch Washington. And you haven't done much about that. It's too partisan, too interest-group oriented, things don't get done. There's too many people up there playing politics."[27]

Emerging from this experience was a swelling demand for term limits and perhaps for a third party, based on two quite remarkable assumptions: 1) that the people elected under such altered conditions will behave notably different from those elected under the present ones; and 2) that voters are somehow being unfairly manipulated when, despite their vigorously expressed cynicism about politicians, they regularly and overwhelmingly reelect incumbents.[28]

When politicians respond to what they think their constituents want they are routinely accused of "pandering to public opinion" and of "doing anything to be elected." When they go in a direction different from what public opinion seems to dictate, they are accused of "ignoring the will of the people" and "pandering to special interests." If they have sharp differences, they are accused of polarizing the situation, "encouraging an 'either/or' politics based on ideological preconceptions rather than a 'both/and' politics based on ideas that broadly unite us."[29] If they manage to agree, they are accused of selling out principle for a Tweedledum and Tweedledee me-tooism. It's a tough racket.

Related is the concern about "negative campaigning." The implication, apparently, is that if politicians can't say something nice about other politicians, they shouldn't say anything at all. As Riker has observed, however, by any standard of what reasonable discourse should be like, there is nothing wrong or indecent about negative campaigning if it helps to differentiate candidates and issues—as it almost always does. Moreover, it is a commonplace in democratic campaigns, never more so than in the intensely contentious ratification campaign for the since-sanctified United States Constitution.[30]

In an important study of political campaigning, Stephen An-solabehere and Shanto Iyengar find that campaign advertising—including negative advertising—"informs voters about the candidates' positions and makes it more likely that voters will take their own preferences on the issues into account when choosing between the candidates." Therefore they conclude that political advertising, particularly television advertising, "actually fosters the democratic ideals of an informed and reasoning electorate."

However, at the same time Ansolabehere and Iyengar become greatly concerned because negative campaign advertising increases the voters' cynicism about the electoral process and because it is taken by some voters, particularly nonpartisan ones, to be "a signal of the dysfunctional and unresponsive nature of the political process itself," causing them to lose interest in voting, thereby "eroding the participatory ethos of the American public." To help "short-circuit this cycle of negativity," they consider several remedies. One might be to encourage journalists and media watchers to police the ads, but they find that this approach gives the negative ads even more play and that the negativity of press coverage of negative ads only adds to the problem. More promising, they suggest, is to charge candidates more for negative ads than for positive ones and to strengthen party campaign organizations on the (highly dubious) grounds that "party-centered campaigns remove the incentive to air personal attacks."[31]

Thus, on the one hand this study finds that negative advertising clarifies and informs; on the other that it alienates some members of the voting public who have, despite hundreds of years of disconfirmation, fallen for the mythical notion that democracy is about Rockwellian deliberative consensus. The fault clearly lies with the myth, not with the reality, but instead of seeking to abandon the endlessly attractive, if thoroughly discredited myth, we are urged to mellow reality in hopes that it will somehow come to resemble it. Interestingly, the most famous sustained instance of negative campaigning was probably Harry Truman's colorful and successful give-'em-hell presidential campaign of 1948, but reformers don't seems to be concerned about that one. It may be that the recent popular cynicism about negative campaigning is being caused not so much by the campaigning itself as by the campaign against negative campaigning.

At any rate, like other democratic values and practices, negativity does seem to be something new democracies pick up with considerable ease. A report from Paraguay after a mere two years of experience with the political form observed that "newspaper, television, and radio reports are filled with mud-slinging worthy of the most mature democracy."[32] That, it seems, is the way democracy is. To be deeply offended by it is fundamentally misguided.

The problem in all this, as John Hibbing and Elizabeth Theiss-Morse have aptly put it, is that people lack "an appreciation for the ugliness of democracy." In fact, "true democratic processes in any realistic environment are bound to be slow, to be built on compromise, and to make apparent the absence of clean, certain answers to important questions of the day." Yet, people want "both procedural efficiency and procedural equity," a sort of "stealth democracy."[33]

Actually, as Bismarck's aphorism may suggest, the unpleasantness is not really peculiar to democracy; it applies to law-making more generally. The problem is heightened in a democracy, however, because all interests can participate, because people are allowed freely to speak their minds—thereby perhaps enhancing its natural disorderliness—and also because the decision-making process is comparatively open in all its chaotic, appalling finery.[34] Reformers and idealists who yearn for Rockwellian consensus and closure only enhance the public's unrealistic and uncomprehending misperception, and consequently they heighten cynicism about the process.

There are a number of potential solutions to this problem, if problem it be. One, of course, is for law-makers simply not to appear to do much of anything, and, indeed, in early 1998 when the most visible accomplishment of the American Congress was to rename an airport, the popularity of the institution soared.[35] But this approach is clearly not feasible overall, and it is hardly desirable from the standpoint of decision making. Nor is an effort to make decision making less grubby likely to be either successful or sensible. Even Hibbing and Theiss-Morse toy with the suggestions that "ways must be found to limit the influence of key actors" like interest groups, and that "important steps need to be taken to reassure people that monied interests are not getting preferential treatment."[36] But the interplay of interests (virtually all of them "monied") is at the very heart of the process, and it simply cannot and should not go away. Moreover, some interests will inevitably get "preferential treatment"—that is, what they want—while others will not.

More hopeful, following another suggestion of Hibbing and Theiss-Morse, might be to seek to educate the public to more nearly understand and appreciate democracy's inevitable and congenital ugliness. However, because of the popular and apparently universal belief—tirelessly fostered by democratic theorists and idealists—that democracy really ought to be much different than it has always and everywhere been, this effort, too, is unlikely to be very successful. Nonetheless, it might be refreshing sometime to hear a politician and even the occasional educator rise above sanctimony for a moment and frankly admit that "special interests," far from being a distorting evil, are what the whole thing is all about, and that, in the words of playwright John Mortimer, "freedom is perpetual fussing."[37]

The Quest for Participation

Democratic theorists, idealists, and image-makers maintain that "democratic states require . . . participation in order to flourish," or that "a politically active citizenry is a requisite of any theory of democracy," or that "democracy was built on the principle that political participation was not only the privilege of every man, but a necessity in ensuring the efficiency and prosperity of the democratic system," or that "high levels of electoral participation are essential for guaranteeing that government represents the public as a whole," or that "to make a democracy that works, we need citizens who are engaged."[38]

But we now have over two hundred years of experience with living, breathing, messy democracy, and truly significant participation has almost never been achieved anywhere. Since democracy exists, *it simply can't be true* that wide participation is a notable requirement, requisite, guarantee, need, or necessity for it to prosper or work. Routinely, huge numbers of citizens even—in fact, especially—in "mature" democracies simply decline to participate, and the trend in participation seems to be, if anything, mostly downward. In the United States, nearly half of those eligible fail to vote even in high-visibility elections and only a few percent ever actively participate in politics. The final winner of a recent election for the mayor of Rochester, N.Y., received only about 6 percent of the vote of the total electorate. (However, he is a very popular choice: if everybody had voted, he would almost certainly have achieved the same victory.) Switzerland is Europe's oldest democracy, and it also boasts the continent's lowest voter turnout.[39]

Statistics like these frequently inspire a great deal of concern—after all, it is argued, "political participation" is one of the "basic democratic ideals."[40] But it may be more useful to reshape democratic theories and ideals to take notice of the elemental fact that democracy works even though it often fails to inspire very much in the way of participation from its citizenry.

And it might also be asked, why, exactly, is it so important for citizens to participate? Most analyses suggest that nonvoters do not differ all that much from voters in their policy concerns, though there are some (controversial) suggestions that leftist parties might do a bit better in some countries if everyone were forced to vote.[41] However, once in office, responsible leftist and rightist parties both face the same constraining conditions and, despite their ideologies and campaign promises, often do not differ all that much from each other in their policies—frequently to the disillusionment and disgust of their supporters who may come to feel they have been conned.

Some hold voting to be important because "of the problem of legitimacy." The idea is that "as fewer and fewer citizens participate in elections, the extent to which government truly rests on the consent of the governed may be called into question"; moreover the "quality of the link between elites and citizens" will erode.[42] Actually, such callings into question seem to happen mostly when a candidate, like Bill Clinton in 1992, gets less than half of the recorded *vote*—and these are principally inspired by partisan maneuvering by the losers to undercut any claim that the winner has a mandate. And in local elections, the often exceedingly low turnout and participation levels rarely even cause much notice: I have yet to hear anyone suggest that the mayor of Rochester is illegitimate or "unlinked" because hardly anybody managed to make it to the polls when he was elected.

Moreover, it really seems to strain credulity to suggest that "if people feel distant from the electoral process, they can take no pride in the successes of the government." *No* pride? It seems that even nonvoters celebrated victory in the Gulf War. Or that nonvoters "avoid responsibility for the problems facing the nation."[43] But nonvoters seem to have no more difficulty than voters in routinely (and sometimes even correctly) blaming the politicians for whatever is wrong. And it is simply too glib to conclude that "if you don't vote, you don't count."[44] If that were true, women would never have gotten the vote, slavery would still exist, and there would never have been prison reform or legislation aiding the homeless.

There are also claims that low turnout levels "contribute to the problem of an unrepresentative policy agenda." But it is difficult to understand what this could possibly mean—or, better, what a "representative policy agenda" would look like. Agendas are set by people actively trying to pursue their interests; they are not out there somewhere in the miasma waiting for us objectively to snap them up. As Steven Rosenstone and John Mark Hansen argue, "political participation is the product of strategic interactions of citizens and leaders." People "participate when politicians, political parties, interest groups, and activists persuade them to get involved." Thus, there will not be an "ideal" or even "normal" degree of participation. Rather, participation will increase when "salient issues reach the public agenda . . . when governments approach crucial decisions . . . when competitive election campaigns stimulate, when social movements inspire."[45]

Hundreds of years of experience, then, suggest that the pursuit of participation for the sake of participation is rather quixotic. Instead, applying a philosophical observation attributed to impresario Sol Hurok, perhaps we should accept the fact that "if people don't want to come, nothing will stop them." Moreover, discontent and cynicism about the system itself (and consequently perhaps nonvoting) are increased when alarmists passionately lament that many people, as they have throughout democratic eternity, freely decide to pursue interests they find more pressing than politics, or manage to come up with more interesting things to do on election day than to go through the often inconsequential ritual of voting. (Sometimes, actually, nonvoters, by the very act of not voting, may be indicating their concerns and preferences more eloquently than those who actually do vote.)[46]

The Quest for an Enlightened Citizenry

"If a nation expects to be ignorant and free," Thomas Jefferson once said, "it expects what never was and never will be."[47] Pretty much ever since those memorable words were issued, the United States has managed to be both, and with considerable alacrity.

Fortunately for America, eternal vigilance has not proven to be the price of democracy—it can come quite a bit cheaper. In ideal democracies, James Bryce once suggested, "the average citizen will give close and constant attention to public affairs, recognizing that this is his interest as well as his duty"—but not in real ones. And Horace Mann's ringing prediction that "with universal suffrage, there must be universal elevation of character, intellectual and moral, or there will be universal mismanagement and calamity" has proven untrue.[48]

Nonetheless, democratic idealists continue to insist that "democracies require responsibility." Or they contend that democracy "relies on informed popular judgment and political vigilance." Or they persist in defining democracy "as a political system in which people actively attend to what is significant."[49] One would think it would be obvious by now that democracy works despite the fact that it often fails to inspire or require very much in the way of responsibility and knowledge from its citizenry. Democracy does feed on the bandying about of information, but that is going to happen pretty much automatically when people are free to ferret it out and to exchange it. Democracy clearly does not require that people generally be well informed, responsible, or actively attentive.

Recent surveys find that around half the American people haven't the foggiest idea which party controls the Senate or what the first ten amendments of the Constitution are called or what the Fifth Amendment does or who their congressional representative or senators are. Moreover, this lack of knowledge has generally increased (particularly when education is controlled for) since the 1940s.[50] A month after the Republican victory in the 1994 election that propelled the vocal and energetic Newt Gingrich into the speakership of the House of Representatives and into the media stratosphere, a national poll found that 50 percent hadn't heard enough about Gingrich even to have an opinion about him. Four months later, after endless publicity over Gingrich's varying fortunes and after *Time* magazine had designated him its "Man of the Year," that number had not changed (so much for the power of the press).[51] In a poll conducted two years later, half were still unable to indicate who the speaker was. Meanwhile, less than 20 percent guessed correctly that over the preceding twenty years air pollution and the number of the elderly living in poverty had declined, and most people were of the wildly distorted impression that foreign aid comprised a larger share of the federal budget than Medicare.[52]

One recent analysis observes that "for the last 200 years the United States has survived as a stable democracy, despite continued evidence of an uninformed public."[53] It also notes that "in theory, a democracy requires knowledgeable citizens." Although it then labels the contradictory condition "the paradox of modern democracy," it seems, rather, that it is the theory that should be called into question, not the reality.

Moreover, it may not be entirely clear why one should expect people to spend a lot of time worrying about politics when democratic capitalism not only leaves them free to choose other ways to get their kicks, but in its seemingly infinite quest for variety is constantly developing seductive distractions. Democratic theorists and idealists may be intensely interested in government and its processes, but it verges on the arrogant, even the self-righteous, to suggest that other people are somehow inadequate or derelict unless they share the same curious passion. Many studies have determined that it is the politically interested who are the most politically active. It is also doubtless true that those most interested in unidentified flying objects are the ones most likely to join UFO clubs. UFO enthusiasts, however, get no special credit by political theorists for servicing their particular obsession, while politics junkies are lauded because they seem to be fulfilling a higher, theory-sanctified function.

In the end, the insistence that terrible things will happen unless the citizenry becomes addicted to C-SPAN can inspire cynicism about the process when it is observed that the Beverly Hillbillies (or whatever) enjoy vastly higher ratings.

Cynicism and Resistance to Demagogues

Cynicism about the process may be a standard pose among citizens in democracies, one substantially inspired by the very people who so passionately bemoan it—democratic theorists, idealists, and image-makers questing after their vaporous democratic ideal. This pose, derived in my view from a fundamental incomprehension about how democracy works, is probably undesirable, and it can certainly become tedious. But I do not wish to argue that cynicism is necessarily in all cases a bad thing.

One of the classic objections to democracy, voiced by Plato and many others, is the supposed susceptibility of the masses to the wily seductions of demagogues. Apathy and commonsense have probably helped solve this potential problem as noted in the previous chapter, but so also has a substantial, if often unfair and undeserved, wariness about politicians. Indeed, in many postcommunist countries a healthy distrust of all politicians has probably been important, as Stephen Holmes suggests, in keeping extremists from gaining much political ground there.[54]

HYPERDEMOCRACY

Tocqueville once observed that "democratic institutions awaken and foster a passion for equality which they can never entirely satisfy."[55] At its extreme this passion has proven to be extremely destructive.

I have argued that under democracy people are inevitably and substantially unequal in their impact on the political system, though individuals retain the freedom to alter their political weight on an issue of concern to them and regularly do so. As part of process, people of wealth or "advantage" have generally been quite capable of using their position to guide—or manipulate—the political system to keep it from confiscating their wealth or severely diminishing their advantages. Thus, as Martin McGuire and Mancur Olson point out, no democracy has ever voted to eliminate private property.[56]

Because of this phenomenon, there seems to be no realistic hope of achieving the ideal of true equality that democratic image-makers often seem to revere—particularly as it relates to economic equality—unless democracy is itself destroyed.

Agitators like Vladimir Lenin—hyperdemocrats, they might be called—have followed exactly this logic. He begins by observing, correctly, that under democracy the same people—rich and well-born like him—tend to retain their privileges, and, citing Marx, he caricatures capitalist democracy as a condition in which the "oppressed" are "allowed, once every few years, to decide which particular representatives of the oppressing class should be in parliament to represent and oppress them." To sever this control he proposes a "modification of democracy" characterized by the "suppression by force" of the capitalist class. This process, he assures us, would ultimately lead to a condition of "equality of labour and equality of wages."[57]

Thus the logic of the democrat's idealistic and romantic emphasis on equality can lead to calls for democracy's suppression. (However, the ultimate irony of all this, as noted in chapter 2, is that under the schemes and devices and mechanisms put together by Lenin and his followers, economic equality was not really reduced.)

In fact, of course, Leninism is profoundly antidemocratic not only in its ultimate conclusions, but in its starting assumptions. In the end, democracy trusts the commonsense and reasonableness of ordinary people, and it leaves them free to think and to contribute as they wish even if this sometimes (or even often) leads to results some might consider ill-advised, even foolish. By contrast, the version of communism that took hold in Lenin's Soviet Union and elsewhere was based on the theory that ordinary people actually *don't* know what is good for them, taking as conclusive proof of this the very fact that rich people are able to maintain much of their advantage in democracies. From this they conclude that ordinary people have had their heads filled with all sorts of devious capitalistic propaganda giving them a "false consciousness" about life and about the class conflict. Accordingly, it was necessary for an elite group of revolutionary, conspiratorial intellectuals, styling itself the "vanguard of the proletariat," to think for the naive, manipulated, and unaware masses, and to organize their activities until they come to their senses.[58]

THE REBELLION OF MINORITIES

The problem of convincing minority peoples to accept democratic rule is heightened by democracy's idealistic association with political equality, majority rule, and active political participation by the mass of people. Taking these three notions at face value, a national or other minority—particularly one that knows it inspires considerable hostility in the majority—can quite logically come to fear persecution in a democratic system since it will obviously be outnumbered by its perceived enemies. This perception can lead to despair, desperation, and rebellion. Democratic image-makers characteristically argue that the minority's only hope is that the majority will somehow treat it with respect, tolerance, and good will—an argument that in many cases will never be remotely persuasive.

As discussed in the previous chapter, democracy has actually had a good, if imperfect, record of dealing with minority issues, particularly when compared to other forms of government. But this is not so much because democratic majorities have been notably tolerant of minority concerns. Rather, it stems from the opportunities that democracy affords minorities to increase their effective political weight—to become more equal, more important, than their arithmetical size would imply—on issues that concern them. This holds even for groups held in considerable contempt by the majority, like homosexuals. Moreover, the fact that most people most of the time pay little attention to politics—the phenomenon of political apathy—helps interested minorities to protect their rights and to assert their interests, particularly when they are reasonably persistent and circumspect about it.

The civil wars in Croatia and in Bosnia-Hercegovina in the early 1990s were triggered, in part at least, because Serbs there did not understand this democratic reality and instead reacted—or over-reacted—to the conventional democratic image. Believing inaccurately that democracy is centrally built around political equality, active participation, and majority rule, they responded to alarmists and propagandists who claimed that they would mainly face persecution in a democracy in which they were outnumbered.[59] (Something similar might be said for Kosovars in Serbia and for Palestinians in, and in areas occupied by, Israel.)

Experience suggests, by contrast, that the Serbs could well have substantially maintained their interests, identity, and dignity if the system had remained essentially democratic. (Although democracy came under substantial assault in war-racked Croatia and Bosnia-Hercegovina, it is remarkable how much of it survived and persisted even under those conditions, and it is reasonable to expect that it would have remained fairly well-developed—in part because of pressures from the West—if war had been avoided.) In the process the Serbs would probably have found that, to a considerable degree, their numerical inferiority was largely an arithmetical technicality. This seems, for example, substantially to have been the experience since 1989 in Bulgaria for the Turkish minority (which had been severely persecuted under the Communists) and in Lithuania of the Polish minority.[60]

However, it must be conceded that there are no certain guarantees. As observed in the previous chapter, a majority that is sufficiently large and determined can at times indeed persecute the minority in a democracy. Obviously, whites in the American South were able for decades to keep blacks from participating effectively in the political system—although, as also noted there, that condition rather quickly broke down when blacks effectively organized. And, even though the American Constitution has a specific guarantee against unreasonable seizures, the property of Japanese-Americans was often summarily confiscated in the United States during World War II. What is impressive, however, is how unusual such arbitrary seizures have been in democracies.

Democracy routinely and necessarily leaves a minority free to organize peacefully to protect itself, and it provides legal mechanisms for the minority to express its views and to pressure the government for recognition and for relief of grievances. There is no such regular, systematic, or necessary assurance in other systems.

THE TROUBLE WITH TRANSITOLOGY

A couple of Polish writers were discussing conditions in their country on a street corner in Warsaw fairly recently. At one point, one reflected, "I think we all must now believe that this is it."

In my view most of the postcommunist countries of central and eastern Europe as well as many of the new democracies elsewhere have essentially completed their transition to democracy: they are already full-fledged democracies by the nonideal standards I have proposed in this book. Judging from two hundred years of experience with democracy, what they have now is, pretty much, *it*. It will, in all likelihood, never get much better.

There will, of course, be continued political change in these countries and some of this will be quite important. Politicians will come and go; some parties will fall and others will rise in voter favor (with luck perhaps the beer-drinkers' party will once again capture seats in the Polish parliament); constitutional and legal structures will undergo development; controversial issues will emerge and decline; economic and trade policies will be reshaped and refined; governmental subsidies will be increased and decreased; tax laws will be altered. But barring some sort of violent upheaval, the time of fundamental change is substantially over in many of these countries, and further developments will take place in environments which are essentially democratic. The societies may become more or less efficient, humane, responsible, productive, corrupt, civil, or effective, but these changes will probably have to come about within (or despite) the present political framework, not through further fundamental institutional transformation.[61]

Accordingly, it may now be sensible to decrease the talk of "transition" and to put a quiet, dignified end to the new field of transitology at least as it applies to countries like Poland. Transitological thinking may cause people in the new democracies in Europe and elsewhere to continue to think that things may become substantially different—hopefully better—in the future.[62] Thus, not only are transitologists sometimes spreading visions that will never come to pass, but their perspective can inspire or reinforce a short-term point of view that is undesirable from a political standpoint and even more so from an economic one.[63]

There may be similar misdirecting mischief in the related notion of "consolidation." Democracies do become more or less democratic, a phenomenon traced in various democracy ratings schemes such as those put out regularly by Freedom House. It is certainly appropriate to keep track of the new democracies and to become concerned by any retreat that might take place—if, for example, opposition leaders are harassed or if organized protesters are forcibly stifled, or if newspapers find it difficult to publish facts the government deems inconvenient. (In my approach, such freedoms are more central to democracy than the existence of elections.) Thus, Peru in the 1990s lost some of its democratic character, and Chile in 1973 abandoned democracy almost entirely for several years. It is sensible to be sensitive to such changes.

But to seek to establish a point at which a country becomes "consolidated" may not be terribly helpful since, as with Chile in 1973, this condition can be overthrown at any time by sufficiently dedicated and effective antidemocrats—some of whom might have even have previously been democrats.[64]

Many new democracies, then, have fully completed their transitions and are about as "consolidated" as any country is likely to get. And, like the older democracies that are their model, the new democracies are unlikely ever to achieve orderly deliberation, political equality, or wide and enlightened participation by the mass of the public.[65]

Rather than urging the new democracies on to impossible perfection, it would probably be better to take the laid-back approach adopted by the Polish writer, Adam Michnik. He suggests that we color democracy gray and notes that it frequently "chooses banality over excellence, shrewdness over nobility, empty promise over true competence." At its core, he points out, democracy is "a continuous articulation of particular interests, a diligent search for compromise among them, a marketplace for passions, emotions, hatreds, and hopes." But it is also "eternal imperfection, a mixture of sinfulness, saintliness, and monkey business." Yet only democracy has the "capacity to question itself" and the "capacity to correct its own mistakes," and "only gray democracy, with its human rights, with institutions of civil society, can replace weapons with arguments."[66]

Only pretty good, perhaps, but, as they'll be quick to assure you down at Ralph's Grocery, that's about as good as it gets.

The Rise of Democracy

I HAVE ARGUED that, contrary to the gloomy and sometimes strident claims of many of its well-wishers, democracy can function remarkably well even when its constituents participate only as moved
to do so and even when they exhibit little in the way of self-discipline, restraint, commitment, knowledge, or sacrifice for the general interest. For democracy to operate, people do not generally
need to be good or noble, nor do they need to be deeply imbued
with some sort of democratic spirit or culture. They need merely
to muse about how they think things ought to be, relying on their
best guesses about what would be in their own best interests or
what they think might be in the general society's best interests,
and, if they happen to be sufficiently moved by these musings, to
express them in nonviolent ways. Maybe someone will listen.

It follows from this perspective that no elaborate prerequisites
or cultural preparations are likely to be necessary for democracy
to emerge, and that an agonizing process of "democratization" is
not required. Indeed, unless democracy is suppressed by thugs
with guns, it seems likely that it can come about rather easily, almost by default, if leaders 1) happen to come to the conclusion
that democracy is the way to go; and 2) put the institution into effect by allowing people generally the freedoms to complain and to
attempt to overthrow the leadership nonviolently.

Accordingly, in this chapter I question the notion, popular
among theorists, that, in part, perhaps, because democracy requires a high degree of participation and deliberativeness, the
form is a difficult, even delicate, one to put, and to keep, in place.
In particular, I question the view that democracy's development is
essentially the result of broader intellectual, cultural, educational,
social, and economic trends. Among other things, that view has
generated a considerable pessimism about the pace at which
democracy can develop in the world, a pessimism that persists even

though recent history strongly suggests that it is singularly unjustified. And it has also provided autocrats with a convenient excuse for neglecting democratic reforms.

Democratic development, it seems to me, has principally been a matter of convincing leaders to do democracy. That is, democracy is merely an idea and its rise has essentially been the result of a two-hundred-year competition of ideas, not the necessary or incidental consequence of grander changes in social, cultural, economic, or historic patterns. It has triumphed not because it was somehow required by wider forces, but because its ideas, ably executed and skillfully promoted—or marketed—at one point in the world's history, have increasingly managed to catch on. This chapter traces that development, and it muses a bit about democracy's prospects.

A DEMOCRATIC DIALOGUE

My perspective on democracy may perhaps be clarified in the following fanciful dialogue between a pair of citizens in a prospective democracy.

"It's been decided: we're going to be a democracy."

"Democracy? What's that?"

"Form of government."

"Mm. What's it about?"

"Well, you're free to say whatever you want."

"You mean, I can complain and stuff?"

"Right. And the government won't do anything to stop you."

"So if I don't like the way things are going, I can scream and holler?"

"Yes. You can organize and publish and petition, too. Form groups, demonstrate, strike. Things like that."

"Sounds fair enough. Can I throw rocks?"

"No. You can't use violence."

"But if I have a gripe I can change things I don't like?"

"Well, you can *try*."

"Try?"

"Just because you have a beef doesn't mean you'll be successful at getting your way."

"You mean I can complain, but nothing will happen?"

"Probably. After all, other people are free too. They can refuse to listen, disagree, call you names—whatever."

"What's the point of complaining if all that happens is that other people call me names?"

"You should have thought about that before you started complaining."

"That's democracy? Anything else?"

"We're going to have elections too. You can decide who you want to run the government."

"You mean, *I* get to decide the whole thing?"

"Well, you and all the other voters. The candidate wins who gets the most votes. You're just one of them."

"How am I supposed to know who to vote for?"

"Up to you. Just choose. Whatever suits your fancy."

"That's it? But what if I don't know anything about the candidates?"

"Doesn't matter. You can vote anyway."

"What about the other voters?"

"Same for them. They can decide however they want."

"How many voters really know what's going on?"

"Beats me. Not many, probably."

"Wouldn't it be better to keep the ignorant and the incompetent from voting?"

"Tried that. Doesn't seem to make all that much difference so they just let everybody vote."

"How do you know you'll get good leaders with all this?"

"Well, actually it seems to work pretty well where it's been tried."

"Amazing. You mean it works even if people don't really know what they're doing?"

"Seems to."

"Can't they be fooled by clever candidates?"

"Sure. But not all of them all of the time."

"That's the hope? That someone somewhere will not be fooled?"

"That's about it."

"Seems pretty slender. You know, this voting stuff seems like it could become a lot of bother, particularly if everybody else gets to vote too. I'm pretty busy a lot of times. Do I have to vote at all?"

"Nope. Fact is, your vote can hardly make any difference to the outcome anyway."

"What's the sense of voting then?"

"Might make you feel good."

"So, with democracy I get to vote for leaders if I want, whether I know what I'm doing or not. And the saving grace is that my vote mostly doesn't matter much anyway?"

"Something like that."

"There seems to be even less here than I thought. What else is democracy about?"

"That's about it. Pretty simple, isn't it?"

"Simple is right. Sounds like any dimwit can do democracy."

"Yeah, that's probably true. Made me think of you somehow."

"Thanks. What else you got?"

THE HISTORICAL MOVEMENT OF IDEAS

As this dialogue suggests, and as Americans should surely know by now, it doesn't take a population of rocket scientists or moral paragons to pull off a democracy. Therefore, about the only prerequisite for democracy is that people—probably only the ones who happen to be in charge at the moment, actually—become convinced to allow it to come into effect.

In practice, democracy seems to be about as difficult to put on as a new suit of clothes, and it has spread so assiduously in recent years not so much because it has been made cosmically inevitable by various economic or social developments, but because it has come into style: it's what just about everyone who is anyone is wearing this season. And indeed, democracy has lately been taken up most effectively not by countries which are necessarily the most economically, socially, culturally, or historically prepared or ad-

195

vanced, but by those with leaders who identify most with, who most admire, and who most want to join, the fashionable company of democracies.

It seems useful, therefore, to consider what Francis Fukuyama has called "the autonomous power of ideas" or what Robert Dahl terms the "historical movement of ideas." As Dahl warns, however, "One can hardly exaggerate how badly off we are as we move into this terrain. If it is difficult to account satisfactorily for the acquisition of individual beliefs, it is even more difficult to account for historical shifts in beliefs." But it seems important to do so: as Dahl continues, "because of their concern with rigor and their dissatisfaction with the 'softness' of historical description, generalization, and explanation, most social scientists have turned away from the historical movement of ideas. As a result, their own theories, however, 'rigorous' they may be, leave out an important explanatory variable and often lead to naive reductionism."[1]

Ideas in this view are very often forces—independent variables—themselves, not flotsam on the tide of broader social or economic patterns. As Ernest Gellner has pointed out, "a great deal can happen without being necessary," without being "inscribed into any historic plan." In the case of democracy, it seems quite possible that the human race could have discovered and developed democracy quite a bit earlier. Or it could have missed or suppressed it, and remained mired in what Gellner calls "the dreadful regiment of kings and priests" for quite a bit longer.[2] Moreover, since it is (merely) about ideas, the process by which democracy has become widely accepted can perhaps be reversed or superseded without notable social or economic change if other ideas come along which seem, or can be made to seem, superior.

In this regard, consider one of the more interesting developments of the last two centuries: the rise of the notion that the venerable institution of slavery ought to be abolished. Substantial efforts have been made by scholars and analysts to use material factors, particularly economic ones, to explain the origin and the amazing success of this once-novel idea. But, as Stanley Engerman has observed, New World slavery never was in economic decline—indeed, at the same time that the abolition movement was taking flight the Atlantic slave trade was entering an extremely profitable phase. Consequently the success of the movement has to be explained by "political, cultural, and ideological factors."[3] The idea of abolishing slavery was successfully promoted at a propitious time, and it seems to have been not only an idea whose time had come, but one which has proved to have considerable staying power.

I am primarily concerned in all this not with the process by which the democratic idea was developed by intellectuals, but rather with the process by which it came to be broadly accepted. Thinkers are always spinning out ideas (that's why we call them Thinkers), but few of these generate wide appeal, however much they may entrance other Thinkers. Ideas take effect when they are widely espoused and accepted, not when they are being formulated by some guy sitting on a rock someplace. At any given time there are always a huge array of ideas around, and only a few of these catch on. Some may be of lengthy pedigree while others may be quite new and original. People sort through this market of ideas and prove receptive to some while remaining immune to others. Their receptivity may not be easily predictable, but it is surely not random.

THE CORRELATES OF DEMOCRACY

Before developing this approach, however, it would be useful to assess another perspective, one that has dominated much of the literature: the notion that the rise of democracy has been principally caused by social or economic developments. As Dahl has pointed out, democracy has been "strongly associated" with a whole series of social and economic characteristics: "a relatively high level of income and wealth per capita, long-run growth in per capita income and wealth, a high level of urbanization, a rapidly declining or relatively small agricultural population, great occupational diversity, extensive literacy, a comparatively large number of persons who have attended institutions of higher education, an economic order in which production is mainly carried on by relatively autonomous

197

firms whose decisions are strongly oriented toward national and international markets, and relatively high levels of conventional measures of well-being."[4]

That such characteristics are more nearly correlates than causes, Dahl observes, is suggested by the case of India where political leaders were able to establish a viable democracy even though "the population was overwhelmingly agricultural, illiterate ... and highly traditional and rule-bound in behavior and beliefs." Or "even more tellingly" there is the case of the United States which took to democracy when it was still "overwhelmingly rural and agricultural."[5]

So it goes with the other supposed relationships—political culture, for example. Democracy may have been established earlier in Protestant countries than in Catholic ones, but once Catholic countries took a notion to become democratic, their religious tradition did not seem to cramp their style very much.

Moreover, modern methods of transportation and communication do not seem to be required even in large democracies: the United States became democratic before the development of the steamboat, the railroad, and the telegraph—that is, when things and information moved scarcely faster overland than in the days of ancient Athens. And democracy has lately been established in large, underdeveloped countries like Botswana, Mongolia, and Namibia, while it remains neglected in such technologically sophisticated societies as Saudi Arabia.

Some analysts have held that a sizeable middle class is necessary for democracy: as Barrington Moore put it, "No bourgeois, no democracy."[6] The cases of India and quite a few other places call that generalization into question, and the recent experience in eastern Europe seems to shatter it.

Accompanying democracy's rise over the last two centuries have been the industrial revolution, enormous economic growth, the rise of a middle class, a vast improvement in transportation and communication, surging literacy rates, and massive increases in international trade. But if these developments somehow "caused" the growth of democracy, they also stimulated its direct opposites: Nazism, fascism, Bolshevism.[7] Moreover, the process of develop-

198

ment was often wildly out of synchronization. Democracy and the industrial revolution may have flowered together in England in the late eighteenth century, but firm democracy did not come to industrial Germany until 1945 (and then it had to be imposed from the outside), and it is only now being developed in industrial Russia.

By the end of the twentieth century it is quite easy to find democracy comfortably accepted in places like Mali, Mongolia, and Namibia that are very poor, have yet to develop much of a middle class, and are still quite backward in industry, literacy, communications, transportation, and trade. Meanwhile, some of the world's richest countries—like the Arab oil states—are also among the least democratic. As Samuel Huntington has pointed out, countries "transit to democracy at widely varying levels of development."[8]

Democracy does indeed correlate with various social and economic characteristics—wealth, capitalism, literacy, and so forth—but these correlations are, in my view, essentially spurious: democracy, after all, is also correlated with the rise of the string quartet. The McDonald hamburger sold first, and continues to sell best, in rich capitalistic, literate, Protestant countries, but it doesn't follow that you have to be rich or capitalistic or literate or Protestant or well-prepared or sophisticated or middle class or industrialized or cosmopolitan or uncontentious to buy one.

The correlation may suggest that certain social and economic developments make democracy more feasible. But this correlation—at best very imperfect—is often extrapolated to the point where the social or economic developments are seen to be *necessary* to democratic development. Thus, Huntington maintains that "economic development makes democracy possible," or that "political leaders cannot through will and skill create democracy where preconditions are absent." Such assertions seem to suggest that, despite the cases of India, Paraguay, Mali, much of the Caribbean, Botswana, Mongolia, and eighteenth-century America, democracy is impossible without economic development. And he suggests that in Haiti in the late 1980s the "obstacles to democracy" would likely "confound even the most skilled and committed democratic leader." But a few years earlier, as Giuseppe Di Palma notes, some might have said (in fact, did say) the same thing about poor, isolated countries like Portugal and Spain.[9] The obstacle to democracy in Haiti seems to have been a group of thugs with guns, not the absence of "preconditions," and it will be interesting to see if the current experiments there take long-term effect as they apparently have in Portugal and Spain.[10]

"General theories correlating democracy with the level of economic development or 'modernization,' or indeed associating it with some particular type of 'political culture,'" Laurence Whitehead observes, "necessarily abstract from" the "unpredictability" of the process. Noting the rise of democracy in southern Europe in the mid-1970s and its decline at the same time in countries where it was well established like Chile and Uruguay, he concludes that "the stock of available theories is of little help in explaining the timing, the longevity, or the geographical incidence of recent experiences of democratization."[11] What good, one might ungratefully be led to ask, are the theories then?

Pessimism about the Pace of Democracy

The notion that various attitudinal, cultural, economic, and atmospheric developments are necessary before democracy can be put in place has regularly led to considerable pessimism about the prospects for the expansion of democracy.

Thus, in a classic article, Dankwart Rustow envisioned the establishment of democracy as a slow, gradual process in which national unity leads to prolonged and inconclusive struggle which leads in turn to a conscious decision to adopt democratic rules followed by habituation to these rules. Applying a similar habituation analysis, Dahl anticipated in 1971 that "In the future as in the past," democracy is "more likely to result from rather slow evolutionary processes" and "the transformation of hegemonic regimes" into democracies is likely to be "measured in generations." In early 1989, on the brink of a major expansion of democracy as the Soviet empire collapsed, he concluded that "it would be surprising" if the proportion of the countries in the world that are democratic "were to change greatly over the next twenty years."[12]

In 1976, specialist Howard Wiarda assessed the possibilities that Portugal might develop a genuinely democratic political system, and, voicing agreement with a study done for the State Department, concluded that this was the "least likely" outcome because of the country's "legacy of authoritarian and autocratic rule," the lack of political experience of centrist parties, and the "absence of a political culture capable of supporting liberal-democratic institutions."[13]

In 1984, in the midst of what he was later to label the "third wave" of democratization, Huntington looked to the future and essentially concluded that democracy could only emerge though economic development or through force: "with a few exceptions, the prospects for the extension of democracy to other societies are not great. These prospects would improve significantly *only* if there were major discontinuities in current trends—such as if, for instance, the economic development of the Third World were to proceed at a much faster rate and to have a far more positive impact on democratic development than it has had so far, or if the United States reestablished a hegemonic position in the world comparable to that which it had in the 1940s and 1950s. In the absence of developments such as these, a significant increase in the number of democratic regimes in the world is unlikely."[14] Neither major discontinuity took place, but democracy surged anyway, and it often did so in countries that quite clearly lacked the supposed requisites.

In 1986, Latin Americanist Robert Kaufman applied a "political-economic perspective" to developments in Argentina, Brazil, Chile, and Uruguay, and found "some room for hope, but little for optimism" that these countries could break "cycles of fragile civilian regimes and prolonged periods of 'exclusionary' military authoritarianism."[15] They were soon to do exactly that.

And, in late 1993, economist Robert Barro, employing an economic model of democratic development on South Africa, came to a confident and decisive conclusion: "Considering the country's level and distribution of income, the ethnic divisions, and the political and economic experiences of most of the countries of Sub-Sahara Africa, this event would perhaps be the greatest political accomplishment in human history. To put it another way, it's not going to happen." When that country unobligingly became a democracy a few months later, an unbent Barro predicted that "The political changes in South Africa in 1994 have probably already overshot the mark, and a substantial decline of political freedom is likely after this year."[16] We continue to wait.

Prerequisitism as an Excuse for Neglecting Democratic Rreform

The prerequisite approach has also supplied a convenient excuse for authoritarian leaders in underdeveloped countries to avoid or "postpone" democratic reform.

Di Palma, for example, points out with some dismay that "a recent carefully drawn propositional inventory of conditions favoring the development or maintenance of democracy in the Third World lists forty-nine demanding conditions—mostly, in fact, preconditions." Some cagy authoritarian leaders in Africa justify their control by sweetly citing theories that democracy can only flourish when a country develops a middle class and sustains economic growth. Such evasions can only be bolstered by assertions that democracy depends on "democratic dispositions," or by authoritative declarations like the one rendered in 1996 by former British Prime Minister Margaret Thatcher: "Democracy needs the right kind of carefully nurtured soil to grow in."[17]

THE MARKETING OF DEMOCRACY

Recent experiences in the postcommunist countries and elsewhere (certainly including South Africa) suggest that democracy is not terribly difficult to institute, that it can come about very quickly, and that it need not necessarily come accompanied by, or preceded by, the social, economic, and cultural clutter that some have found necessary. This in turn suggests that the pessimism of some of democracy's analytic well-wishers may be very substantially overdrawn and that the agile excuses of authoritarian foot-draggers are invalid.

Democracy, in my view, is essentially a governmental gimmick, not a logical or empirical consequence of other factors. As Dahl points out, the role of beliefs is "pivotal" for the rise of democracy: it is difficult to see, he notes, how democracy could exist "if there is a weak commitment to democratic principles among the political activists." By the same token, it seems to me that a country can quite easily become democratic—*fully* democratic—without any special historical preparation and whatever the state of its social or economic development if elites or political activists generally come to believe that democracy is the way things ought to be done and if they aren't physically intimidated or held in check by authoritarian thugs.[18] For example, it is likely that about the only thing keeping isolated, backward, impoverished, prerequisite-free Burma from being democratic is a group of thugs with guns.

As an alternative to elevating correlates to causes, it seems to me important, in Dahl's words, to "treat the beliefs and ideas of political activists as a major independent variable."[19] The remarkable rise of democracy over the last two centuries appears chiefly to be the result of successful efforts by idea entrepreneurs who have actively sought to promote—or market—the concept to political elites around the world. I use the notion of "marketing" substantially as a metaphor or analogy of course, and its chief advantage is that it may allow one to begin to come to grips with the historical movement of ideas.

In modern times the idea of democracy took hold first primarily in Britain, the United States, and northern Europe, areas that have proved in many respects over the last two centuries to be fashion leaders—watched, admired, and then imitated. The wealth and vigor of these countries have not been irrelevant to the appeal of their ideas: advertisers always picture admirable, attractive people using or modeling their products. But the message is not that you must *be* admirable and attractive in order to buy the

203

product, but rather that you will *become* admirable and attractive *if* you buy it.

At one time Paris was the center of fashion for women's clothes. Designs shown there soon filtered to other areas in the world in a fairly predictable pattern: cities and areas that were with it copied Paris quickly, those less with it took longer or avoided infection entirely. For the most part, Paris was imitated most quickly by people in other large urban areas in the developed world. Paris fashions did well in New York not because New York is a large city like Paris, but because New Yorkers were more anxious to be with it than people in rural areas—or indeed than people in other large cities like Los Angeles or Atlanta. There is a strong, if imperfect, correlation between Paris fashion and urbanization. But the essential determinant, the one that explains the diffusion best, is not city size, but rather the degree to which people are tuned in to fashion cues coming out of Paris.

The diffusion of democracy seems best explained by a similar analysis. After a long marketing process, democracy has been selling well, particularly lately, even in such isolated and backward places as Burma. Like soccer and Shakespeare and fast food and the cotton gin and the airplane and the machine gun and the computer and the Beatles, it caught on first in one corner of the world and is in the process, except where halted by dedicated forces, of spreading worldwide. Eventually, I suppose, it could fall from fashion, but for now things look pretty good.

The process by which a product—or an idea—is successfully marketed can be quite complicated. And, although those who have sought to promote democracy have been successful, it does not follow that their triumph derives simply from their own manipulative cleverness. As any knowledgeable marketeer will admit, no amount of promotion can guarantee that a product will sell: if marketing alone could assure the success of a product, we'd all be driving Edsels. Careful planning and adept promotion are important, but so are happenstance and luck.

A sketch of the tactics and strategies applied by democracy's promoters might include several components.[20]

Undermining the Competition

First, they needed to undermine the competition, to seize upon, and to bring out its defects. When democracy emerged it had first to contend with hereditary monarchy, and later with other forms of authoritarianism.

Some reasons why democracy is superior to, or less inferior than, the competition were arrayed in chapter 6. But, although democrats were able to show as time went by that democracy is inherently a good—or pretty good—product, and also that it is markedly superior in several important respects to the competition, this was not enough to assure success. Inherent superiority has never guaranteed that a product will come to dominate a market. Most objective experts agree that Beta is superior to VHS for home video recording; yet VHS captured an overwhelming share of the market. As noted in chapter 3, Apple fans passionately argue that something comparable is happening, or has happened, in the computer field. To be sure, it is easier to peddle a pretty good product than a pretty bad one, but products rarely sell themselves: they need to become available at the right time and to be pushed in the right way.

Until around 1800 (and even after) the most common form of government was the hereditary monarchy—an authoritarian arrangement in which succession was determined by the fate of birth. Associated with it was a two-tiered class system in which leadership positions were generally reserved for those of appropriate birth: talented people who did not spring from approved loins were artificially excluded. This institution presumably came about because it seemed to be a sort of sensible expansion of the smallest natural social unit, the family. Certainly kings, emperors, czars, sultans, kaisers, and other such potentates have regularly adopted a paternalistic pose and have been hailed as father figures by their subjects. Very often, too, monarchy has been closely allied with religion—the divine right of kings and all that—and this artfully developed connection enhanced its acceptance.

But, as discussed in chapter 6, hereditary monarchy is a remarkably defective form of government, and democracy's chief initial competitor was thus something of a pushover. Monarchy's amazing longevity over the millennia and in all corners of the globe was probably due chiefly to the fact that it simply had no effective competition as a form of government. Once formidable alternatives were fabricated—chiefly highly flawed democracy—monarchy faded out in rather short order—over a century or so—particularly in the developed world.

Creating Demand for Congenial Values

Second, democracy's advocates needed to create demand for values which, if embraced, would rather automatically aid the acceptance of their product. For example, democracy will be helped (but its success will not necessarily be assured) if the notion becomes accepted that the government owes its existence and its perpetuation not to the dictates of God as expressed in the genetic process, but to the general consent and approval of the people at large. Or that political freedom is a natural, supreme right of all. Or that the class system, restricting political office to members of a limited gene pool, is unwise and unjust and that all people are created—that is, born—equal.

While the gradual acceptance of such concepts aided in the growth of democracy, it was quite possible to accept them without necessarily embracing democracy itself—indeed, the concepts have often been promoted by people who were antidemocrats. However, as crusaders for clean air necessarily aid the promoters of nuclear energy, so those who espoused theories about the importance and validity of the consent of the governed, about the injustice of the class system, and about the virtues of freedom and tolerance necessarily assisted the cause of those who wanted to promote democracy.

For example, although the influential Voltaire assiduously propagandized for freedom of thought and for tolerance of diverse opinion, he was not a democrat: he advocated rule by enlightened philosopher kings (preferably witty ones, I suspect), not by the people, whom he dismissed as "stupid and barbarous" and in need of "a yoke, a cattle prod, and hay." Isaiah Berlin has suggested the possibility of a liberal-minded despot—Voltaire's ideal, presumably—and has argued that there is a sense in it which it could be said that liberty is not "logically connected with democracy or self-government." In time, however, democracy's promoters were able to demonstrate that the liberal-minded despot is something of an illusion. In fact, if the individual's liberty includes the freedom to organize to attempt peacefully to replace the leadership, the notion of the liberal despot is a fundamental contradiction in terms. The best, and perhaps ultimately the only, system that actually guarantees individual freedom is democracy, or as Huntington puts it, "liberty is, in a sense, the peculiar virtue of democracy. If one is concerned with liberty as an ultimate social value, one should also be concerned with the fate of democracy."[21] Voltaire, a nondemocrat, was playing into the hands of democracy's promoters by helping to create demand for a commodity that, ultimately, only democracy could fully and reliably supply.[22]

A similar sort of intellectual evolution took place in the 1960s when the Catholic Church adopted the notion that it ought to seek to promote "social change" and to protect "basic personal rights." These conclusions did not particularly stem at the time from a new found love for democracy, but from a need to respond to various then fashionable forms of "liberation theology," some of which were totalitarian (and violent) in nature. By the late 1980s, however, things had importantly evolved: the pope still specifically denied that he had become an "evangelizer of democracy," but he now argued that, since he was "the evangelizer of the Gospel" to which "of course, belong all the problems of human rights," it followed that democracy "belongs to the message of the Church" because, he had now come to believe, "democracy means human rights."[23]

Market-Testing the Product

Third, the product had to be market-tested—put into practice somewhere to show it could actually work. Rather remarkably, and very much contrary to the anticipations of such influential antidemocrats as Plato, it soon became clear, as discussed in chapter 6, that democracy was, comparatively speaking, a rather effective method for choosing and reviewing leaders, and that it does not necessarily lead to a vast social leveling, the persecution of the rich and other minorities, or rule by mobs, incompetents, and demagogues.

The American experiment, as R. R. Palmer observes, demonstrated that ideas of liberty, class equality, responsible citizenship, popular sovereignty, religious freedom, free speech, separation of powers, and deliberately contrived written constitutions "need not remain in the realm of speculation, among the writers of books, but could be made the actual fabric of public life among real people, in this world, now."[24] And, even as the United States showed that one could have a quite respectable country without kings and without a traditional hereditary aristocratic class, the market test in Britain demonstrated that a country could move from monarchy to democracy in an orderly fashion without physical destruction of the aristocratic class.

A key issue in the growth of democracy concerned the size of the electorate. Reasonable questions about the competence of ordinary people to review the policies and activities of their leaders had been raised for thousands of years. Effectively, those market-testing democracy had a simple experimental solution to this problem. Initially they restricted the vote to the best and the brightest (and the richest). When that proved to work out pretty well, they gradually broadened the electorate to see if special problems would emerge as suffrage was expanded. Political and social pressure—particularly by feminists—also enhanced this process. It seems likely that those in authority soon learned that political clout was only imperfectly measured by the strict, simple arithmetic of the ballot box: those in the minority could still usually generate substantial influence through position, money, and organization. Thus suffrage expansion rarely was terribly problematic as long as the system remained democratic.[25]

Luck and Timing

Finally, there is the matter of luck and timing. Good promoters always stand ready to use fortuitous events and circumstances to advance their product, and successful promotion is often less a matter of artful manipulation than of cashing in on the tides of history or of being in the right place at the right time. One must be there when opportunity knocks, and one must be prepared to lurch into productive action while the sound of the knock is still reverberating.

Admirable market tests: fashion leadership. Promoters of democracy were lucky that they first test marketed their product in Britain and America (in the United States it was explicitly called "the American experiment") because, in the process, democracy came to be associated with countries which were held to be admirable—that is, which became fashion leaders or role models—for reasons that were often quite irrelevant to the institution itself.

It was probably the British experiment, not the American one, that was most influential in democracy's competition with monarchy. During the nineteenth century democratic Britain became the strongest and most important country in the world. It ruled the seas, developed the world's dominant economy, established a vast and impressive overseas empire, and was the scene of a substantial intellectual renaissance in philosophy, literature, and science. It was led in these endeavors by democratically selected politicians, such as Benjamin Disraeli and William Gladstone, who would be considered exceptional by the standards of most any age. Even more to the point, it was difficult to imagine that Britain could have attained all this if things were run, as in days of old, by its monarch, in this case the fussy and simple Queen Victoria.

The disastrous French Revolution. Democracy's promoters were also lucky that the French Revolution came after, rather than before, the substantial establishment of democracy in the United States and Britain. As Thomas Jefferson wrote in 1795, "What a tremendous obstacle to the future attempts at liberty will be the atrocities of Robespierre!"[26]

The French experience may have helped to spread democratic ideology across Europe, but its excesses, including expansionary war, probably acted, on balance, to slow democratic progress as conservatives banded together throughout Europe to bar a repetition of the French disaster. For example, Catherine the Great of

Russia, once a liberal reformer, became convinced by the experience that "equality is a monster."[27] In fact, it seems entirely possible that the French experience could have permanently discredited democracy had there not been the more congenial British and American examples to suggest that its excesses were not an inevitable consequence of democracy.

In Germany over a century later, democracy also degenerated into chaos, the rise of a dictatorship, and then aggressive, continent-wide military expansion. In the wake of that war, however, the Western victors blamed chaos (particularly economic chaos) for the phenomenon, not democracy, and they advocated democracy as a remedy.

The disastrous American Civil War. There was also luck for democracy in that the spectacular, if temporary, failure of democracy in America—the Civil War—didn't happen earlier. In the preface to the 1848 edition of his *Democracy in America,* Alexis de Tocqueville proclaimed the United States to be the "most stable of all the nations on earth" because, "while all the nations of Europe have been devastated by war or torn by civil discord, the American people alone in the civilized world have remained at peace."[28] Thirteen years later (and three years after Tocqueville's death), unable democratically to resolve central issues of slavery and the right of states to secede, the United States descended into four years of catastrophic civil war, an event that many saw as a crisis not only for American democracy but for democracy generally. Accordingly, as Abraham Lincoln put it (a bit overdramatically perhaps) in one of history's most famous speeches, it was imperative that after the war the nation should "have a new birth of freedom" in order that democracy—that is, "government of the people, by the people, for the people"—"shall not perish" not only from America, but "from the earth."

The American Civil War showed, soberingly, that democracies, like other governmental forms, were perfectly capable of cascading into the calamity of internal warfare. But the successful reestablishment of democracy after that disastrous interregnum (and perhaps the subsequent absence of any serious possibility of a repetition) could be taken by democrats to be heartening. Riker suggests, perhaps only a bit too rhapsodically, that "the present world-wide ascendancy of democratic theory is in no small part a consequence of the fact that American democracy survived its civil war."[29]

The World Wars. Democracy's ancient competitor, monarchy, was in well-deserved decline in Europe throughout the nineteenth century. World War I proved useful, though perhaps not essential, to the rise of democracy in that it spelled the final demise of the three remaining effective European monarchies. They were taken principally to have been responsible for initiating the catastrophic conflict either through desire (Germany) or through bumbling incompetence (Austria-Hungary, Russia).

The chief winners of World War I were all democracies, and in the war's wake a slew of new, rather imitative, democracies emerged in Europe. But then important governments sprang up that were virulently antidemocratic: Fascist Italy, Falangist Spain, theocratically nationalist Japan, and Nazi Germany and Austria. Moreover, in the 1930s these regimes often seemed to be on the upswing—fashion leaders, even—and their decisiveness and apparent virility made them widely attractive, particularly when compared to the stodgy, meek, economically troubled, indecisive democracies of Britain, France, and the United States.

As it happened, however, the authoritarian leaders of Italy, Japan, and Germany had secretly built international war and conquest into their ideology and agenda. At least in Europe, war was decidedly unpopular among the people, and it seems unlikely that Germany and Italy would have gone to war if a democratic debate had been allowed.[30] Without that constraint, however, the authoritarian masters were able to plunge their countries into cataclysm. As European monarchy had met its demise in World War I, Fascism and Nazism, together with Japanese militarism, died, bloodied and discredited, in World War II.

At the war's end the democracies, once again victorious, set about foisting their form of government upon the portion of Germany they occupied and upon Italy, Austria, and Japan. This, despite the fact that none of the countries would seem to have been very well prepared for it. Japan had had only limited and sporadic

211

experience with democracy—or with liberal thought in general. Democracy in Italy, Germany, and Austria had never been very strong or satisfying, and in each case it had proved powerless to prevent a takeover by vicious and destructive antidemocratic forces. To the people of each country, however, it must have seemed that even democracy at its worst was better than the alternative that had just brought catastrophe upon them, and they took up—or lapsed into—democracy without a great deal of apparent effort.

EXAMINING THE THIRD WAVE

In the aftermath of World War II, then, modern democracy had been on the market for less than two centuries. During that time it had been suitably tested, refined, and packaged to increase its appeal; it had rebounded from such potentially discrediting calamities as the Reign of Terror in France and the Civil War in America; and it had seen its comparative appeal and credibility enhanced as it survived two wars in which several of its major competitors had been destroyed. All the countries of West Europe except for Spain, Portugal, and perhaps Greece were now solidly in the democratic camp. And except for some shaky moments in a few of these countries, particularly France, democracy has generally proved quite robust there—and in Japan as well. Together with the United States, Canada, New Zealand, Iceland, and Australia, these countries represented then, and now, the vast majority of the world's wealth, and they had considerable potential for fashion leadership.

It seems unlikely that the rise of democracy was inevitable. If democracy had been badly marketed—if, for example, the British and American democratic experiments had become negative role models by degenerating into the mob violence and expansionary war that characterized France after its putatively democratic revolution of 1789—the world might never have adopted democracy at all, no matter how much economic or social development took place at the same time. On the other hand, since literacy, economic development, and modern communications do not seem to be required for a country to become democratic, the world—or substantial portions of it—could have become democratic centuries earlier if the right people at the right time had gotten the idea, had deftly promoted and market-tested it, and been graced by the right kind of luck.

It may be useful to apply such considerations to what Huntington in an important study has labeled the "third wave" of democratization. By his reckoning, the first two waves took place in 1828–1926 and 1943–64, and the third began around 1975. Since that time, not only has one competitor—hyperdemocratic communism—died out, but a more traditional competitor, the strong-armed dictatorship, has also been very considerably weakened.

It seems to me that about the only requirement for a country to become a democracy in this period, as in earlier ones, is the more or less general desire to do so. That is, for a country to become a democracy it has been a necessary and sufficient condition that the country—or perhaps only its political elite—find the idea attractive, that it catch the bug.

In assessing the rise of democracy during the third wave, Huntington does acknowledge "the beliefs and actions of political elites" as "probably the most immediate and significant explanatory variable." He concludes, however, that, while this may be "a powerful explanatory variable, it is not a satisfying one. Democracy can be created even if people do not want it. So it is not perhaps tautological to say that democracy will be created if people want democracy, but it is close to that. An explanation, someone has observed, is the place at which the mind comes to rest. Why do the relevant political elites want democracy? Inevitably, the mind wants to move further along the causal chain." As his mind moves further along, he clings to the concept of economic preconditions, but his other explanations for the recent democracy wave stress persuasional and promotional elements that fit nicely into a marketing approach: democracy's stylishness and the influence of fashion leaders (or what he calls "demonstration effects" or "snowballing"), changes of doctrine in the Catholic Church, the role of key converts like Gorbachev, the failures of the competition, and patterns of imitation.[31]

213

In a more recent article, Huntington continues to contend that economic development "has a strong positive effect on democratization." But he ends up concluding that "democratic development occurs when political leaders believe they have an interest in promoting it or a duty to achieve it."[32] In my view, as the democratic dialogue above suggests, this is just about the only requirement.

The View in 1975

Despite the postwar advances, democracy didn't seem to be in good shape in 1975. Many democracies or near-democracies had recently been taken over by authoritarian forces, including Greece in 1967, the Philippines in 1972, and two of Latin America's oldest democracies, Chile and Uruguay, in 1973. Then in 1975 democratic Lebanon descended into virulent civil war, and India, the world's largest democracy, became an authoritarian state (only for a couple of years, as it turned out), while communism, substantially contained since 1949, began to gain market share: it picked up Cambodia, Vietnam, and Laos in 1975, and was to add Angola in 1976, Mozambique and Ethiopia in 1977, South Yemen and Afghanistan in 1978, and Nicaragua and Grenada in 1979.

Many western democrats were plummeted by those developments into deepest gloom. The usually ebullient Daniel Patrick Moynihan, then the American envoy to the United Nations and a former ambassador to India, proclaimed in 1975 that democracy "increasingly tends to the condition of monarchy in the 19th century: a holdover form of government, one which persists in isolated or peculiar places here and there" but "which has simply no relevance to the future." In a similar mood, Germany's Willy Brandt was reported to believe at the time that "Western Europe has only 20 or 30 more years of democracy left in it; after that it will slide, engineless and rudderless, under the surrounding sea of dictatorship."[33]

Actually, even from the perspective of 1975 this gloom was a bit excessive. Democracy may have been clobbered by the competition in many areas of the globe, but it was alive and thriving not merely "in isolated or peculiar places," but in most of the major countries of the world. And then, quite remarkably, as if in conspiracy to embarrass Moynihan and Brandt—or to cheer them up—the world launched itself into something of a democratic binge that has been going on ever since. Democracy became all the rage.

Decolonization

Since 1975 just about every country that has received independence from Western colonizers—mainly small island republics in the Caribbean, but also such unlikely contenders as Papua New Guinea (1982) and Namibia (1989)—has adopted democracy. For many ex-colonies, former British overseership may have aided the democratic process. However, overall, as Huntington pointed out in 1984, most "former British colonies have *not* sustained democracy."[34] That is, it appears that the difference is not so much British preparation as the fact that these countries were decolonized in a period in which democracy was beginning to be the way things were done.

Southern Europe

The real tide of democracy seems to have begun in the three remaining nondemocracies in Europe outside the communist bloc. Even before Moynihan's gloomy prognosis was in print, Greece had moved from military dictatorship to democracy: after a failed venture in Cyprus, the discredited Greek leaders resigned in favor of civilian rule and Greece again became a democracy. Then in 1975 the focus shifted to Portugal where a struggle took place between democratic and communist forces in the wake of the collapse of an authoritarian dictatorship. For months the communists were on top, and they were clearly moving to consolidate their control. When they tried to close the country's last noncommunist newspaper, however, massive street demonstrations erupted, the cabinet shifted direction, and free elections in 1976 put a noncommunist government in control. In short order a similar transformation took place in Europe's last noncommunist nondemocracy, Spain, after the death of its long-time dictator.

The crucial dynamic in all this seems to have been essentially one of imitation, not one of economic or social necessity. By 1975 dictatorial Portugal and Spain had become something of anachronisms in the neighborhood. Released from old-fashioned authoritarianism, they shopped around for role models and found them in solidly, contentedly, and prosperously democratic Western Europe; as Huntington puts it, there was a "pervasive desire to identify their countries with Europe."[35] Portugal, in particular, had little previous experience with democracy and Spain's experiment with it in the 1930s had devolved into a disastrous civil war. Nevertheless both took to democracy well.

Latin America

Democracy's growth in Latin America since 1975 has been particularly impressive—by 1990 almost the entire area had turned democratic. This sweeping change over such a short period of time is difficult to credit to objective forces such as increasing wealth, a rising middle class, or burgeoning literacy rates. Indeed, over the period most countries in Latin America probably became *worse* off in many material ways—the rise of democracy there took place during a very substantial debt crisis.[36]

Nor can the democratic trend be readily credited to American pressure or salesmanship. For a century and a half the United States has repeatedly and often evangelically urged democracy upon its neighbors to the South, and it has often been quite prepared to use money (and sometimes military force) to gild the philosophic pill. These policies seem rarely to have made much lasting difference. For example, in 1913 President Woodrow Wilson dramatically declared the United States to be the "champion" of democracy in the Americas. To show he meant business, he dispatched U.S. troops to Nicaragua, Haiti, and the Dominican Republic to champion the democratic process. All three countries subsequently lapsed into extended dictatorships.[37]

The promoters improved neither the product nor the packaging. What changed was the receptivity of the customers: democracy caught on, at least among political elites, as an idea whose time had come.

The gradual acceptance of democracy by the Roman Catholic Church may have been helpful in this process as discussed above. But probably more important was the fact that each of the converted countries had been run by a military dictatorship—a form of government very familiar in the area—that in many cases had become discredited because of corruption and because of murderous suppression policies, usually against violent leftist insurgencies. The experience showed that military dictatorship, unchecked by public opinion, often led to excessive violence, and that it was generally less effective—or at any rate no more effective—at confronting the rebellions than civilian democracy. In Argentina, in addition, the military had led the nation into a failed, if brief, war against Britain over some nearly barren islands in the South Atlantic.

In olden days, of course, a discredited authoritarian regime would characteristically be replaced not by an effective democracy, but by another military dictatorship. By the 1970s, however, military leaders throughout Latin America appear to have become convinced that the military dictatorship was a thing of the past, and they often seem to have been embarrassed that their countries were so out of fashion. They had once subscribed to an almost "messianic self-image as *the* institution ultimately interpreting and ensuing the highest interests of the nation," in the words of Guillermo O'Donnell and Philippe Schmitter. But, partly because of the destruction the military had wreaked, Latin American societies came to reject that image, and gradually the military came to accept, and to facilitate, transitions to civilian democratic rule. Increasingly, the generals began to realize that they actually might do better under democracy where they "don't have to answer the hardest questions." As a result, a consensus has emerged that constitutional rule is the future of Latin America. When a clumsy coup effort was launched in Argentina in 1990, the country's president reacted not so much with alarm as with contemptuous dismissal. He labeled the effort "ridiculous antics" and, as one observer noted, he "just said no and it was over in a matter of hours."[38]

At the same time, and not unrelated, was the increased willingness of leftist groups to eschew violence and to seek to advance their cause through peaceful democratic means. As one reporter put it in the 1990s, "the Latin American left's 30-year obsession with armed struggle as a means to revolution has come to an end."[39]

Perhaps the most spectacular case of a new, instant democracy created during the third wave is Paraguay, a country that had never known any kind of government except Jesuit theocracy or rigid military dictatorship. In 1989 Paraguay's guiding autocrat, entrenched since 1954, was overthrown by a man who had been one of his chief henchmen and who had become fabulously wealthy in the process. The new leader, however, was sensitive to the fact that democracy is what everyone is wearing nowadays—that "despots have gone out of style," as a reporter from the *Economist* put it. Accordingly he held fair elections and promised that, if elected president, he would guide the country to full democracy in four years. Paraguayans, in the first free election in their grim history, took him at his word, and on schedule in 1993 another election was held and another man became president.[40]

That military leaders still had (and have) the physical ability to maintain themselves in office is suggested by a couple of counterexamples to this trend. In Panama in 1989 General Manuel Noriega, in classic Latin American fashion, calmly stole an election that went against him and was deposed only by an American military invasion. Liberated from this anachronistic tyrant, the country became a democracy. In the 1990s, a somewhat similar process took place in Haiti.

Asia

In 1984, Huntington observed correctly that "democratic regimes that last have seldom, if ever, been instituted by mass popular action."[41] The rise of democracy in Portugal might have been taken to be an exception at the time, but soon such exceptions were to proliferate enough to disprove the rule.

Demonstrations in the Philippines in 1986, together with pressure from the United States, forced a dictator from office, and democracy was established there. And in 1987 demonstrations, with far less American pressure, pushed the government of prospering South Korea toward democracy.

Most remarkably, massive prodemocracy demonstrations erupted in 1988 in Burma, one of the poorest and most isolated places on the globe. Somehow the people there had gotten the message: clearly, neither prosperity, economic growth, a burgeoning middle class, nor frequent and close contact with the West were necessary for the democratic idea to find receptive minds. The democracy movement was put down by force, but some moderately free elections were held in 1990—although the military then refused to let the newly elected government take office.

Meanwhile, the regime in Taiwan, seeing the light, liberalized substantially, and a somewhat rocky democracy was established in Pakistan in 1988. Advances were also made in Thailand and Malaysia and, in the late 1990s, Indonesia.

Of particular interest in this regard was the remarkable absence of military coups during the very considerable economic crises in the area that began in 1997. This is a change that strongly resembles the one that has taken place in Latin America. In Thailand, for example, where the military had ousted civilian leaders no less than seventeen times since 1932, most recently in 1991, the army's commander in chief had come by 1998 to believe that "The coup d'état is outdated. The more time passes, the more it is obsolete. My soldiers must stay completely out of politics." A similar realization seems to be dawning in Pakistan.[42]

Soviet Communism Implodes

Communism, a hyperdemocracy established by Lenin in the Soviet Union, was viscerally devoted to the proposition that democracy, or at any rate Western democratic capitalism, should, and eventually would, perish from the earth through internal revolution and through "wars of national liberation."[43] In result, a virulent and sometimes violent contest between the promoters of democracy and those of communism took place as each group sought to peddle its wares—to win hearts and minds—using agitation, propaganda, demonstration projects, and caustic disparagement of the competition.[44]

Communism's sales efforts were substantially aided by the Soviet Union's apparent economic progress and by its dramatic launch in 1957 of the first artificial space satellite. In America, the hastily assembled, if august and authoritative, President's Commission on National Goals declared the democratic world to be in "grave danger" from communism's "great capacity for political organization and propaganda" and from the "specious appeal of Communist doctrine to peoples eager for rapid escape from poverty." Meanwhile, the Central Intelligence Agency alarmingly calculated that the Soviet gross national product might be triple that of the United States by the year 2000.[45]

By the late 1970s or early 1980s, however, it was becoming clear to a few Soviet officials and intellectuals that the Soviet social and economic system was stagnating under the weight of a stifling and cynical bureaucracy, an irrational and often erratic planning mechanism, and an incompetent and sometimes vicious ideological apparatus.[46] Moreover, it was becoming increasingly clear that many of the problems came about *because* the Soviet Union wasn't democratic, or at any rate, free. The all-encompassing secretiveness and suspiciousness of the ruling elite meant that the flow of information was severely hampered, new ideas were routinely stifled, suggestions for improvement were casually ignored, and attempts at protest were forcibly suppressed. Devices that might weaken the system's control of information, like personal computers, photocopying machines, home videotape recorders, and telephone books were strictly regulated.

Most importantly, blunders went unappreciated, unexamined, and uncriticized. For a decade and probably much more, no one at the top seems to have understood what was going on with the economy. Not only was it increasingly unproductive and uncompetitive, but the leadership was mindlessly straining it by expanding the defense budget and gathering to its embrace a collection of costly overseas dependencies (the ten countries that fell into its orbit between 1975 and 1979) to add to its older ones, like Cuba.

Meanwhile, its colonies in east Europe, particularly Poland, were becoming more of a psychic and economic burden—the empire was striking back.[47] Added to this was war: in 1979, without discussing the decision widely or apparently considering it very carefully, the Brezhnev regime sent tens of thousands of troops into neighboring Afghanistan to prop up a faltering friendly regime there, and costs and casualties mounted.

Meanwhile, communism was failing in the outer reaches as well. For decades it had preached that successful revolution would be followed by social, political, and economic bliss. But successful Communist revolutionaries repeatedly led their countries instead into civil war, economic collapse, and a state of severe social injustice, most horrendously in Cambodia where Communist romantics found that their revolutionary theory required them to commit genocide, killing over a million people.[48]

By contrast with all this, democratic reform began to look pretty good—or at least less bad than the obvious alternatives. Wherever there was a suitable contrast, noncommunist countries were doing comparatively well economically: East Germany versus West Germany, North Korea versus South Korea, Hungary versus Austria, Vietnam versus almost any noncommunist country in Southeast Asia. As in Latin America, it was economic decline, not economic development, that was leading to calls for democracy.

Mikhail Gorbachev was one of those insiders who had begun to see the defects in the system. After assuming leadership in 1985, he quickly garnered an increasing appreciation for the appalling mess he had inherited, and he tried to free up the system. As he did so the democratic idea flared up throughout the Communist empire in east Europe. In country after country demonstrators demanded democracy, the removal of despised leaders, and ultimately the overthrow, through elections, of Communist domination. A key element in the success of this movement in 1989 was the suggestion from Gorbachev that, unlike his predecessors, he would not use force to suppress independent democratic developments in the area.

That the Soviet Union might eventually tire of its troublesome and dependent east European empire and allow it to wriggle free was perhaps predictable.[49] The astounding speed of the transformation was not, however, as Communist authorities gave in, with various degrees of reluctance, to a seemingly unstoppable force. Remarkably, communism yielded to democracy more smoothly, and far more quickly, than had monarchy, first in East Europe, and then in Gorbachev's USSR when peaceful, but massive, street demonstrations helped undercut a coup by Communist hardliners in 1991.

Actually, some of this development might have been at least partly anticipated. In 1956, Hungary declared it planned instantly to become a multiparty democracy, and in 1968 there came a similar glimmer in Czechoslovakia. Both ventures were crushed by Soviet tanks, but the 1989 experience suggests that most of the countries in eastern Europe (and probably those on the Baltic Sea) would have been democratic but for the artificial dictates of the occupying forces of the Soviet Union.[50]

However, it had generally been assumed that Communists, who had heretofore never relaxed their control over any of their acquisitions, were dedicatedly tenacious. Reflecting this perspective, Huntington concluded in pre-Gorbachev 1984 that "The likelihood of democratic development in Eastern Europe is virtually nil" and that democratization could occur there "only if either the Soviet Union were drastically weakened through war, domestic upheaval, or economic collapse (none of which seems likely), or if the Soviet Union came to view Eastern European democratization as not threatening to its interests (which seems equally unlikely)."[51] The Soviet Union did weaken, though not "drastically," but it did come to fear democracy less.

THE FUTURE OF DEMOCRACY

After two hundred years of development—with a considerable burst after 1975—democracy may be ripe for some setbacks. Indeed, as Larry Diamond and Charles Gati point out, democracy has not actually taken—that is, authoritarian rulers have taken over—in some of the postcommunist countries, particularly those in Asia.[52] However, although democracies have often reverted to authoritarian rule historically, this does not mean that democracy is a peculiarly fragile form: any government can be overthrown by a sufficiently large and dedicated group of thugs with guns, and it is not at all clear that authoritarian governments—fraught with histories of coups and countercoups, and with endless battles for succession—are any less fragile. The problem seems to be one of definition. When a democracy gets overthrown we say it has failed, but when one dictator topples another we sometimes see this as persistence of form and a kind of stability.

What will be most likely to foster democracy in countries that do not now have it, and what is most likely to maintain democracy in ones that do, will not be economic or social development, but rather the desire of ruling elites to emulate the established democracies. The leaders of, say, Poland want very much to join the West, and, since democracy is clearly the price of admission, they will willingly pay it. The leaders of, say, Turkmenistan or Afghanistan, on the other hand, may find neither the goal nor the price to be of much interest.

China

One important setback to democratic development took place in China in 1989 when democracy demonstrators with rather mild demands were forcibly put down. This suppression was carried out by aging Communist leaders who concluded, probably correctly, that to give in to the movement could eventually result in the demise of Communist Party control: the freedom to speak and petition implies, and sets into motion, the potential for the replacement of regimes even if the formal mechanism of elections is not in place.

China is still given the lowest possible score on Freedom House's democracy rating scheme, but there clearly has been vast liberalization from the totalitarian days of Mao (when China also received the lowest possible score, of course). In fact, as economist Gale Johnson stresses, "The greatest improvement in civil rights the world has ever seen occurred in China when the communes were abolished. Virtually every day, people living in the communes had no civil rights; the commune controlled the economy, their lives as workers, the political and police powers. That all disappeared overnight, and 700 million people were released from domination by a bunch of bureaucrats."[53]

In a 1996 assessment, Henry Rowen observes that although the Communist Party retains its authoritarian control, there have lately been three notable, if underreported, democratic developments: the emergence of semicompetitive democratic elections at the village level, the growth of a viable legal system, and an increasing liberalization in the media.[54] Rowen, however, remains something of an economic determinist, and he concludes that it will take until around 2015 before China is wealthy enough to become a democracy.

But it seems to me that the key determinant in China and elsewhere is more likely to be the mentality of the leadership. There is a possibility that Chinese rulers are becoming embarrassed by their political backwardness, very much like Latin American military leaders in the 1970s and 1980s. Moreover, the observation that President Jiang Zemin is reportedly given to reciting from the American Declaration of Independence and the Gettysburg Address at public functions (as well as mysteriously singing "Kiss Me Once, Kiss Me Twice, and Kiss Me Once Again") suggests he is being influenced by Western fashion leaders. There is also the potentially subversive acquisition of democratic, liberal Hong Kong in 1997 and the clear desire in Beijing eventually to bring democratic Taiwan into the fold, something that is likely to happen only if the Taiwan Chinese can be persuaded that their interests and life-style will be preserved in a united China. Strands like these suggest Rowen could prove to be a pessimist.

Islam

Democracy has yet to penetrate Islamic countries very deeply. Indeed, of the fifty-three countries rated "not free" by Freedom House in its 1996 ratings, twenty-nine were Muslim.

As Huntington has observed, Islam often associates democracy

224

with the Western influences many in the religion oppose.[55] Thus the elites in many Islamic countries specifically do *not* find the Western democracies to be attractive fashion leaders, even as those in, say, Hungary, do. Consequently, although many Islamic states are far overdue for democracy from an economic determinist's standpoint, even rich Islamic states have adroitly managed to resist the trend.

But this again demonstrates that it is the mindset of the elites that matters, not economic or social preparation. Where Muslim leaders have allowed elections, as in Algeria and Iran in 1997, the voters displayed considerable ability to differentiate and express themselves even though the choice of candidates and the freedom of speech were limited. And some Muslim states, such as Mali, Turkey, Pakistan, and Qatar have certainly been able to move substantially toward democracy.[56] The Islamic countries are kept undemocratic not by the necessary dictates of their culture or by the state of their economic development, but by the will of their leaders.

Africa

In Africa, there has been notable democratic progress in quite a few places. The most spectacular case, of course, is South Africa, but there has also been democratic development in Tanzania, Botswana, Malawi, Namibia, Mozambique, Ghana, Benin, Kenya, Zimbabwe, Zambia, Madagascar, Gambia, Nigeria, and Senegal.

Most impressive is impoverished, isolated Mali—Africa's Paraguay perhaps. By becoming democratic it stands as an embarrassment to those leaders in other African states who self-servingly excuse their authoritarian ways by blandly serving up the notion from classic transitological literature that democracies can only flourish where there is a middle class and sustained economic development.[57]

One-party and dictatorial authoritarian regimes have generally performed as badly in Africa as in Latin America, while many of the continent's democracies or near-democracies are comparatively serene and prosperous. And there appears to be a substantial exhaustion with mindless sloganeering and with aging, ineffectual ideology. Quite a few African dictators began nervously whistling in the dark after the dramatic east European events of 1989. To justify their tenure, they continue to insist that only a one-party system can provide unity against the potentially centrifugal forces of tribalism and ethnicity. But given their failures, a little democratic disunity begins to take on a certain appeal. As a citizen of once-democratic Kenya put it, "Since the multiparty system works elsewhere and has previously worked in Kenya, one would like to know the aspect of our human nature which rendered us incapable of making it work after 1982."[58]

Prospects

Although there may well be some softness in the democratic trend of the last decades of the twentieth century, the prospects seem generally rather favorable for further democratic development. In very substantial portions of the globe democracy has become all the rage, and it could well capture an even greater market share in the future. As Fareed Zakaria puts it, "there are no longer respectable alternatives to democracy; it is part of the fashionable attire of modernity."[59]

Democracy is, of course, entirely capable of making colossal mistakes. But, as Machiavelli observes hopefully, "the people are guilty of fewer excesses than the prince," and their errors "are of less importance, and therefore more easily remedied."[60] The advantage may be merely comparative but, as democracy's competitors become discredited, people increasingly seem to have come to conclude that it is real. And, quite possibly, they are right.

Democracy is an intellectual construct that has been on the market for quite a while, has an intrinsic appeal, has a fairly good track record, has proved in market tests to be notably better (or less bad) than the competition, and, despite some occasional overeager and inflated claims, has been rather well marketed and packaged by its promoters who, after several lucky breaks and after two hundred years of patient, persistent salesmanship and judicious product modification, are now cashing in. In general, economically advanced countries have tended to buy this idea (as well as many other related ones) comparatively earlier, but it is the exertions of idea entrepreneurs that have been more determining of the pace of democratization than the correlated wealth of their customers.

CONCLUSION

*

Democracy and Capitalism

CONNECTIONS AND DISCONNECTIONS

IT HAS been a running theme of this book—its bottom line, in fact—that there is a considerable disconnection between democracy and its image and between capitalism and its image. This chapter includes an assessment of the connections, if any, between democracy and capitalism themselves.

Democracy and capitalism, it seems, are actually quite independent: each can exist without the other. However, democracy may benefit on balance from its (erroneously alleged) association with capitalist prosperity, and both institutions, on the other hand, are often unfairly associated with crime, something that could undermine their acceptance.

Moreover, although capitalism does not require democracy to function effectively, democracy probably does enhance capitalist economic growth by reducing the threat of government confiscation, by helpfully establishing a reasonably coherent rule of law, by maintaining a fundamental bias toward openness and transparency, by allowing *all* interest groups (rather than a privileged subset) to enter the political fray, by providing a process for ousting failed leaders, and, lately at least, by gaining a perhaps undeserved association with stability and predictability.

Finally, there seem to be a number of conceptual connections, or at least similarities, between democracy and capitalism, not the least of which is their ability to function even when their constituents generally do not appreciate them very well.

CAPITALISM WITHOUT DEMOCRACY, DEMOCRACY WITHOUT CAPITALISM

While it is no news to observe that capitalism can exist without democracy—quite a few countries have managed that quite effectively—it is commonly maintained that a country must be capitalist in order to become a democracy. Thus, for Charles Lindblom, "only within market-oriented systems does political democracy arise." And Peter Berger maintains that "capitalism is a necessary but not sufficient condition of democracy under modern conditions," while Milton Friedman finds that "history suggests" that "capitalism is a necessary condition for political freedom." Robert Dahl observes that "it is a historical fact that modern democratic institutions . . . have existed only in countries with predominantly privately owned, market-oriented economies, or capitalism if you prefer," and then extrapolates this historical regularity: "it looks to be the case that market-oriented economies are necessary to democratic institutions."[1]

Both the generality and the logic of such declarations could bear some analysis, however. To begin with, until the rise of real command economies in communist countries in this century, nearly all countries in the modern world have been capitalistic in some reasonable sense of the word—ill-managed, perhaps, or foolishly restrictive, but nonetheless basically capitalistic. That is, outside the communist world all democracies have been capitalistic, but so also have just about all nondemocracies.

In this circumstance, the only way a noncapitalist democracy could have arisen would be for a democracy to abandon capitalism. However, after a capitalist country becomes democratic, successful capitalists and other people of wealth, although a minority of the population, have been able to use democratic opportunities to keep the government from substantially confiscating their wealth, a process discussed in chapter 6. This has been true even in countries controlled by important democratic socialist movements that have been explicitly devoted to creating a command economy. For example, in 1918 Britain's Labour Party pointedly adapted a clause in its constitution (one not removed until the 1990s and then only after a furious internal battle) that called for "common ownership of the means of production, distribution, and exchange."[2] The party was never able to carry out this anticapitalistic stipulation, however, even though it ruled the country with a substantial parliamentary majority for many years.

Thus, democracies have generally been established in capitalist countries and, because of the democratic process itself, they have remained essentially capitalist. Since a capitalist democracy cannot by its nature become noncapitalist, then, a noncapitalist democracy could emerge only if democracy were imposed upon a country that was neither capitalist nor democratic. This became a possibility only after 1989 when many countries with command economies took up democracy in the aftermath of the collapse of communism. And that experience seems to do considerable damage to the commonly accepted and previously unassailable notion that democracy cannot exist in a noncapitalistic economy.

Many of the postcommunist countries, particularly in central Europe, successfully became democracies even though the vast majority of their people continued to work for the government, even though the economy continued to be centrally planned, and even though most property continued to be state-owned. Politicians in these countries have worked (and continue to work) to change that of course, but only because the old economic system has become discredited, not because the process of democracy mandates it.

Bulgaria appears to furnish the clearest case in point. For various political reasons, very little meaningful economic reform took place for several years after 1989—all the important sectors of the economy remained controlled by the government and most everyone remained its employee. Moreover, prices were substantially controlled, peasants were actively dissuaded from farming privately, bankruptcy remained unknown, state-owned enterprises continued to be heavily subsidized, privatization was very limited, and the government stubbornly rejected all the reform conditions proffered by the International Monetary Fund. Yet, although Bulgaria's politics were often tumultuous, they remained free and open—that is to say, fully democratic. People remained free to speak, publish, and organize, and fair elections were held every couple of years. Eventually, fed up with the hugely mismanaged economy, massive, but peaceful, street protests brought down the government at the end of 1996, and a subsequent, duly elected government finally began to institute meaningful economic re-

233

forms.[3] But for the better part of a decade, democracy worked quite well in the effective absence of capitalism.

Analysts who argue that democracy can only flourish in a capitalist economy have generally pointed to the importance of independent money. Thus William Riker argues that "when all economic life is absorbed into government, there is no conceivable financial base for opposition."[4] Friedman follows a similar line of reasoning. If "all jobs are under the direct control of political authorities" it would take "an act of self-denial" for the government "to permit its employees to advocate policies directly contrary to official doctrine." Moreover, he questions whether those in opposition would be able to "finance their cause. . . . How could they raise the funds?" But just that sort of "self-denial" clearly did take place in Bulgaria, and the opposition was able to come up with the necessary means to launch its successful protest. (Indeed, in many countries, protest against government policies has often come from students even though many of them are entirely dependent on government stipends for their livelihood.) Friedman also finds it difficult to imagine that the government might help finance "subversive propaganda."[5] But in many democracies that is exactly what happens as opposition parties are automatically guaranteed, and regularly receive, governmental funds if they can make a plausible case that they represent even 2 or 3 percent of the population.

History no longer suggests, it seems, that capitalism is a necessary or logical condition for democracy.

Democracy's Connection with Capitalist Prosperity

I have argued that democracy is merely an idea, one that has been peddled with increasing success by idea entrepreneurs over the last couple of centuries. A potential danger to democratic development is that democracy may have been oversold by these promoters in some important respects. In particular, democracy may have been bought by many people, especially lately, because it seemed to be associated with capitalist prosperity.

While prosperity and democracy seem to have gone hand in hand in the developed Western world, prosperity certainly did not accompany democracy in India or the Philippines, and some may eventually be led to notice that much of the present prosperity of Spain, South Korea, and Taiwan was achieved under authoritarian regimes.[6] Moreover, since, as discussed in chapter 5, successful economic development does not inspire people to acknowledge they have become happy, some disillusionment is likely, and it is possible disappointed democracy-embracers might start shopping around for other forms of government.

There is another prospect, however. As was also suggested in chapter 5, capitalist prosperity has been on a roll in much of the world for quite some time now for various reasons including the rise of wealth-enhancing business virtue. Moreover, this economic expansion will likely not only accelerate but spread much more broadly around the world in the future (particularly in the absence of major war) because of the ascent of the politically incorrect one-handed economist: economists now essentially know what they are talking about, speak with something resembling one voice, and, despite the politically painful nature of much of their advice, increasingly are being heeded by policymakers. This burgeoning prosperity has not been crucially caused by the rise of democracy, nor will it be in the future—the key to prosperity both for democracies and nondemocracies is to adopt sound economic policies. But the rise of democracy happens to have been accompanied by the capitalist prosperity surge, and democracy may benefit because it will be given undue credit for that surge. And, if the surge continues, such fellow-traveling credit will likely continue to be given.

DEMOCRACY'S CONNECTION TO CAPITALIST GROWTH

Although capitalism can certainly exist without democracy, although it now appears that democracy can exist without capitalism, and although nondemocracies are entirely capable of adopting sound economic policies which can cause them to prosper,

235

democracy may nonetheless, on balance, be beneficial to economic development in several ways.

First, as noted in chapter 6, democracy in practice, if not in Plato's imaginings, does give to property owners a certain confidence that they can protect themselves from arbitrary seizure of their property—or at any rate that they will have recourse if such seizure does take place. Insofar as that confidence is necessary to encourage innovation and capital investment and the beneficial effects these activities have on economic growth and efficiency, democracy will have an economic leg up on authoritarian regimes—or at least on those of the more absolutist sort.[7] Rosenberg and Birdzell point out that "it was not until the nineteenth century that merchants developed enough confidence in governments to invest in large, immobile factories rather than in bills of exchange, ships, and moveable stocks of goods," an important phenomenon that accompanied the rise of democracy and may possibly have been partially caused by it.[8]

Second, although I argued at the end of chapter 4 that quite a bit of capitalist development can take place without much of a legal system as in China today, effective legal systems still do have an economic benefit where they exist—that is, China's economic development would be on even better ground if it had a viable legal system. Insofar as democracy is associated with the rule of law—and, of course, the absence of violence—this association will aid capitalist development. However, if the courts are mainly enforcing business-discouraging laws and regulations as in India for much of its postindependence history, this benefit will be minor.

Third, as noted in chapter 2, businesses which are open and transparent enjoy, on average, a competitive advantage since others are more likely to be willing to deal with them. Therefore an economy with routine and comprehensive openness is likely to develop more prodigiously than one where secrecy prevails. It is certainly possible under democracy to have private business dealings that are secret and opaque, but democracy does foster an atmosphere of openness, whistle-blowing, public prying, and transparency that can be helpful to capitalist development.

Fourth, despite initial appearances, democracy may be better than other forms of government at handling interest-group pressures that can harm the economy. Many economists have bemoaned the economically perverse effects that interest-group politics can have in a democracy. Thus Rosenberg and Birdzell argue that an "adverse political response to organizational innovation is inherent in democratic politics" because an innovation or development that benefits a wide and a diverse group of consumers often threatens existing firms and their employees who are then likely to organize for political action.[9] Although this phenomenon certainly occurs in democracies, it also takes place in non-democracies. The difference is that in a democracy *all* specially interested people and groups, not just those who happen to be favored by the ruler or the ruling group, are admitted into the fray and may freely seek to manipulate governmental policy to their benefit. Some interests in a democracy do enjoy special privileges, but this is nothing compared to the perks traditionally graced upon preferred groups like the army, the aristocracy, the landed gentry, or the nomenklatura in nondemocracies. In a democracy, interests which are not officially preferred have at least a fighting chance of undercutting favored interests and getting some of the gravy for themselves.

Fifth, democracy, as discussed in chapter 6, is better than other governmental forms at getting rid of failed leaders whereas authoritarian governments, including monarchies, very frequently are incapable of accomplishing this elemental task. For example, it is conceivable that in a democratic China a leader like Mao might have been able to put into place a fanciful economic policy like the Great Leap Forward, but it is inconceivable that he could have remained in office after the policy produced disastrous results including an induced famine in which some fifteen to thirty million perished. In democratic Bulgaria by contrast, the bums were summarily, and peacefully, thrown out in 1996 when their economic policies had merely reduced wages by a factor of ten in a single year and caused the banking system to collapse, wiping out 80 percent of all personal savings in the process.[10] The miserable citizens of mismanaged autocracies like Iraq and Cuba or North Korea do not have the same opportunity. Even where failed leaders are not removed from office in a democracy, their tenure is generally limited by something other than their physical health or their caginess at undercutting coups, so they can often be waited out. Democratic leaders may do dumb things, but their errors—including economic ones—are more likely to be corrected.

Sixth, democracy has come to garner a reputation for stability, and this can enhance the prospects for economic development. Although democracy has not always been known historically as a stable form of government—quite the reverse sometimes— several recent developments may combine to help democracy overcome that image, whether fully deserved or not. Among these are the exhilarating ascendance of democracy of late, the comparative instability recently shown in Communist and military autocracies, the association of democracy with such overwhelmingly, even tediously, stable states as Switzerland and Britain and the United States and Japan, and the clear intention of rich, powerful democracies to assist struggling like-minded countries with their economic development. Since wealth-enhancing investors and entrepreneurs tend to be congenitally fond of stability and predictability, countries held to exhibit those characteristics are accordingly more likely to prosper, something that has greatly benefited impoverished Mali, for example, after it became an effective democracy in 1992 against all transitological odds.[11]

THE CONNECTION OF DEMOCRACY AND CAPITALISM WITH CRIME

Although democracy and capitalism do not, by definition, allow for violence, they may be damaged if they come to be causally (and casually) linked to crime, especially in postcommunist countries. People often look with alarm at the United States where colorful stories of criminal mayhem abound, never at capitalist democracies like Canada, Japan, or Switzerland where crime is low.

Two responses to this concern are unlikely to be very helpful. One is to observe (correctly) that crime in many of the new democracies is, for the most part, actually still quite low, especially compared to that enjoyed in the exemplary United States. The other is to suggest that they must grin and bear it because Western standards of justice require that, essentially, it is better to let a lot of criminals roam free than to imprison a few innocent people. This latter notion merely reinforces the connection of democracy with crime, and the understandable response is to suggest that the choice actually then is between locking up a few innocent people or locking up all of them as, out of fear, they place themselves essentially into house arrest. What good, people may well ask, is "freedom" if one no longer feels free to walk the streets? People are now far freer to speak their minds in the new democracies of course, but not that many people ever say things that anyone, even the most paranoid of dictators, would want to suppress, whereas everybody uses the sidewalks.

Concern about crime has, of course, also been very high at times in the United States, and it can be a hot topic with voters as was shown in the 1994 elections there. An important difference, perhaps, is that concern about crime does not translate in the U.S. into demands to get rid of democracy and capitalism; in some new democracies it conceivably could. Alarmist Hitler analogies should be avoided, but it was the demand for order (in that case from street fighting by political gangs) as much as economic instability that helped him into office.[12]

Obviously, efforts to improve police work could help with this concern. But, as in the United States, the fear of crime is often essentially psychological—concern about crime burgeoned in 1994 even though crime had actually been going down at the time for more than ten years.[13] Moreover, with a free capitalist press, crime, which sells papers everywhere, is more likely to be reported and dwelled upon—often in gruesome detail—and it is likely to be handled in the usual incompetent, anecdotal manner so common in America.[14]

CONCEPTIONAL CONNECTIONS BETWEEN DEMOCRACY
AND CAPITALISM

It has been pointed out at various points in this book that there are a number of conceptual connections between democracy and capitalism. Both rely more on the individual than on the collective; both question authority in one way or another and work best when it is restrained; both allow people the freedom to put an enterprise or a sitting government out of business if they become dissatisfied with its performance; both are notably, if often clumsily, self-correcting; and both leave people substantially free for individual pursuits even though this generally leads to a considerable inequality of result and to a sort of (nonviolent) disorderliness that some find distasteful. Both are also founded on the fundamental—even breathtaking—assumption that it is best, in the end, actually to trust people to understand and to act upon their own interests, and on the related assumption (or hope) that, in the end, you can't fool everybody every time.

Moreover democracy and capitalism are conceptually linked in that each has a kind of "emptiness at the core," as Francis Fukuyama has put it. This quality can be unpleasantly unsatisfying at least to people who aspire to grander goals and who have higher visions: there is, it often seems, no *there* there. What Yergin and Stanislaw say about capitalism can be said about democracy as well: "a system that takes the pursuit of self-interest and profit as its guiding light does not necessarily satisfy the yearning in the human soul for belief and some higher meaning beyond materialism."[15] And it must be granted that democracy and capitalism, at least in the form suggested by the perspective of Ralph's Pretty Good Grocery, really do lack any sort of snappy answer to such great philosophical themes as what is truth? what is good? and what, after all, is the meaning of life? To queries and expostulations about such matters, there is a tendency to shrug, and, like Voltaire's Candide, to suggest exhaustedly, if good-naturedly, "That is well said, but we must cultivate our garden."

Finally, the institutions of democracy and capitalism share a conceptual connection in that both seem routinely to inspire in their constituents a curious incomprehension about the way they work.

Both in mature democracies and in new ones many still cling to a fuzzy, romantic, Rockwellian image that, centuries of experience suggest, is quite fantastic. Democracy, I have argued, is not about active mass participation, enlightened citizen vigilance, heartwarming consensus, or majority tolerance, but the notion that it *ought* somehow to be that way still persists and even prevails.

Similarly, a common view of capitalism, one often held even by capitalists when they trouble to generalize about it, maintains that capitalism is somehow vicious and reprehensible or at least devoid of virtue. This view prevails even though the daily business experience of people in advanced capitalist countries—where they are treated overwhelmingly with honesty, fairness, civility, and even compassion by acquisitive proprietors and deal-makers—constantly belies the negative image. For example, in polls conducted in 1990, the residents of capitalist New York tended to agree with those in still communist Moscow that it is "unfair" for an entrepreneur to raise prices merely because demand increases, and New Yorkers were, if anything, *less* tolerant of economic inequality, *more* distrustful of "speculators," and *less* appreciative of the importance of material incentives. And, although the overwhelming majority of economists insist otherwise, generous portions of the public in capitalist America continue to maintain that downsizing is bad for the economy, that foreign trade agreements cost domestic jobs, and that gasoline prices result mainly from the quest for profits by Big Oil rather than from the normal play of supply and demand.[16]

However, on the brighter side, these faulty popular perspectives—that democracy ought somehow to be much better than experience has shown it to be and that capitalism deep down is somehow really much worse than experience routinely suggests—do not seem to have greatly hampered the fundamental workings of either institution at least in advanced capitalist democracies of late. In operation democracy is far from ideal, but it seems to be the best (or least bad) form of government. And in operation capitalism, for all its real and imagined flaws, seems the best (or least bad) way to run an economy for the greatest benefit of the greatest number.

Hence, although there probably ought to be *some* guiding minds at work for democracy and capitalism to be properly instituted and maintained, it does not appear necessary for people in general fully to appreciate them, or even to believe in them, for them to work. For societies striving to embrace the gains—however limited, modest, and at best pretty good—of democracy and capitalism, that somewhat perverse message could be the most hopeful of all.

* *Appendix* *

AN INVENTORY OF PROPOSITIONS

CAPITALISM

UNDER CAPITALISM, virtue is considerably more than its own reward: contrary to its image, capitalism tends, all other things being equal, systematically, though not uniformly, to reward business behavior that is honest, fair, civil, and compassionate, and it inspires a form of risk-taking behavior that can often be credibly characterized as heroic.

Moreover, since phonies can usually eventually be spotted, people who are genuinely honest, fair, civil, and compassionate are more likely to succeed in business than those who simply feign such qualities.

Since a nice guy will feel bad (punish himself) if he lets somebody down, it is sensible, all other things equal, to prefer to deal with nice guys. As a result, nice guys, on average, have a competitive advantage over non-nice guys and accordingly will tend to prosper—that is, to finish first.

When people generally expect to be treated dishonestly, unfairly, or discourteously in business they will tend to avoid making transactions, and hence there will be less growth because there will be less economic activity.

Virtuous business practices may be financially beneficial in the long term, but in part because of capitalism's traditional image, this reality may not be obvious to the very capitalists who stand to benefit from them. It has apparently often taken an effort for people to grasp the concept of enlightened, long term, economic self-interest.

Since the business virtues are economically advantageous, they can arise and flourish through normal competitive pressures. What seems to be required is the establishment of an important business innovation: since the profitability of virtuous business behavior is apparently often not obvious, a business innovator must discover the economic value of virtue and then act upon this important discovery. Other businesses, noticing the success of the innovator, follow suit.

When dishonest business practices are common, courts or regulatory systems will be swamped. But when honesty is the norm, the courts and regulators will be capable (strongly encouraged by the many honest businesses) of enforcing the comparatively rare infractions, and consequently further encouraging economic growth. It seems likely, then, that effective institutions are more the result of virtuous norms than the cause of them.

As an elaborated, self-conscious principle, the notion that honesty, fair dealing, civility, and compassion bring wealth seems to have been generally discovered, or to have been made clearly explicit, only in the nineteenth century or so. P. T. Barnum's mid-century tract, *The Art of Money-Getting,* may be the earliest publication in which the profitability of virtuous business behavior is specifically and extensively laid out.

The rise of business virtue seems very much to have coincided with the remarkable economic rise of the West in the last two centuries, and probably importantly helped cause it.

The invasion of institutions like McDonald's and K-Mart can have a very beneficial impact on the business climate because such businesses furnish examples of how to prosper through the routine and prominent application of established and tested procedures of honesty, fairness, civility, and compassion to business practices.

Where trust has arduously, and profitably, been built up, efforts to further guarantee honesty by mechanical legalistic devices could actually be counterproductive.

It is desirable to have effective antifraud legislation, but as a practical matter the swindled have very little chance of ever getting their money back even where there is a highly developed and substantially incorruptible court system.

When demand outstrips supply and the seller is unable to raise the price, customers become supplicants, and there is no economic disincentive to incivility, surliness, and arrogance.

The remarkable, historically unprecedented economic expansion of the past two centuries has taken place substantially by accident or default. It was not notably guided by government policy—indeed, it frequently took place *despite* government policy—because it occurred when economists often didn't know what they were talking about or fundamentally disagreed over policy, or, when they could agree, were often ignored by decision makers who were pursuing divergent agendas, were mesmerized by faulty economic folk wisdom or ideology, or were paralyzed by political cowardice.

The random politician or governmental official consulting the random economist only a generation ago might well have gotten the wrong advice. It would have been better, on average, to consult a reader of tea leaves or an astrologer. Now, however, economists appear to have reached a substantial and probably correct (though not necessarily theory-based) consensus about how economies work, and the advice they render is likely—or more likely than not—to be sound.

Moreover, although it is very often politically painful and counterintuitive to act upon such advice, policymakers increasingly are willing do so.

In the process, economists and like-minded idea entrepreneurs seem substantially to have managed to get across four highly consequential and enormously controversial ideas: the growth of economic well-being (as opposed, for example, to the quest for otherworldly eternity and the quest to maintain inborn differences as expressed in class structure) should be a dominant goal; wealth is best achieved through exchange rather than through conquest; international trade should be free; and economies do best when the government leaves them substantially free.

These elemental propositions in combination not only hold the formula for a huge expansion of economic well-being, but they suggest the demise of such central human institutions as empire and war.

War is unlikely if countries take prosperity as their chief goal *and* if they come to believe that trade is the best way to achieve that goal. Thanks in part to the success of economists, both propositions have now gained wide currency.

If people with business motivations had actually been running the world, its history would have been quite a bit different (and generally better).

Free trade furnishes the economic advantages of conquest without the unpleasantness of invasion and the sticky responsibility of imperial control.

Although Kant and many others have posited that increased trade enhances the prospects for peace, history does not suggest that this proposition has much validity: most wars, after all, are civil conflicts, fought between groups which know each other only too well and trade with each other only too much. But a good case could be made for the opposite causal proposition: peace often leads to, or at any rate facilitates, trade.

Advances in economic well-being do not necessarily cause people to think they are happier. Rather, each improvement seems quickly to be taken in stride, and standards are continually raised to compensate. In an important sense, then, things never get better.

However, this curious phenomenon may have a kind of intellectually invigorating quality of its own, and the seemingly unquenchable quest for economic improvement may be useful—crucial, even—for economic advance.

Capitalism is, in an important respect, profoundly irrational. Speculators do worse on average than those who simply and almost randomly buy the market across the board. At the same time, capitalism requires that speculative investment money be generally transferred from bad enterprises to good ones. Therefore, at base, capitalism depends on the self-lacerating thrill of the gamble, and many capitalists effectively act as altruists—that is, they knowingly and systematically take a financial loss in order to better the economic condition of their fellow human beings.

DEMOCRACY

Perfect democracy is an oxymoron.

Democracy, like God, works in mysterious ways its wonders (such as they are) to perform—ways that call into question many theories, hypotheses, expectations, and images generated both by supporters and by opponents about how the institution really ought to work.

Democracy is a form of government in which people are left (equally) free to become politically unequal. It is characterized not by political equality, active participation by the citizenry, and something resembling majority rule and consensus, but by political inequality and substantial apathy—effectively, by minority rule and majority acquiescence.

Democracy is an admirable form of government not because it furnishes a guide to atmospheric and unreachable ideals, but because it is a governmental form, generally compatible with a vigorous and productive society, that functions rather well when people manage, on average, to be no better than they actually are or are ever likely to be: flawed, grasping, self-centered, prejudiced, and easily distracted.

Long experience with democracy suggests that it is scarcely possible to change things a great deal. Inequality, disagreement, apathy, and ignorance seem to be normal, not abnormal, in a democracy, and to a considerable degree the beauty of the form is that it works despite these qualities—or, in some important respects, because of them.

Democracy clearly does not require that people generally be well informed, responsible, or actively attentive. Eternal vigilance has not proven to be the price of democracy—it can come quite a bit cheaper.

Although the advantage is only comparative, democracy seems to do better than other governmental forms at generating effective governments, choosing leaders, addressing minority concerns, creating a livable society, and functioning effectively with real, flawed human beings.

Democracy is a form of government which is necessarily and routinely (though not necessarily equally) responsive. It comes about when the people effectively agree not to use violence to replace the leadership, and the leadership leaves them free to try to dislodge it by any other means: because people are free to develop and use peaceful methods to criticize, pressure, and replace the leadership, the leaders must pay attention to their critics and petitioners.

There are plenty of nonviolent methods for removing officeholders besides elections, and much of what goes on in a democracy comes from petition and pressure, not from elections and legislative voting.

Indeed, it is possible, though not necessarily desirable, to have an effective, responsive democracy even without elections. Like any political device, elections will tend to protect some interests more than others. Moreover, their policy message is almost always ambiguous and often utterly undecipherable.

People excluded from participation in elections, like the feminists of the nineteenth century, have often have nevertheless profoundly affected policy if they have had the right to petition and protest.

247

Some people, because of their manipulative skills, social position, or sheer luck will do much better under the system than others. Unlike other systems, however, democracy gives to all the opportunity, without regard to social status or ideological conviction, to seek to manipulate the system in their favor.

Because of this characteristic, democracy has been able to survive a potential defect that theoreticians for millennia had concluded was terminal: it allowed democracy to coopt, rather than to alienate, the rich.

While democracy may open up the competition for leadership to all, changes in leadership have not usually been terribly revolutionary: voters have often been inclined to support rich people for office. Democracies, like monarchies, have largely been run by the well connected and the well born.

It is no easy task to persuade free people to agree with one's point of view. What is most difficult of all is to get them to listen in the first place.

Only democracies generally have been able to establish effective review and succession arrangements and thereby solve an elemental problem of governance.

Because of apathy, people, sometimes despite their political predispositions, are often effectively tolerant.

The patent and inevitable contrast between the hopelessly ideal images of democracy and its rough and ready reality often inspires the very cynicism about the democratic process that the idealists continually bemoan and profess to want to reduce.

The quests for equality, for deliberative consensus, for active participation, and for an enlightened citizenry, while not necessarily undesirable, are substantially hopeless.

It is a fundamental property—and perhaps defect—of democracy that citizens may watch laws being made, and when they do so they often compare democracy to its image and then reject the actual process with righteous disdain, even outrage, opaquely dismissing it as bickering and correctly, but uncomprehendingly, labeling it "politics as usual." Effectively, however, politics as usual is the same as democracy in action.

The undisciplined, chaotic, and essentially unequal interplay of "special interests" is a crucial and central part of democracy, not a distortion of it.

The overselling of equality by democratic idealists has encouraged the rise of a destructive and profoundly antidemocratic form when this ideal is transferred to the economic realm. In order really to plunder the propertied it has been necessary to abandon democracy.

Even granting that political cynicism may have risen in recent decades, the quality itself seems more nearly to be a constant than a variable quality in politics. And while this rise of cynicism may be mostly undesirable, it is hardly terminal.

As the futile struggle for campaign finance reform in the United States suggests, people who want or need to influence public policy are very likely to find ways to do so no matter how clever the laws that seek to restrict them.

By just about any standard of what reasonable discourse should be like, there is nothing wrong or indecent about negative campaigning, particularly if it helps to differentiate candidates and issues—as it almost always does.

Democratic theorists and idealists may be intensely interested in government and its processes, but it verges on the arrogant, even the self-righteous, to suggest that other people are somehow inadequate or derelict unless they share the same curious passion.

Democracy does often persecute minorities but, unlike other forms of government, it routinely allows the persecuted to work to change things, a process that has often been remarkably effective even for tiny minorities which are regarded with disgust and contempt by the majority.

Adherence to the democratic image can logically lead some minorities to fear that, if the form is actually about equality, majority rule, and active participation, they stand to be persecuted in a democracy. They can be led to rebel in misguided desperation if they take the democratic ideal too seriously.

Contrary to the ideal image—an image which has often inspired a considerable pessimism about its prospects and one which can furnish authoritarian leaders with a convenient excuse for neglecting reform—democracy is really quite a simple and easily graspable form of government.

Democracy is essentially a governmental gimmick, not a logical or empirical consequence of other factors. A country can quite easily become fully democratic without any special historical preparation and whatever the state of its social or economic development if elites or political activists generally come to believe that democracy is the way things ought to be done and if they aren't physically intimidated or held in check by authoritarian thugs.

Accordingly, the world could just as well have embraced democracy centuries earlier. Or the world could have missed entirely, and we'd still be living, like most of the human race for most of its existence, under the capricious rule of queens and kings and eunuchs.

Democracy's growth has not been the result so much of broader economic, social, or cultural developments. Rather, it has been the consequence of a sort of marketing process that has been characterized by product testing, by luck, by fashion leadership, by the convenient self-destruction of competing institutions, and particularly by the effective propaganda ministrations of idea entrepreneurs—politicians, writers, and organized activist groups.

It was necessary to market-test democracy—to put it into practice somewhere, to show it could actually work. Very much contrary to the anticipations of antidemocrats, it soon became clear that democracy was a rather effective method for choosing and reviewing leaders, and that it does not necessarily mean rule by mobs, incompetents, and demagogues, lead to the persecution of the rich and other minorities, or precipitate a vast social leveling.

Monarchy's amazing longevity over the millennia and in all corners of the globe was probably due chiefly to the fact that it simply had no effective competition as a form of government. Once formidable alternatives were fabricated—chiefly highly flawed democracy—monarchy faded out in rather short order, particularly in the developed world.

Promoters of democracy were lucky that they first test-marketed their product in Britain and America because, in the process, democracy came to be associated with countries which were held to be admirable—that is, which became fashion leaders or role models—for reasons that were often quite irrelevant to the institution itself.

The Islamic countries are kept undemocratic not by the necessary dictates of their culture or by the state of their economic development, but by the will of their leaders.

Most of the post-Communist countries of central and eastern Europe as well as many of the new democracies elsewhere have essentially completed their transition to democracy: they are already full-fledged democracies. That is, judging from two hundred years of experience with democracy, what they have now is, pretty much, it.

An overemphasis on the details of democratic transition may cause people in new democracies to continue to think that things may become substantially different—hopefully better—in the future. Thus, not only are transitologists sometimes spreading visions that will never come to pass, but their perspective can inspire or reinforce a short-term point of view that is undesirable from a political standpoint and even more so from an economic one.

Democracies do become more or less democratic, but to seek to establish a point at which a country becomes "consolidated" may not be terribly helpful since, as with Chile in 1973, this condition can be overthrown at any time by sufficiently dedicated and effective antidemocrats—some of whom might even have previously been democrats.

What is most likely to foster democracy in countries that do not now have it, and what is most likely to maintain democracy in ones that do, will not be economic or social development, but rather the desire of ruling elites to emulate the established democracies.

Democracies have often reverted to authoritarian rule historically, but this does not mean that democracy is a peculiarly fragile form: any government can be overthrown by a sufficiently large and dedicated group of thugs with guns. The problem seems to be one of definition. When a democracy gets overthrown we say it has failed, but when one dictator topples another we sometimes see this as persistence of form and a kind of stability.

Although there may well be some softness in the democratic trend of the last decades of the twentieth century, the prospects seem generally rather favorable for further democratic development. In general, economically advanced countries have tended to buy this idea (as well as many other related ones) comparatively earlier, but it is the exertions of idea entrepreneurs that have been more determining of the pace of democratization than the correlated wealth of their customers.

251

CAPITALISM AND DEMOCRACY

Both democracy and capitalism rely more on the individual than on the collective; both question authority in one way or another and work best when it is restrained; both allow people the freedom to put an enterprise or a sitting government out of business if they become dissatisfied with its performance; both are notably, if often clumsily self-correcting; and both leave people substantially free for individual pursuits even though this generally leads to a considerable inequality of result and to a sort of (nonviolent) disorderliness that some find distasteful.

Both are founded on the fundamental—even breathtaking—assumption that it is best, in the end, actually to trust people to understand and to act upon their own interests, and on the related assumption (or hope) that, in the end, you can't fool everybody every time.

Capitalism and democracy are in important respects viscerally unequal and unfair at the systemic level, if not at the personal level, a condition that stems rather naturally and inevitably from the related facts that both institutions leave individuals free to pursue their interests and that some will simply do better at the pursuit than others.

Capitalism will emerge if people are left free to be acquisitive, and democracy can come about if people are left free to complain (and to organize complainants). Neither quality, it seems, is terribly difficult to inspire.

Democracy and capitalism are quite independent. While capitalism can exist without democracy as has often been noted, recent experience in some post-Communist countries suggests that democracy can exist without capitalism as well.

The undeserved association of democracy with capitalist prosperity could lead to destructive disillusion in some places, but it might also help democratic development if the world is really in the process of massive economic improvement.

While democracy may not be necessary for capitalism, democracy probably does benefit capitalist growth by furnishing property owners some potential remedy against governmental confiscation, by establishing the rule of law, by routinely encouraging openness and transparency of information, by allowing *all* interest groups (rather than just a privileged subset) to attempt to influence government policy, by providing a mechanism for removing failed leaders, and, at least lately, by gaining a perhaps undeserved association with stability and predictability.

Democracy and capitalism are conceptually linked in that each has a kind of bland emptiness at the core, a quality that can be unpleasantly unsatisfying to people who aspire to grander goals and who have higher visions.

The faulty popular perspectives that democracy ought somehow to be much better than experience has shown it to be, and that capitalism deep down is somehow really much worse than experience routinely shows it to be, do not seem to have greatly hampered the fundamental workings of either institution, at least in advanced capitalist democracies.

Thus, democracy and capitalism are similar in that they can work pretty well even if people generally do not appreciate them very well, a paradoxical quality that may be one of their most important strengths.

✻ *Notes* ✻

CHAPTER ONE
CAPITALISM AND DEMOCRACY: IMAGES AND IMAGE MISMATCHES

1. Address to a Joint Session of the United States Congress, 21 February 1990.

2. Delli Carpini and Keeter 1996, 22.

3. Kennedy 1964, 539.

CHAPTER TWO
CAPITALISM'S IMAGE

1. Rosenberg and Birdzell 1980, 235. Another definition is: "an economic system with private ownership of land and capital, the individual rights to his (or her) own labor, and the frequency of competitive markets in the determination of prices and quantities for goods and services and for factors of production" (Engerman forthcoming).

2. Macaulay 1963, 63. Stigler 1982, 22. McCloskey 1994, 186. Franklin: *Poor Richard's Almanac,* entry for May 1740. Kavka: quoted in Klein 1997c, 105. See also McCloskey 1994, 183; Wilson 1995, 52–53. On reputational effects, see also Kreps 1990, Axelrod 1984, Klein 1997a, Hardin 1991, Frank 1988, ch. 4.

3. Emden 1939, 17. For a discussion see Nevaskar 1971, especially pp. 219–22. As Nevaskar observes, the same phenomenon characterizes another pacifist group, the Jains of India. See also Klein 1997b, 5. Max Weber once found that Baptists in some areas of the United States had a similar advantage: see Klein and Shearmur 1997, 30.

4. Nevaskar 1971, 130.

5. See Saxon 1989, 334–37.

6. Plowden 1967, 66.

7. Quoted, Weeks 1993, 13. See also Plowden 1967, 67–68.

8. Barnum 1871, 498–99. Of course, such conclusions only hold when governmental policies make it possible to profit honestly.

9. On this issue in postcommunist Europe, where taxi drivers "understand the rules of capitalism in a negative way: as the absence of any rules," see Drakulič 1997, 62–63.

10. See Ramirez 1995.

11. See Klein 1997c, 122–27. On John D. Rockefeller's obsessive concern about protecting the quality of Standard Oil products, see Chernow 1998, 253.

12. Autry 1991, 17. Drucker 1974, 456, 462.

13. Rockefeller: Chernow 1998, 146. Stigler 1975, 179. Barnum 1871, 496. On fairness, see also Brams and Taylor 1999.

14. McCormack 1984, 73, 42, 40; McCormack 1989, 191–92.

15. Kahneman et al. 1986, 738; see also Frank 1988, 176.

16. Thaler 1985, 211–12.

17. The hotels have sometimes found that one acceptable way around this problem is to impose a three-day minimum stay (Thaler 1985, 211).

18. Barnum 1871, 496–97.

19. Barnum 1871, 496.

20. Appel 1930, 55.

21. Peters and Waterman 1982, 29, 157 (emphasis in the original). Cringely 1992, 270. Steinhauer 1998. Templeton: *Wall Street Week with Louis Rukeyser,* PBS, 10 January 1997.

22. Peters and Waterman 1982, 238. See also Schleh 1974, ch. 15; Autry 1991, 122–26; Drucker 1974, 463; Peters 1994, 145; Bittel 1972, 180–214; Vaill 1989, ch. 9; Deep and Sussman 1992, 79–81 and ch. 7. On the honest respect Barnum showed toward his employees, including his many performing freaks, see Saxon 1989, 119.

23. McCormack 1989, 3, 135.

24. H. Smith 1976, 67. Landes 1998, 306n. See also Wilson 1995, 51; Passell 1998.

25. There are remedies against mistreatment by government agencies in a democracy, but they are awkward and indirect: an ill-treated customer can pressure an elected representative who in turn can lean on the agency to treat its customer/supplicants with more civility. (On this issue more generally, see Hirschman 1970.) Among private businesses in the United States, the Toyota experience may most nearly approximate the Soviet one. For quite a while, demand for this car outstripped supply as customers were practically buying them off the boat. Prices rose, but, for various reasons, not to a market-clearing point. Sales approaches developed during that heady time seem to have persisted: in a questionnaire returned by 120,000 car buyers for *Consumer Reports* (April 1995, 270), Toyota placed dead last in expressed satisfaction with the car-buying experience.

26. McCormack 1989, 121. "The pride of man," warns Adam Smith, "makes him love to domineer" (1976, 388 (III.ii)). In his book on man-

agement, James Autry discusses such behavior and supplies a quote from T. S. Eliot: "Half the harm that is done in this world is due to people who want to feel important" (1991, 150). The "harm" in instances like these is to the manager's own bottom line.

27. Barnum 1871, 497. Saxon 1989, 171, 252.

28. Boston CEO (Chad Gifford): *NewsHour With Jim Lehrer,* PBS, 29 April 1997. Cohen and Greenfield 1997, 31.

29. Steckel and Simons 1992, ch. 1. Hood 1996, ch. 2. Advertising's effect: Clancy and Shulman 1994, 140.

30. McCormack 1984, 199–200. Autry 1991, 113.

31. Dunlap 1996, 172–74; emphasis in the original.

32. Quoted, Reder 1994, 7.

33. Failure rate: Clancy and Shulman 1994, 8, 140. It is conventionally estimated that 90 percent of high-tech start-ups fail, though people who have carefully looked at the phenomenon suggest the ratio may be more like 95 percent. Cringely 1992, 232.

34. Nevins 1945, 678. Nevins 1940, 712.

35. Gilder 1984.

36. Wilson 1991, 147. Stigler 1982, 24–25. On this approach in Kant's thought, see Machan 1996, 36.

37. Wilson 1993, 102. Drucker 1974, 462. On this issue, see also Frank 1988, 134–35; Akerlof 1983.

38. McCormack 1984, 4.

39. Autry 1991, 17 (emphasis in the original). For a review of the literature on the malpractice issue, see Levinson 1994.

40. McCormack 1984, 115.

41. Drucker 1974, 456, 462. Saxon 1989, 16.

42. In addition, if the friendship is genuine—that is, if both friends derive some benefit from it—the offended friend can punish the offending friend by withdrawing from the friendship.

43. McCormack 1984, 42 (emphasis in the original). See also McCormack 1989, 2.

44. McCormack 1989, 192.

45. Wilson 1995, 52. Smith 1896, 255.

46. Smith 1976, 898 (V.ii.k). Tilly 1993, 184. A similar moral disconnect can be seen in the behavior of American college students: a student who is known to cheat at exams may well find others doubting the student's general honesty; but one who steals street signs to decorate a dormitory room often will not.

47. Somewhat along the same lines, people who are fundamentally vir-

tuous in their business dealings can also often seek to use government to protect them from competition without necessarily dampening their business reputations, an issue that will be discussed again in chapter 4.

48. Engerman forthcoming. For debate on the business cycle issue, see Kuznets 1961, Lebergott 1964, Romer 1986a, Romer 1986b.

49. Stigler 1984, 149, 155.

50. Tawney 1962, 284. Creating needs: see, for example, Barber 1995, 59.

51. Simon 1995, Rosenberg and Birdzell 1986, Easterlin 1996, Bailey 1995, Stigler 1975, 179.

52. Marshall 1920, 6.

53. Smith 1976, 612 (IV.vii.c). Rockefeller: Chernow 1998, 469.

54. Weeks 1993, ch. 8.

55. Rosenberg and Birdzell 1986, 13.

56. Rickey quoted, Will 1990, 246. Chernow 1998, 101, 133, 197, 284, 557; see also Yergin 1991, 52.

57. One member of the board went along, saying: "I guess I can take the risk if you can," an absurd piece of self-puffery since Rockefeller was clearly taking all the risk himself. Chernow 1998, 285–88.

58. Rockefeller, however, was not always lucky. He made a number of extremely bad, even naive, investments, including the payment of six million dollars for a Colorado company that was not only a money loser, but brought him years of grief and labor turmoil (Chernow 1998, 343, 367–70, 382–85, 556, 571).

59. Cringely 1992, 128–32. Barnum 1871, 476.

60. Nevins 1940, 712.

61. For the bias in full flower, see Brandeis 1934. See also Chernow 1998, 288–89. On the long-term views of large firms, see Chandler 1977, 10.

62. On this issue, see Mueller 1989, 267–69.

63. Barnum 1871, 499. See also McCloskey 1994, 189.

64. Chernow 1998, 467.

65. Rohter 1998.

66. See Bergson 1984; Friedman and Friedman 1980, 146–48; Dye and Zeigler 1988; Kuteinikov 1990; Stigler 1984, 156; Rosenberg and Birdzell 1986, 324; Drucker 1974, 369–72.

67. Ludwig von Mises cites the observations of an eighteenth-century German writer, Justus Möser: "Life in a society in which success would exclusively depend on personal merit would, says Möser, simply be unbearable. As human nature is, everybody is prone to overrate his own worth

and deserts. If a man's station in life is conditioned by factors other than his inherent excellence, those who remain at the bottom of the ladder can acquiesce in this outcome and, knowing their own worth, still preserve their dignity and self-respect. But it is different if merit alone decides. Then the unsuccessful feel themselves insulted and humiliated. Hate and enmity against all those who superseded them must result" (1972, 10–11). Möser therefore advocated promotion by blood lines—though, as the revolutions which began at the end of the eighteenth century were to attest, his method of quality-free promotion actually did inspire quite a bit of resentment.

68. See Malkiel 1996, especially chs. 6, 7, and the bibliography on pp. 492–96. See also Solman 1997, Zweig 1997, and McCloskey 1990, chs. 8–9.

Chapter Three
Sources of Capitalism's Negative Image

1. Peters 1994, 81.

2. Rosenberg and Birdzell 1986, 181. On this issue see also Hayek 1954, and for a related, balanced discussion of contemporary "sweat shops," Rohter 1996a.

3. A rare exception might be the popular film, *It's a Wonderful Life*. Its economics, however, are bit difficult to dope out. Its good guy businessman hero seems simply to give away money (which, however, saves him in the end since it inspires a charity lovefest in his honor) while the bad guy businessman prospers even though all his customers hate him. Moreover, the plot hinges ultimately on a contrived theft.

4. Many of the businessmen who went bankrupt trying to compete with Rockefeller had it even worse, of course. As the daughter of one of them wrote, "Father went almost insane over this terrible upset to his business. He walked the house day and night. . . . [He] left his church and never entered a church afterward. His whole life was embittered by this experience" (Chernow 1998, 148).

5. Chernow 1998, 121, 122, 260, 319–21, 335, 342, 343, 430, 556.

6. Alger 1876, 312. On this issue, see Scharnhorst 1980, 41–43, 142–44; Scharnhorst 1985, 149–50; Trachtenberg 1990, vi–vii. In his 1980 book Scharnhorst makes a wonderfully wry commentary on the Alger hero in the dedication: "To Sandy, who, though not a banker's daughter, I would save from drowning, if I could swim."

7. Clancy and Shulman 1994, 81–82. On the importance of the pro-

ducer, rather than the various directors, in establishing the Astaire-Rogers phenomenon of the 1930s, see Mueller 1985, 8.

8. Rosenberg and Birdzell 1986, 258. Cringely 1992, 207, 235.

9. Kristol 1978, xi.

10. Stigler 1982, 32. Plato: Machan 1996, 36. McCloskey 1994, 188. Graña 1964, 162. See also Schumpeter 1950, 145–55; Mises 1972, 12–14; Holmes 1993, ch. 13; McCloskey 1998.

11. Havel 1995, 36. See also Gallagher 1990.

12. Jouvenel 1954, 118–21.

13. Havel 1995, 37.

14. Boesche 1988. China: Rosenberg and Birdzell 1986, 88.

15. There seems to be an edge of condescension even in a business magazine, *Fortune,* when it characterizes the operating principles of a successful company ("excellence of quality, reliability of performance, and loyalty in dealer relationships") as a "version of the Boy Scout law" (quoted, Peters and Waterman 1982, 171).

16. Bittel 1972.

17. Kenner 1936, xiii–xiv; emphasis in the original.

18. Graña 1964, 159. Oddly, however, none of this prevents many intellectuals and artists (Lillian Hellman, Charles Dickens, Pablo Picasso, and Bertolt Brecht, for example) from engaging in sharp business practices—even sometimes wallowing in what might be called greed—when their own financial interests are involved.

19. Nozick 1997, 285, 289. He points out that the same mechanism can be used as well to explain the alienation of intellectuals in a communist system (290).

20. Wilson 1991, 139. Smith 1896, 257, 259. Gilder 1984, 16; see also 260. Keynes 1963, 369. Schumpeter 1950, 131; for a critique, see McInnes 1995, 94–97. Fukuyama 1989, 18. On capitalism's supposed alienating and repressive effects on the human personality, see Hirschman 1977, 132.

21. St. Augustine: Hirschman 1977, 9. Stigler 1984, 150.

22. *New York Times,* 3 May 1991, A10.

23. McCloskey 1994, 189. See also Hirschman 1977.

24. Weber 1958, 56. Graña 1964, 172–79.

25. McCormack 1989, 135. Wright 1937, 260–61.

26. Incapable: Smith 1976, 782 (V.i.f). Merchant risk-taking: Smith 1976, 411 (III.iv). Effeminate: Smith 1896, 257–59. Noblest: Smith 1976, 697 (V.i.a).

27. Boesche 1988, 39. Kant 1952, 113.

28. Treitschke readily acknowledged that war had its unpleasant side,

but these defects, he held, were overwhelmed by its many virtues: "War, with all its brutality and sternness, weaves a bond of love between man and man, linking them together to face death, and causing all class distinctions to disappear. He who knows history knows also that to banish war from the world would be to mutilate human nature" (1916, 1:15, 66–67, 2:395–96). Bernhardi 1914, 26. While not a proponent of war, H. G. Wells at times saw considerable virtue in military organization: "When the contemporary man steps from the street of clamorous insincere advertisement, push, adulteration, underselling, and intermittent employment, into the barrack-yard, he steps on to a higher social plane, into an atmosphere of service and co-operation and of infinitely more honorable emulations" (1908, 214–15).

29. Spencer 1909, 664–65. Lea 1909, 45.

30. On this issue more generally, see Mueller 1989, ch. 2.

31. Samuelson: McInnes 1995, 91. Vargas Llosa: Gallagher 1990.

32. Drucker 1974, 373–74; emphasis in the original.

33. On Friedman and philanthropy: Hood 1996. On Hayek: McInnes 1998.

34. Hirschman 1977, 71. Tawney's list is: diligence, moderation, sobriety, thrift (1962, 245).

35. For a balanced account, see Easterbrook 1995. See also Yergin and Stanislaw 1998, 385–86.

36. See also Yergin and Stanislaw 1998, 362, 364. After being ignominiously defeated by Blair's Labour Party, Britain's Conservative Party leader William Hague got around in 1997 to proclaiming at a party conference that "Conservatives ca-a-a-re." Hoggart 1997; White 1997.

37. McCormack 1989, 121.

38. Schulz: Yergin and Stanislaw 1998, 368. Landes 1969, 7.

39. Marshall 1920, 8.

40. Johnson: Burrough and Helyar 1990; the snappy aphorism is prominently displayed on the jacket of the book's hardcover edition. Nevins 1945, 678; see also Hidy and Hidy 1955, 34. Rockefeller accusations: Chernow 1998, 145–48, 168.

CHAPTER FOUR
THE CONSEQUENCES OF CAPITALISM'S IMAGE
FOR ECONOMIC DEVELOPMENT

1. Weber 1958, 57.

2. As Rosenberg and Birdzell put it: "If we take the long view of human

history and judge the economic lives of our ancestors by modern standards, it is a story of almost unrelieved wretchedness. The typical human society has given only a small number of people a humane existence, while the great majority have lived in abysmal squalor. We are led to forget the dominating misery of other times in part by the grace of literature, poetry, romance, and legend, which celebrate those who lived well and forget those who lived in the silence of poverty. The eras of misery have been mythologized and may even be remembered as golden ages of pastoral simplicity. They were not" (1986, 3; see also Marshall 1890, 2–4).

3. Bairoch 1981, 3, 8. Data in figure 4.1: Bairoch 1993, 95

4. Jones 1987. Landes 1969, 19.

5. Rosenberg and Birdzell 1986. McCloskey 1994, 189. See also Landes 1998.

6. North 1990, 123–24.

7. North 1990, 124.

8. They also suggest—wittily, but a bit too ingeniously perhaps—that the "very contempt in which the clergy and the older aristocracy held the rising merchant class could only have encouraged the merchants to develop a code of honor pivoting on scrupulous care in timely payment of debts and on loyalty to superiors—both points of striking weakness in the aristocratic code" (1986, 124–26, 128).

9. Gerschenkron 1962, 48.

10. North 1990, 101. Gerschenkron 1962, 48–49.

11. North 1990, 123.

12. Though, as Richard Tilly has pointed out, this process can also be used to facilitate collusion among businesses and to restrict competition (1993, 200). On the competition-stifling effects of guilds, see also Rosenberg and Birdzell 1986, 51, 174; Landes 1998, 242–45.

13. North 1990, 87.

14. Landes 1998, 493; Rosenberg and Birdzell 1986, 151–53, 159–63, 258.

15. Rosenberg and Birdzell 1986, 11.

16. North 1990, 112–17.

17. Appel 1930, 50–52, 370–73. Barnum's recollection of business in the early part of the century stresses that "sharp trades" and "dishonest tricks and unprincipled deceptions" occurred both in the cities and in the country (Barnum 1855, 39). This observation suggests it may be unwise to assume that transaction costs in the small-scale village are necessarily low because "trade exists within a dense social network" (North 1990, 120).

18. Appel 1930, 54. On the rise of set prices in England, see Alexander 1970, 173–74. There were other advantages to setting prices: a business did not have to rely on an employee's bargaining ability (in contemporary auto sales, the sales manager is usually consulted before a haggled sale is consummated), one could hire less expensive sales clerks, and the process was less time-consuming.

19. Barnum 1871, 496.

20. Haggling also persists in the purchase of houses, but here the amateur usually hires a professional—an attorney and/or a realtor—to check over the deal before it is consummated.

21. McAneny and Moore 1994. On efforts by the National Automobile Dealers Association to "buff the industry's greasy image," see Bennet 1995.

22. *Consumer Reports,* April 1995, 270–71.

23. There are difficulties, however, because new car transactions have traditionally, if illogically, been combined with the purchase by the dealer of a traded-in vehicle for which setting a price is generally impossible (see Wilson 1995, 53n). Also, some auto dealers, unlike Wanamaker, are apparently failing to set their prices low enough, allowing other dealers, in a *New York Times* business reporter's evocative phrase, to "ruthlessly undercut them to capture sales" (Bradsher 1996). To some unsentimental customers, however, it is possible that such "ruthless" behavior might instead look suspiciously like a good deal.

24. McGuire and Olson 1996, 72–73, 76. De Long and Shleifer 1993, 699.

25. McGuire and Olson 1996, 80. De Long and Shleifer 1993, 699.

26. Montesquieu: Hirschman 1986, 107. Smith 1896, 253, 255. Wilson 1991, 148. Klein 1997c, 105. Scottish historian: Hirschman 1977, 61.

27. Smith 1976, 612–13 (IV.vii.c).

28. In his essay, "Advice to a Young Tradesman," Franklin observes, "He that is known to pay punctually and exactly to the time he promises, may at any time, and on any occasion, raise all the money his friends can spare. This is sometimes of great use. After industry and frugality, nothing contributes more to the raising of a young man in the world than punctuality and justice in all his dealings; therefore never keep borrowed money an hour beyond the time you promised, lest a disappointment shut up your friend's purse for ever" (1856, 88). And the entry for May 1740 in Franklin's *Poor Richard's Almanac* declares, "Tricks and treachery are the practice of fools that have not wit enough to be honest."

29. For discussions of such informal institutions in action, see Greif 1993, Benson 1997. See also McCloskey 1994, 183–84.

30. Defoe 1727, 2:34.

31. However, Smith's observation about probity is found not in his published work but rather in notes from earlier lectures taken down by students and published a century after his death. An observation by Defoe, an experienced international trader, essentially suggests that Smith may have been biased because he was living in a comparatively advanced capitalist area: "Our tradesmen are not, as in other countries, the meanest of men" (1727, 1:305).

32. McCormack 1989, 3, 8.

33. Aware that a reputation for bilking the gringos is bad for the economy more generally, the Mexican government has established tourist police to help foreigners maneuver the unfamiliar uncertainties of the marketplace and perhaps to keep them from being taken.

34. Banfield 1958, 64, 79, 93–94. See also Putnam 1993.

35. Rosenberg 1975, 379. Tilly 1993, 188. Poland: Blobaum 1995, 81.

36. Yet Peters and Waterman note that the condition persists in some quarters. They quote a chief of naval operations who says the U.S. Navy assumes "that everyone below the rank of commander is immature," and cite an underground poem circulated among General Motors workers complaining that the company treats them as if they were inmates in an "overgrown nursery" (1982, 235).

37. Tilly 1993, 188–89. Strikes: Greenhouse 1996. Particularly in contrast with General Motors, the Ford Motor Company enjoyed cordial company-union relations in the 1990s, something it considered a competitive advantage (Bradsher 1998). Standard Oil was a generally well-run company, but its antipathy to unionization was so intense as to become economically irrational: see Chernow 1998, 576–81.

38. See Mayo 1933.

39. Peters and Waterman 1982.

40. Defoe concludes by urging that the shopkeeper "should not make a common whore of his tongue" but rather that there exists a "happy medium" in which "the shop-keeper, far from being rude to his customers on the one hand, or sullen and silent on the other, may speak handsomly and modestly of his goods what they deserve, and no other." He goes on to argue that this "way of discoursing to a customer, is generally more effectual, and more to the purpose, and more to the reputation of the shop-keeper, than a storm of words, and a mouthful of common shop-language, which makes a noise, but has little in it to plead, except to here

and there a fool that can no otherwise be prevailed with" (1727, 1:251–56).

41. Frank 1988, 165. There are eerie reflections of Defoe in an article about training schools recently set up by the automobile industry, a retail business that still haggles with customers. When asked, "All buyers are— what?" the salespeople (being trained to become "sales professionals") instantly reply, "liars." The article observes, "Once the negotiating begins, so does the lying . . . every customer suspects the salesman of being slime." To enhance sales, the students are urged to tell the truth, however: it is in their interest to be honest and not to "high gross" their customers: "sacrificing some profit now will yield referrals and repeat business" (Bennet 1995).

42. Tilly 1993, 183–84, 201 n. 13.

43. Marshall 1890, 7.

44. Tilly 1993, 182, 185–86, 199, see also 195. Circus: Plowden 1967, 104; Culhane 1990, 175.

45. Stigler 1982, 23–24. For a history of early efforts, see Kenner 1936. On Underwriters' Laboratories, see Brearly 1997.

46. Gerschenkron 1962, 19.

47. Specter 1995. This process may resemble the adjustments of traditional arrangements that occurred when Japan, China, and Korea were confronted with western capitalism; see Fukuyama 1995, 349–50. On China's efforts to deal with the lingering incivility problem, see Faison 1995; or for East Europe, see Perlez 1993.

48. Tilly 1993, 182, 199–200.

49. Abramovitz 1989, 14–15.

50. Rosenberg 1964, 58–60. See also McCloskey 1998, 311–14.

51. Peters and Waterman 1982, 29.

52. Tilly 1993, 201 n. 10.

53. Marshall also argues that "in every age poets and social reformers have tried to stimulate the people of their own time to a noble life by enchanting stories of the virtues of the heroes of old." Yet, "adulteration and fraud in trade were rampant in the middle ages to an extent that is very astounding when we consider the difficulties of wrong doing without detection at the time." In addition, "No traders are more unscrupulous in taking advantage of the necessities of the unfortunate than the corn-dealers and money-lenders of the East" (1890, 6–7).

54. Quoted, Jones 1987, 235.

55. Klein 1997b, 1. Macaulay 1963, 61, 66. See also Ellickson 1991.

56. Standard Oil: Chernow 1998, 114. Macaulay 1963, 65–67. McCor-

mack, a lawyer himself, contends that "Fights between law firms on be-half of clients are often mere vehicles for firms to charge time and earn money. I feel that if you can put the two parties in most legal disputes in a room by themselves—even two years into the legal dispute—the mat-ter will get resolved, certainly more cheaply, and probably a lot more eq-uitably" (1984, 207).

57. For a similar observation, see Holmstrom and Kreps 1996.

58. Another area in which the courts are likely to be next to useless is the stealing of often unwritten and rarely copyrighted jokes by stand-up comedians. The industry is effectively policed by a newsletter which ac-tively reports on such unsavory business behavior, and performers who get a reputation for lifting the material of others are very likely to lose gigs.

59. Merchant law: Benson 1997. Rosenberg and Birdzell 1986, 116–17; emphasis added. Smith 1976, 412 (III.iv). See also Ellickson 1991.

60. See Wang forthcoming; Yergin and Stanislaw 1998, 206–7.

CHAPTER FIVE
DEVELOPMENT, HAPPINESS, AND THE RISE OF THE POLITICALLY
INCORRECT ONE-HANDED ECONOMIST

1. See, for example, Simon 1995; Easterlin 1996, 84, 153; Lebergott 1993; Rosenberg and Birdzell 1986, 333; Jones 1987; Jones 1988; Wat-tenberg 1997; Landes 1998, ch. 29; Landsburg 1997.

2. Henderson: Gregg 1956, 13. Osler 1932, 123–24. On this issue, see also Kunitz and Engerman 1992.

3. Consumers were quick to respond to the success: by 1929, the amount Americans spent on medicine was nearly seven times higher than in 1900; by 1990 it was seven hundred times higher. Initially in the cen-tury, however, life expectancies were raised less by medicine (or "dosing") and surgery than by improved public health—in particular, by better sewage and water supply—and by better housing which reduced the number of germ-carrying people sleeping in the same room (Lebergott 1993, 36–37, 122–23). On the placebo effect, see Blakeslee 1998.

4. For discussions, see Lebergott 1993, Simon 1995, Easterlin 1996. Data in figure 7.1: Sweden and England, Preston 1995 and correspon-dence with Preston; more developed and less developed countries, Bai-ley 1995, 403.

5. See, for example, Engerman 1997.

6. For an extended philippic against economic theory, see Cassidy 1996.

7. Summers 1992, 12. Privatization: Yergin and Stanislaw 1998, 114–15.

8. Hellman 1998, Yergin and Stanislaw 1998.

9. Stigler 1975, 57.

10. Brody 1997.

11. Weinstein 1997.

12. Stigler 1975, 57.

13. Kuznets 1966, 12–14. Rosenberg and Birdzell 1986, 309.

14. Wright 1968, 463. Pogge von Strandmann 1988, 97. For an extensive discussion of the varying role of economics as a motivation, or excuse, for war, see Luard 1986.

15. See Jäckel 1981.

16. Russett 1972, 58–60. As Samuel Eliot Morison points out, "The fundamental reason for America's going to war with Japan was our insistence on the integrity of China" (1963, 45). Melvin Small notes that "the defense of China was an unquestioned axiom of American policy taken in along with mother's milk and the Monroe Doctrine. . . . One looks in vain through the official papers of the 1930s for some prominent leader to say, 'Wait a second, just why is China so essential to our security?'" (1980, 238–39). Warner Schilling observes crisply, "At the summit of foreign policy one always finds simplicity and spook," and suggests that "the American opposition to Japan rested on the dubious proposition that the loss of Southeast Asia could prove disastrous for Britain's war effort and for the commitment to maintain the territorial integrity of China—a commitment as mysterious in its logic as anything the Japanese ever conceived" (1965, 389). See also Mueller 1995, 103–8.

17. See Mueller 1993; Mueller 1995, ch. 2; Rush 1993.

18. Mueller 1994a, ch. 8.

19. See also Hirschman 1977; McCloskey 1994, 180–82.

20. Urquhart and Berkowitz 1987.

21. For A. A. Milne's perspective on such thinking, see Milne 1935, 4, 222–23.

22. Buckle 1862, 154, 157. See also Friedman and Friedman 1980, 1–2; Smith 1976, 429–51 (IV.i).

23. On this issue, see also Crawford 1993; Nadelmann 1990; Rosenberg and Birdzell 1986, 17. Beginning in 1908, Angell argued that "It is a logical fallacy to regard a nation as increasing its wealth when it in-

creases its territory." Britain, he pointed out, "owned" Canada and Australia in some sense, yet it certainly did not get the products of those countries for nothing—it had to pay for them just as though they came "from the lesser tribes in Argentina or the USA." The British, in fact, could not get those products any cheaper than the Germans. Thus, he asked, "If Germany conquered Canada, could the Germans get the wheat for nothing? Would the Germans have to pay for it just as they do now? Would conquest make economically any real difference?" He also argued that the popular notion that there were limited supplies in the world and that countries had to fight to get their share was nonsense: "The great danger of the modern world is not absolute shortage, but dislocation of the process of exchange, by which alone the fruits of the earth can be made available for human consumption" (1914, 31; 1933, 108, 175). A half-century later, Malthusian alarmists once again joined in a debate on the issue of scarce resources though they did not advocate conquest as an antidote. For a discussion, see Arndt 1978.

24. Kant 1957, 24; see also Hirschman 1977, 79–80, 134–35. Buckle 1862, 157. Peace activists of the nineteenth century were quick to take up Kant's argument, and often with a similar sense of optimism. Particularly prominent were two Englishmen, Richard Cobden and a Quaker, John Bright, who saw international peace as one of the benefits of free and unfettered trade. And in 1848 John Stuart Mill concurred: "It is commerce which is rapidly rendering war obsolete" (Howard 1978, 37). On booty as an important, though usually not primary, motive for medieval war, see Kaeuper 1988.

25. Mahan 1912, 131. A nation's "wealth, prosperity, and well-being . . . depend in no way upon its military power," Angell argued, noting that the citizens of such war-avoiding countries as Switzerland, Belgium, or Holland were as well off as the Germans, and much better off than the Austrians or Russians (1951, 165; 1933, 89–92, 230; 1914, 36.)

26. Rosecrance 1986, 16, 24. For a discussion of the mechanism by which attitudes toward war have been reshaped, and particularly of the crucial role of World War I in this process, see Mueller 1989 and especially Mueller 1995, ch. 9.

27. Jefferson 1939, 263. The rise of successful capitalism might also affect religion. Modern science and medicine have been destructive of two of religion's once-popular appeals: its ability to explain the physical universe and its ability to heal. (On religion's once-presumed ability to explain the physical universe, see Barr 1987.) And the notion, at one time accepted even by atheists, that religion is vital because it supplies a moral

code, is being undercut when, apparently for the first time in history, many areas in formerly pious Europe have developed societies that are orderly, moral, and generally admirable despite the fact that religion, particularly organized religion, plays little effective part. Now, the newly emerging unselfconscious acceptance of material gain as a dominant goal may tend to devalue another of the church's appeals. As suggested in chapter 3, religion attained prominence in human life in part because it can sometimes supply spiritual uplift as a sort of relief from material woes and fates and because it seeks to give higher meaning to a dreary and difficult life. But if people become primarily materialistic and rich, they may come to feel they need religion less. Of course, in other areas, such as portions of the Islamic world, religiosity may have actually heightened in recent years, and it certainly retains a considerable degree of force in the United States. Thus, whether Europe is a true harbinger remains to be seen. For the argument that it is not, see Berger 1996/97. For the argument that religion is weakest where it is state-dominated, and strongest where there is a vigorous competitive market for religion, see Iannaccone et al. 1997.

28. Actually, to be complete about this, there may be something of a clash between this and the previous proposition. Logically, an ardent free trader should favor conquest—at least ones where damage is minimal and where long-term resentments are not stirred up—since this would expand the free-trade zone to the general benefit. For example, free traders would presumably hold that North Americans would generally benefit if Canada were painlessly and benevolently to conquer the United States, making it, perhaps, its eleventh province.

29. Drew 1994, 338–46.

30. On Nixon and China, see Mueller 1989, 184–85.

31. For a discussion of a somewhat similar development in the 1930s, which depended crucially on the mind-set of a key player, the secretary of state, and on President Franklin Roosevelt's "reliance on economists," see Goldstein 1988, 70–71.

32. Legal restrictions forbidding foreign countries or interests from contributing to political campaigns are, to that degree, unwise policy. See Passell 1998b.

33. Hayek 1988, 45. On the once central, but now abandoned, quest in India for "self-sufficiency" and in Latin America for freedom from "dependency," see Yergin and Stanislaw 1989, chs. 3, 9.

34. Stigler 1975, xi; see also Buchanan 1990. On this process more generally, see also Goldstein 1988.

35. Krugman quoted, *Investor's Business Daily,* 24 August 1998, A6. Friedman and Friedman 1984, 129. However, in the 1930s Keynes advised against the "economic entanglements" of trade (Sachs 1998, 102–3, 110).

36. Waltz 1979, 138.

37. Lip service is often given in the United States to reducing its dependence on oil supplies imported from the politically unstable Middle East, but absent a clear crisis, these warnings have not been very effective. The dependence remains. On the national security imperative Japan once saw in maintaining a domestic oil-refining capacity, see Yergin and Stanislaw 1989, ch. 6.

38. Yardeni forthcoming.

39. Schumpeter 1950, 417; see also Lipset 1993a, Yergin and Stanislaw 1998, 22. Hirsch 1976, 1. Friedman: Hartwell 1995, 165.

40. Heilbroner 1993, 97. Hartwell 1995, 191. On this issue, see Stigler 1959, Yergin and Stanislaw 1998. The Mont Pelerin Society, a group of free-market advocates founded in 1947 to "slow down and stop the march down the road to serfdom," voted "decisively" in 1972 that the world was "still threatened" by such tendencies. However, it happily discovered in the 1990s that its goal was now to "encourage a march down the road to freedom." A role that had been "largely negative and critical" could now be "positive and creative" (Hartwell 1995, 158, 216–17). In 1980, Friedman was willing to suggest that "the tide is turning," while still fearing that the trend "may prove short-lived" (1980, 283).

41. Keynes: Skidelsky 1996, 117. India and Latin America: Yergin and Stanislaw 1998, 215, 234; see also Sachs 1998, 101. Judt 1997.

42. Yergin and Stanislaw 1998, 138. See also Sachs 1998, 99.

43. See Heilbroner 1997; Yergin and Stanislaw 1998.

44. Yergin and Stanislaw 1998, 137.

45. On the once-dominant notion of the "just price" and the "just wage," see Rosenberg and Birdzell 1986, 38. Nixon: Yergin and Stanislaw 1998, 62. In 1973, Milton Friedman warned that "If the U.S. ever succumbs to collectivism, to government control over every facet of our lives, it will not be because the socialists win any argument. It will be through the indirect route of wage and price controls" (Friedman and Friedman 1980, 305).

46. There also seems to be an increasing belief that it may be wise judiciously to regulate the financial system itself because, as one economist has put it, "There's more of a stake in keeping the financial sector honest than there is, for instance, in cosmetics." Yergin and Stanislaw 1998,

373, 349; see also Denny 1997. On the successes of governmental efforts to deal with environmental concerns in the last few decades, see Easterbrook 1995. See also Passell 1998c.

47. Yergin and Stanislaw 1998, 317.

48. See Rosenberg and Birdzell 1986, 119–23; Jones 1987; Weingast 1997; McGuire and Olson 1996; De Long and Shleifer 1993; North and Weingast 1989.

49. For Margaret Thatcher's ready acceptance of this role, see Yergin and Stanislaw 1998, 124.

50. India: Yergin and Stanislaw 1998, 216.

51. Simons 1997, Cohen 1997.

52. It is common to calculate government spending as a percentage of gross domestic product and to conclude that, since this figure has risen in the last decades in most developed countries, governmental "control" over the economy has risen. But most government spending in these countries has not been in consumption but rather in subsidies and transfers, items that do not enter the GDP calculation (Crook 1997, 8). What purports to be a "percentage," therefore, is actually a ratio. Moveover, in assessing "control" of the economy, the rise of transfers may well be far less significant than declines in regulation, in confiscatory taxation, and in once-popular wage and price controls. On this issue, see Nye 1997, 138–41.

53. Aristotle: quoted, Campbell 1981, 56. Slovak film: *Je lepšie byt' bohatý a zdravý, ako chudobný a chorý* by Juraj Jakubisko. Pearl Bailey: quoted, Kunitz and Engerman 1992, 29; Murray (1988, 68) attributes this pithy observation to Sophie Tucker.

54. Easterlin 1974, 90–96, mostly using data and analyses from Cantril 1965. On this issue, see also Murray 1988, ch. 4.

55. Diener 1983, 553. See also Campbell 1981, 241; Easterlin 1974, 99–104; Easterlin 1996, 133–35; Murray 1988, 66–68; Inglehart and Rabier 1986, 22–23. People in wealthy countries may be happier on average than those in poorer ones, but the association is often weak and inconclusive. See Inglehart and Rabier 1986, 40, 44–50; Easterlin 1974, 104–8; Easterlin 1996, 138; but see also Veenhoven 1991, 9–12.

56. Smith 1979; Easterlin 1995, 136, 138; Campbell 1981, 27–30.

57. Veenhoven 1991, 19. Data for Britain and France: Veenhoven 1993, 146–47. See also Murray 1988, ch. 4.

58. Easterlin 1995, 136–40, using data from Veenhoven 1993, 176–77. See also Inglehart and Rabier 1986, 44. Japanese economy: Sullivan 1997.

59. Easterlin 1974, 111–16.

60. Campbell 1981. See also Campbell, Converse, and Rodgers, 1976; Murray 1988, ch. 4.

61. In seeking to explain why professions of happiness did not rise between 1946 and 1977 in the United States, Stanley Lebergott points to a different consideration: the ominous simultaneous expansion in nuclear megatonnage. The considerable increases in measured real incomes during that time, he suggests, could not offset fears of "collective suicide" or of concerns over "poverty, civil rights, nuclear plant explosions, the environment" (1993, 14). The problem with this explanation is that people seem to respond in very personal terms when they are asked about happiness; political considerations like those suggested by Lebergott scarcely enter the happiness calculus unless the question specifically asks about concerns for the nation itself (see Easterlin 1996, 134). Moreover, at the same time the problems Lebergott mentions were rising in the United State, others were dissipating—concerns about food shortages or labor disputes, for example. Even more pointedly, there was actually a considerable decline in fears of atomic war with the relaxation of international tensions that began with the signing of the partial test ban treaty of 1963 (see Mueller 1977, 326–28.).

62. Scitovsky 1992, vi–viii, 4. In like spirit, a letter to the *New York Times* from Latvia worries that youth is being worn down by "grinding affluence" (5 January 1998, p. A24). On the "horrors of prosperity," see Waugh 1986, 49–51.

63. Smith 1976, 782 (V.i.f). Tocqueville 1990, 263. Schumpeter 1950; see also McInnes 1995. See also Keniston 1960.

64. Charles Murray, in line with this proposition, argues that job satisfaction has declined in the U.S. (1988, 134–35). But poll data do not support this conclusion: see, for example, Niemi et al. 1989, 238.

65. Mises 1972, 3. See also Murray 1988, 68–69; Whitman 1998.

66. Lebergott 1993, 15; and, for his authoritative calculation on flies and horse manure, p. 24n. For a rare exception to myopic recollection, see Bettmann 1974.

67. Stanley 1995.

68. For a discussion of ever-rising standards of cleanliness and personal hygiene (at one time people routinely went around encrusted in dirt, rarely washed, and, well, smelled), see Schor 1991, 89–91.

69. Baker 1994–95. See also Whitman 1998, ch. 7.

70. Air quality: Easterbrook 1995, Ellsaesser 1995. People think: *Wash-*

ington Post/Kaiser Family Foundation/Harvard University Survey Project, "Why Don't Americans Trust the Government?" 1996.

71. Rosenberg and Birdzell 1986, 6, also 265. However, improvement was evident to economist Alfred Marshall when he published the first edition of his classic textbook in 1890 (pp. 3–4).

72. Woolsey 1993.

73. Kraus 1962, 394.

74. Data: Mueller 1995, 23.

75. For additional doomsaying on international issues, see Kennedy 1987, 1993; Brzezinski 1993. For an extended critique, see Mueller 1994b.

76. Overchoice: Williams 1990. Buridan's ass comparison suggested by Stanley Engerman.

77. Rosenberg and Birdzell 1986, 5. Hume 1955, 14. For Pope John Paul II's very contrasting take on all this, see Elshtain 1995, 13–14.

78. Easterlin 1996, 153. Hume 1955, 21; see also Murray 1988, ch. 7.

CHAPTER SIX
IMAGES AND DEFINITIONS

1. Lindberg 1996, 42.

2. See also Schmitter and Karl 1991, 84–85.

3. Huntington 1991, 7. In other places (1991, 16), however, Huntington uses as a democratic criterion the requirement that 50 percent of adult males be eligible to vote. James Bryce similarly gets entangled in the suffrage issue when he attempts to define democracy (1921, ch. 3).

4. Dahl 1971, 1. Riker 1965, 31. Wiebe 1995, 263–64. Mencken 1920, 203. See also Schmitter and Karl 1991, 76.

5. A similar approach is adopted by Linz 1978, 5–6. For a critique of the rather murky "civil society" or "civic culture" concept, concluding that the "norms of a civic culture are better thought of as a *product* and not as a producer of democracy," see Schmitter and Karl (1991, 83, emphasis in the original). See also Laitin 1995.

6. Riker 1965, 25.

7. Pomper 1974, 37.

8. Bailey 1950, 237.

9. Vote communication: Verba, Schlozman, and Brady 1995, 13. Contract: CBS News/*New York Times* Poll release, 14 December 1994; Toner 1995.

10. Almond and Verba 1963, 37, 473. Mexican observer (Rodrigo Gar-

cía Treviño) quoted, Scott 1959, 298. Needler 1990, 3, 130–31. Scott 1959, 15. See also Yergin and Stanislaw 1998, 252–53.

11. See Scott 1989, Mosher 1991.

12. On this issue, see Fenno 1973; Schlozman and Tierney 1986; Rosenstone and Hansen 1993.

13. Plato 1957, 316.

14. On this issue, see also Riker 1982, 7–8. "Not the privilege": Riker 1965, 20. Locke 1970, 322.

15. There is also the issue of equality before the law (see Riker 1982, 14–15). Thus an aristocrat who killed someone in a drunken brawl would be held as accountable as a commoner who did so. But it seems entirely feasible to have that sort of legal equality under an authoritarian system— it might have been achieved as much in Nazi Germany or Communist Russia as in democratic England or America.

16. Jefferson 1939, 126–27. Pericles: Thucydides 1934, 104.

17. For a discussion, see Dahl 1956, 112–18; Fishkin 1995, 35–36.

18. See also Schmitter and Karl 1991, 83–84; Dahl 1956, ch. 4.

19. Another way to look at all this would be as follows. Opposition and petitioning cost time and money. Democracy takes effect when the government does not increase this cost by harassing or jailing the petitioners and the opposition, or by imposing additional economic or other sanctions on them. The costs of opposition and petition are not equal because some people have more time, money, or relevant skills than others. Elections do have something of an equalizing effect because the cost of this form of political expression is much the same for everybody. However, the political impact of a single vote is so small that unless one gets a psychological charge out of the act, it makes little sense to go through the exercise.

20. Plato 1957, 316, 325–27; see also Elshtain 1995, 96–104. James Madison's solution to the Platonic puzzle was typically gimmicky and institutional and, moreover, highly unlikely to convince Plato. Should a majority yearn for an "improper or wicked project" such as paper money or an equal division of property, such yearnings could be adequately finessed, he proposed in *Federalist Paper* number 10, if the country were large and if governing were done by representatives rather than directly by the passionate masses.

21. On this issue, see also Popkin 1991, 21; McGuire and Olson 1996, 94.

22. Plato 1957, 328. Mencken 1920, 221. Mark Antony's demagogic fu-

neral oration in Shakespeare's *Julius Caesar* illustrates the same process, as do the developments in Henrik Ibsen's *Enemy of the People*.

23. This statement is usually credited to Abraham Lincoln, but there is no conclusive evidence that he ever said it (see Woldman 1950, 74). Intriguingly, the statement has also been attributed to that great showman, prince of ballyhoo and humbug, and hero of the capitalism part of this book, Phineas T. Barnum, who is also (erroneously) alleged to have said, "There's a sucker born every minute." The connection is intriguing because the two statements are quite congruent and might be seen to spring from the same mentality. In tandem they make up a cautionary tale: there are a lot of suckers who can be fooled all the time, they suggest, but be careful—there are a lot of nonsuckers out there too, and eventually, if left free, they'll see through the most artful of frauds, demagogues, and humbugs.

24. Morgan 1988, 147–48.

25. See Pessen 1984. Snobs, too, have been quite safe because social and class distinctions often remain substantially unruffled. Thus, Gilbert's crisp slander against equality, "If everybody is somebody, then nobody is anybody," has not been borne out.

26. See Wasilewski 1998; Rosenberg 1993.

27. Przeworski 1986, 63.

28. As Berelson, Lazarsfeld, and McPhee suggest in a classic study, "The apathetic segment of America probably has helped to hold the system together and cushioned the shock of disagreement, adjustment, and change" (1954, 322; see also Berelson 1952, Weissberg 1998). It almost seems that the only time many people even consider the issue of civil liberties is when they are being queried about it in public opinion surveys (Mueller 1988, 21).

29. During the Cold War, sugar policy was ardently opposed as well by U.S. foreign policy officials because it harmed sugar-producing countries in the Caribbean, thereby making them more vulnerable to the siren song coming from Castro's Cuba. On the continuing political triumph of beekeepers in the United States, see Passell 1995.

30. Madison 1788.

31. Forster 1951, 69–70. The most famous expression of this sentiment comes from Winston Churchill who, referring perhaps to Forster, observed in a House of Commons speech in November 1947 that "It has been said that Democracy is the worst form of government except all those other forms that have been tried from time to time" (1950, 200).

Twenty years before Forster, William Ralph Inge had put it this way: "Democracy is a form of government which may be rationally defended, not as good, but as being less bad than any other" (1919, 5).

32. Dostoyevsky 1945, 305–6.

33. Tocqueville 1990, 235.

34. For a discussion, see Hess 1987.

35. West 1941, 1097. Jefferson 1944, 604. Louis XIV: Chodorow and Knox 1989, 561.

36. Jefferson 1939, 241.

37. Niccolò Machiavelli, not commonly known as an ardent democrat, observes that "a prince who knows no other control but his own will is like a madman." He acknowledges that a people uncontrolled by laws "will hardly be wise," but even under that highly undesirable circumstance, "the people are guilty of fewer excesses than the prince," and "the errors of the people are of less importance, and therefore more easily remedied. For a licentious and mutinous people may easily be brought back to good conduct by the influence and persuasion of a good man, but an evil-minded prince is not amenable to such influences, and therefore there is no remedy against him but cold steel" (1950, 265).

38. When Louis XIV died, the throne went to his great-grandson, aged five, who grew into an indolent adult and reigned ineffectually for over fifty years: he "did not govern himself," Stanley Chodorow and MacGregor Knox have observed, and "he largely prevented others from governing" (1989, 625). Things can be even worse if the king leaves no obvious heir, a conundrum that often sets off vicious intrigue or is resolved by principles that find justice in blood lines, not competence. Even in the comparatively stable monarchical system in England between 1066 and 1702, contested successions were considerably more likely than uncontested ones (De Long and Shleifer 1993, 698–99). One organization that has solved the succession problem is the Catholic church, though it continues to grant unreviewed life-time tenure to occupants of its top office.

39. That certainly seems to have been Machiavelli's belief: "as regards prudence and stability, I say that the people are more prudent and stable, and have better judgment than a prince" (1950, 263). Riker 1982, 244–46.

40. Pateman 1970, 4n.

41. For data see Yang 1997 and Sherrill 1996. On this issue, see also Weissberg 1998, ch. 5. Sherrill concludes from surveys conducted from 1984 to 1994 that "No other group of Americans is the object of such sus-

tained, extreme, and intense distaste" (p. 470). Actually, an earlier survey applying the same measures suggests that Vietnam War protesters inspired admiration ratings that were even lower (Mueller 1984, 152).

42. In an article published in September 1961 James Q. Wilson lamented that "the prospects of vigorous, extensive, and organized Negro protest in large Northern cities are poor." Relevant organizations, he and many others observed at the time, "lack the capacity for mass leadership." He accounted for the "apparent absence of concerted protest action," by "the nature of the ends sought, the diffusion of relevant targets, the differentiation of the Negro community along class lines, and the organizational constraints placed on Negroes as they enter into partial contact with the white community" (1961, 298, 302).

43. See also Schmitter and Karl 1991, 79.

44. For a discussion, see Barany 1998.

45. Riker 1965. Dahl 1989, 311.

46. Forster 1951.

47. Smith 1956, 323–24. Smith could work up quite a bit of enthusiasm for arithmetic. As he put it in a letter to a child in 1835: "Lucy, dear child, mind your arithmetic. You know, in the first sum of yours I ever saw, there was a mistake. You had carried two (as a cab is licensed to do) and you ought, dear Lucy, to have carried but one. Is this a trifle? What would life be without arithmetic but a scene of horrors?" (1956, xiii).

48. For a discussion of this trait in Greek liberalism, see Havelock 1957, 123.

49. Machiavelli was quite confident of this ability: "as to the people's capacity of judging things, it is exceedingly rare that, when they hear two orators of equal talents advocate different measures, they do not decide in favor of the best of the two; which proves their ability to discern the truth of what they hear." In another place he approvingly quotes Cicero: "The people, although ignorant, yet are capable of appreciating the truth, and yield to it readily when it is presented to them by a man whom they esteem worthy of confidence" (1950, 263, 120). Popkin (1991) extensively discusses what he calls "low-information rationality"; see also Page and Shapiro 1992.

CHAPTER SEVEN
CONSEQUENCES OF THE DEMOCRATIC IMAGE

1. Verba and Nie 1972, 1.

2. Hibbing and Theiss-Morse 1995, 150.

3. Sandel 1996, 4, 294–97. Putnam 1995a, 1995b. See also Morin and Balz 1996, Uslaner 1993, Elshtain 1995.

4. Sandel 1996, 323.

5. Table data from *Wilson Quarterly,* Spring 1997, p. 121; Niemi et al., 1989, 303; Mueller 1973, 13. The rise in the 1965 data in the first table may be a lingering effect of the John Kennedy assassination of 1963. On turnout see Nardulli et al. 1996. On confidence in Congress: Hibbing and Theiss-Morse 1995, 34–35. Golden years: Altschuler and Blumin 1997. On the 1960s rise, see also Schudson 1998, 302.

6. Sense of mastery: Sandel 1996, 202. On the considerable effects of the Korean War on public opinion, see Mueller 1973; Mueller 1977; Mueller 1979, 314–15; Mueller 1989.

7. Levin 1960, 58, 61. Keniston 1960, 161–62. President's Commission on National Goals 1960. On this issue, see also Schudson 1998, 300.

8. Dionne 1991, 355. Nelson 1995, 72.

9. Sandel 1996, 6, 318, 334–35, 351.

10. Putnam 1995a, 77; see also Elshtain 1995, ch. 1; and Madison 1788. For a valuable analysis of many of these issues, see Whitman 1998.

11. On some of these issues, see also Schmitter and Karl 1991, 83–84.

12. This problematic expansion may have stemmed in part from the gradual, and mostly painless, extension of suffrage on a one-person-one-vote basis until it embraces almost the entirety of the adult population, a process that may have furnished the illusion that all people should be, or could be, about equal in their political impact. At times, however, democratic philosophers have advocated weighting the vote: for example, John Stuart Mill suggested that smart people like him should be given extra votes to make things work out a bit better.

13. Verba, Schlozman, Brady, and Nie 1993, 267, 314. Mansbridge 1997, 423.

14. Troy 1997, 28, 31. Bennett: Rosenbaum 1997. On this issue, see also Samuelson 1995, Heard 1960, Sorauf 1988.

15. Broder and Johnson 1996, 630. For an excellent discussion of this issue, see Schlozman and Tierney 1986, ch. 15.

16. Verba, Schlozman and Brady 1995, 13. See also Broder and Johnson 1996, 630–31. Without full explanation, Lindblom simply and casually labels this phenomenon "undemocratic" (1977, 169).

17. Dahl 1989, 271, 279.

18. Dahl 1989, 322, 339.

19. Dahl 1989, 339. Almond 1950; see also Neuman 1986.

20. Dahl 1989, 340. On efforts to set up something of a device like this,

see Fishkin 1995; for a critique of the results, see Merkle 1996. On the use of random methods to choose leaders in Greek democracy, see Dahl 1989, 19.

21. In Russell Baker's modest estimation, Capra's "Mr. Smith Goes to Washington" is a "childish slur on the American political system" and "the worst movie ever made about a politician." "The portrait of the Senate is absurd and vicious. Mr. Smith himself is a boob so dense that he should never have been allowed to go to Podunk, much less to Washington" (1998).

22. Dionne 1991, 354.

23. This process is central to Riker's analysis of democracy (1982).

24. See Patterson and Magleby 1992, 544; Mueller 1994a, 180; Hibbing and Theiss-Morse 1995, 14.

25. See Toner 1994.

26. Broder and Johnson 1996, 628.

27. Berke 1994.

28. Nelson observes that "in 1992, the same voters who in 14 states imposed term limits on members of Congress reelected all but six of the 116 incumbents who were running for reelection in their states, including 70 who had been in office longer than the term limit those voters were imposing" (1995, 76).

29. Dionne 1991, 15.

30. Riker 1996, ch. 5; see also Popkin 1991, 234–36.

31. Ansolabehere and Iyengar 1995, 8–9, 12, 14, 16, 145, 150–56.

32. *Economist*, 16 May 1991, 48.

33. Hibbing and Theiss-Morse 1995, 18, 19, 157.

34. In general, local television news is more highly evaluated and trusted than national television in surveys in the United States, a difference that may arise from the fact that local news tends to avoid controversy while national news frequently wallows in it.

35. For data: *Gallup Poll Monthly*, February 1998, 16. On this phenomenon more generally, see Hibbing and Theiss-Morse 1995, 36.

36. Hibbing and Theiss-Morse 1995, 81, 105.

37. Hibbing and Theiss-Morse 1995, 157. Mortimer quoted, Harrison 1997.

38. Lienesch 1992, 1011. Delli Carpini and Keeter 1996, 224. Junn 1991, 193. Ansolabehere and Iyengar 1995, 145. Fishkin 1995, 176.

39. Lijphart 1997, 5. Conway 1991, ch. 1. Switzerland: Teixeira 1992, 8; Lijphart 1997, 5; Burnham 1987, 107.

40. Lijphart 1997, 5.

41. Teixeira 1992, 101. Lijphart 1997, 2–5.

42. Teixeira 1992, 101–3.

43. Ansolabehere and Iyengar 1995, 145.

44. Burnham 1987, 99.

45. Policy agenda: Teixeira 1992, 102. Rosenstone and Hansen 1993, 228–29; see also Rothenberg 1992.

46. Some analysts, like Putnam, argue for participation more broadly and contend that the key to making democracy work is not so much political participation as the presence of "dense networks of social exchange." (Actually, however, he seems to be arguing that such networks may be more helpful for effective government than for democracy itself when he concludes that *"good government"* is a "by-product of singing groups and soccer clubs" [1993, 172, 196, emphasis added; see also Laitin 1995, 173].) Putnam has extrapolated these conclusions, developed from an analysis of Italy, to the United States, but fails to demonstrate that the lamented decline in such things as PTA membership and the rise of television viewing has had detrimental policy consequences (1995a, 1995b; for critiques, see Lemann 1996; Norris 1996; Ladd 1996; *Economist,* 18 February 1995, 21–22; Schudson 1998, 294–314).

47. Quoted, Delli Carpini and Keeter 1996, 1.

48. Bryce 1921, 1:48. Mann quoted, Sandel 1996, 165.

49. Lienesch 1992, 1011; Lakoff 1996, 326; Bellah et al. 1991, 273. One observer urges rather improbably that America will get back on the road to the democratic ideal "only when we have figured out how to use television to teach the essence of citizenship, the virtues of individual sacrifice in the common good and the nobility necessary to make democracy work" (Squires 1990).

50. Delli Carpini and Keeter 1996. See also Berelson 1952, 318.

51. CBS News/*New York Times* Poll release, December 14, 1994. Toner 1995.

52. *Washington Post*/Kaiser Family Foundation/Harvard University Survey Project, "Why Don't Americans Trust the Government?" 1996. See also Morin 1996.

53. Delli Carpini and Keeter 1996, 22. As so often happens, this statement ignores the country's notably unstable Civil War.

54. Holmes 1996, 33–34.

55. Tocqueville 1990, 1:201.

56. McGuire and Olson 1996, 94. Reviewing several studies of new democracies, Nancy Bermeo observes, to her dismay, that "in every en-

during case, dramatic redistributions of property were postponed, circumscribed, or rolled back" (1990, 365). See also Przeworski 1986, 63.

57. Lenin 1932, 73, 82. See also Meyer 1957, 66–70.

58. See Meyer 1957, 19–56, 92–103; Cook 1991, 248–56.

59. For a discussion, see Cohen 1995, 131, 246; Bennett 1995, 137–42; Woodward 1995, 228, 241, 279.

60. See Gordon and Troxel 1995; Ganev 1997; Châtelot 1997; Stokes 1993, 701.

61. See also Stokes 1993, 701–4; Marody 1997.

62. None too surprisingly, cynicism about democracy has flourished in the new democracies of eastern and central Europe. See Gati 1996. Of course, politicians there have to deal daily there with messy issues that are hugely difficult and painful: in the early 1990s, as American politicians agonized over whether flag burning should be banned or whether the gasoline tax should be raised a few cents, politicians in Poland alone privatized more businesses than had previously been privatized in the entire history of the human race and created a banking system in less time than it takes in the West to train a bank examiner (Fischer and Gelb 1991, 99, 100). For all that, however, cynicism may not be much greater than in the "mature" democracies of the West. One analyst is shocked at a poll showing that 79 percent of the Romanian population feels politicians were "ready to promise anything to get votes" while 65 percent say politicians are more interested in strengthening their own parties than in solving the country's problems (Shafir 1993, 18)—disapproval rates likely to be found in the West as well. Another asserts that Russian voters have "lost their faith in all politicians" (Rutland 1994/95, 6). However, while only 6 percent of polled in Russia in 1994 said they trust political parties (Rose 1994, 53), a poll in the United States in the same year discovered only 10 percent willing to rate the "honesty and ethical standards" of congressmen as "very high" or "high," tidily placing them twenty-fifth on a list of twenty-six, just ahead of car salesmen (McAneny and Moore 1994, 2–4), and a 1995 poll in Britain found that 73 percent of Britons considered the ruling Conservative Party to be "very sleazy and disreputable" (*Harper's,* February 1995, 11). Richard Rose argues that "the communist regime has left a legacy of distrust" (1994, 53), but, as noted earlier, there is plenty of evidence to suggest the United States has managed to pick up the legacy without that experience. He also concludes that "An election produces a representative government if those elected are trusted representatives of those who voted for them. The current Russian govern-

281

ment is democratically elected but distrusted" (Rose 1994, 53), but much the same could be said for the United States at almost any point in its history. On a scale of political distrust developed from polls conducted in the 1990s, Japan scored highest; Poland, Russia, and Estonia registered on the same plane as Britain; East Germany, Bulgaria, and the Czech Republic were all a bit lower than West Germany; and Slovenia was level with the United States (Mason 1995, 69).

63. On this issue, see also Holmes 1996. Actually, the theory-derived notion that low participation implies low legitimacy can be dangerously self-fulfilling. For example, a romanticism about political participation has helped lead to the rather bizarre and even potentially disruptive legal requirement in some postcommunist countries that at least 25 or 50 percent of the electorate must participate for an election to be valid. If this were the law in the United States, of course, huge numbers of elected offices would be vacant.

64. There can also be definitional turmoil. By the definition used by Higley and Gunther in one able effort to deal with this tricky concept (1992), it seems likely that Canada could not be considered to be a "consolidated" democracy since devoted secessionists are numbered among its political elite.

65. Actually, if broad political participation is an important standard, many postcommunist countries are *more* democratic than the United States. For example, in the 1994 parliamentary elections in Ukraine some 5,833 candidates competed in the country's 450 electoral districts, and of these, 62 percent were put forward by "simple groups of voters." Moreover, turnout "reached a surprisingly high average of about 75 percent" (*RFE/RL Daily Report*, 1 March 1994; 29 March 1994). And, by contrast with the American public's impressive ignorance about who Newt Gingrich might be, a poll conducted in Slovakia in October 1993, when the country was only ten months old, asked its respondents about a long list of thirty-one politicians, many of them quite obscure, and found only eight cases in which the Slovak public's ignorance level reached that of the Americans' about Gingrich (FOCUS 1993, 10–11).

66. Michnik 1997, 18.

Chapter Eight
The Rise of Democracy

1. Fukuyama 1989, 6; Dahl 1971, 181–82.
2. Gellner 1988, 3–4.

3. Engerman 1986, 339. See also Drescher 1987, Eltis 1987.

4. Dahl 1989, 251. See also Burkhart and Lewis-Beck 1994, Inglehart 1997, ch. 6.

5. Dahl 1989, 253; Dahl 1971, 186.

6. Moore 1966, 418. See also Huntington 1984, 204.

7. As Huntington observes, in 1981 almost all countries with per capita gross national products over $4220 were *either* democratic *or* Communist (1984, 202).

8. Huntington 1984, 200.

9. Huntington 1991, 108, 316; see also Lipset 1993a, 1993b. Di Palma 1990, 6–7.

10. For some analysts, however, this will take a long time: looking at Spain a full twenty-one years after it became a democracy, Harry Eckstein acknowledges that the country "seems well on the way to becoming a stable democracy," but still insists that "the returns are not yet all in" (1996, 24).

11. Whitehead 1986, 38.

12. Rustow 1970, 361; for a more recent expression of this perspective, scc Eckstcin 1996. Dahl 1971, 45, 47. Dahl 1989, 264. By contrast, see Plattner 1988.

13. Wiarda 1976, 51–52.

14. Huntington 1984, 218; emphasis added.

15. Kaufman 1986, 85.

16. Barro 1993, 1994. On the pessimism issue, see also Fukuyama 1992, ch. 1; Muravchik 1992, ch. 6.

17. Di Palma 1990, 4. African leaders: French 1996. Democratic dispositions: Elshtain 1995, 2. Thatcher: speech presented on C-SPAN, 29 December 1996.

18. Dahl 1989, 260, 262. See also Dahl 1971, 126. On elite transformations, see Higley and Gunther 1992.

19. Dahl 1971, 188.

20. On this process, see also Mueller 1995, ch. 10.

21. Voltaire: Chodorow and Knox 1989, 609. Berlin 1969, 129–30. Huntington 1991, 28.

22. A related development took place with respect to the democracy-enhancing fiction that the government owes its authority to the consent of the governed. In some self-serving battles with the king in the seventeenth century, the English Parliament sought to undermine the monarchy's putative direct connection to God by repackaging and selling the ancient notion that government actually owed its existence and legiti-

macy to the consent of the people (who, in turn, somehow embodied the voice of God). But Parliament's objective in all this was, as Edmund Morgan observes, "to magnify the power not of the people themselves, but of the people's representatives." Then the monarchists helped to bring out the democratic implications of the fiction: zeroing in on an apparent weakness in the Parliament's self-serving conceit, they argued that if the people could revoke the King's powers, they could also revoke those of the Parliament. The monarchists took this tack in part because they believed, probably correctly, that in any straight electoral contest with the Parliament, the king would win. But in the process, observes Morgan, "they expanded the dimensions of the fiction and contributed to its future success as the basis of modern government." Thus, by 1650 the notion of the consent of the governed had been substantially accepted, a fiction that could later be used to imply democracy (Morgan 1988, 17, 56, 58, 62, 63).

23. Huntington 1991, 78, 84.

24. Palmer 1959, 239–40.

25. On this process, see also Geoghegan 1983, 156.

26. Jefferson 1939, 279.

27. Seward 1991, 85. Catherine: O'Connor 1994.

28. Tocqueville 1990, xx–xxi.

29. Riker 1965, 12. It is possible, however, that democracy's crisis in America was not all that deep. If the South had won the war or if it had been allowed peacefully to secede, it seems likely that the major portion of the country would have continued to be a democracy.

30. On the unpopularity of war in Germany, see Mueller 1989, 64–68; Mueller 1991; Steinert 1977, 40–41, 315, 341; Kershaw 1987, 122–47, 229, 241. On the unpopularity of war in Italy, see Mueller 1989, 62–63; Knox 1982. On Japan, see Mueller 1989, 71–77.

31. Huntington 1991, 36, 45–46.

32. Huntington 1997, 5, 10.

33. Moynihan 1975, 6. Brandt: Crozier et al., 1975, 2. On these issues, see also Plattner 1988.

34. Huntington 1984, 206; emphasis in the original.

35. Huntington 1991, 88; see also Gershman 1989, 127–28.

36. See Yergin and Stanislaw 1998, ch. 9.

37. Whitehead 1986, 6.

38. O'Donnell and Schmitter 1986, 31, emphasis in the original. Hardest questions: Schemo 1997. Ridiculous antics: Kamm 1990.

39. Rohter 1996b. See also Brooke 1990.

40. *Economist,* 18 May 1991, 48. Brooke 1993.

41. Huntington 1984, 212.

42. Thailand: Kahn 1998. Pakistan: Dugger 1998.

43. The role of the Soviet Union in this enterprise, declared Josef Stalin, was to serve as a "base for the overthrow of imperialism in all countries" or as a "lever for the further disintegration of imperialism." He concluded that "The struggle between these two centers for the possession of the world economy will decide the fate of capitalism and Communism in the whole world," and he would often quote Lenin on such matters: "the existence of the Soviet Republic side by side with the imperialist states for a long time is unthinkable. In the end either one or the other will conquer." As Lenin had also vividly put it, "as soon as we are strong enough to fight the whole of capitalism, we shall at once take it by the neck." Meanwhile, the official Party history proclaimed its "confidence in the final victory of the great cause of the party of Lenin and Stalin, the victory of Communism in the whole world" (Historicus 1949, 198, 200, 203–4; Leffler 1994, 17).

44. For a discussion and an assessment, see Mueller 1989, chs. 5–9.

45. President's Commission on National Goals 1960, 1–2. CIA: Reeves 1993, 54. On the Soviet Union's apparent economic strength at the time, see also Yergin and Stanislaw 1998, 22, 272.

46. For contemporary Western analyses, see H. Smith 1976, Pipes 1984, and Bialer 1986. See also Kennedy 1987, 488–514.

47. See Bunce 1985.

48. As late as the 1970s quite a few people—not only Communists— were still working up enthusiasm for violent, undemocratic revolution. For example, in her multiple-award-winning book about Vietnam, *Fire in the Lake,* American journalist Frances Fitzgerald fairly glowed with anticipation at what successful revolutionaries could bring to Southeast Asia: "when 'individualism' and its attendant corruption gives way to the revolutionary community," she breathlessly anticipated, "the narrow flame of revolution" will "cleanse the lake of Vietnamese society from the corruption and disorder of the American war" (1972, 589–90). Neither corruption nor disorder were eradicated when revolution's narrow flame sliced through Vietnam, and evils far worse were perpetrated.

49. See Mueller 1986; Mueller 1989, 262.

50. On this point, see also Dahl 1989, 263; Huntington 1984, 214. The 1989 experiences also suggest that, from his standpoint, Brezhnev was correct in 1968 when he sent tanks forcefully to stifle Czechoslovak liberalization on the grounds that, although its leaders protested much to

the contrary, the country was on the slippery slope out of the Soviet bloc and into Western democracy.

51. Huntington 1984, 217.

52. Diamond 1996, Gati 1996. See also Zakaria 1997.

53. Collins 1997, 19. The trend toward democracy is also understated when one calculates democracies as a percentage of all countries (as in Diamond 1996, for example). The Soviet Union garnered a rank zero, of course, but the territories it once constituted now make up not one, but fifteen countries which are free to various degrees. To make things comparable it might be sensible to recalculate, counting the old Soviet Union not as one unfree country, but as fifteen unfree ones.

54. Rowen 1996. See also Manion 1996; Pei 1998; Yergin and Stanislaw 1998, 231; Collins 1997; Harding 1998, 12–13. At the end of 1997, it was announced that democracy would be advanced to the township level. In many areas, people can complain all they want, as long as they do not organize: Faison 1998.

55. Huntington 1984, 216.

56. On Qatar, see Jehl 1997. On Iran, see Bakhash 1998.

57. See French 1996.

58. Perlez 1990a; see also Legum 1990; Perlez 1990b, 1990c.

59. Zakaria 1997, 42.

60. Machiavelli 1950, 265.

CHAPTER NINE

DEMOCRACY AND CAPITALISM: CONNECTIONS AND DISCONNECTIONS

1. Lindblom 1977, 116, see also 161–69. Berger 1986, 81. Friedman 1962, 10. Dahl 1990, 80. See also Kristol 1978, xi; Huntington 1984, 204–5, 214. For a useful overview of aspects of this issue, see Almond 1991.

2. Yergin and Stanislaw 1998, 25, 366.

3. See Ganev 1997, Hockstader 1997.

4. Riker 1982, 7.

5. Friedman 1962, 16–18.

6. See, for example, Barro 1993. See also Schmitter and Karl 1991, 85.

7. Mueller 1992a, 990; Olson 1993; *Economist* 1994, 17.

8. Rosenberg and Birdzell 1986, 121–22.

9. Rosenberg and Birdzell 1986, 309. See also Barro 1993, Olson 1982, Buchanan 1990.

10. China: Ashton et al., 1984; Riskin 1995, 414. Bulgaria: Ganev 1997, 131, 136.

11. French 1996. On the foreign policy of the wealthy democracies, see Mueller 1996b. See also Friedman 1997.

12. Bullock 1993, 309–10.

13. See Warr 1995. Although Mayor David Dinkins could correctly point to statistics that showed crime had gone down in New York City during his tenure, this did him little good in his reelection campaign: for example, *New York Times* columnist A. M. Rosenthal actually referred to the "trivializing statistics" that "are supposed to convince us that crime is going down" (1993). For data showing that crime peaked in New York in 1990 and declined steadily thereafter, see *New York Times*, 19 February 1998, A16.

14. For example, buried in a sensational story in *USA Today* about "driveway robberies" in Dallas was the observation that, actually, violent crime had dropped 32 percent in that city in the previous two years (Potok 1994).

15. Fukuyama 1989, 14. Yergin and Stanislaw 1998, 389.

16. Moscow and New York: Shiller et al., 1991, 1992. Economists and the public: Brossard and Pearlstein 1996. When gasoline prices soared during the Gulf War crisis, the public overwhelmingly blamed manipulation by the oil companies, not normal market forces (Mueller 1994a, 151–52, 346 n 10). Much of the outrage against Standard Oil in the nineteenth century stemmed from a similar economic perspective: see Chernow 1998, ch. 12.

* References *

Abramovitz, Moses. 1989. *Thinking About Growth and Other Essays on Economic Growth and Welfare.* New York: Cambridge University Press.

Akerlof, George A. 1983. Loyalty Filters. *American Economic Review* 73, no. 1 (March): 54–63.

Alexander, David. 1970. *Retailing in England during the Industrial Revolution.* London: Athlone.

Alger, Horatio, Jr. [1876]. *Shifting for Himself or Gilbert Greyson's Fortunes.* New York: A. L. Burt.

Almond, Gabriel A. 1950. *The American People and Foreign Policy.* New York: Harcourt Brace.

———. 1991. Capitalism and Democracy. *PS: Political Science & Politics* 24, no. 3 (September): 467–74.

Almond, Gabriel A., and Sidney Verba. 1963. *The Civic Culture: Political Attitudes and Democracy in Five Nations.* Princeton, N.J.: Princeton University Press.

Altschuler, Glenn C., and Stuart M. Blumin. 1997. Limits of Political Engagement in Antebellum America: A New Look at the Golden Age of Participatory Democracy. *Journal of American History* 84, no. 3 (December): 855–85.

Angell, Norman. 1914. *The Great Illusion: A Study of the Relation of Military Power to National Advantage.* London: Heinemann.

———. 1933. *The Great Illusion 1933.* New York: Putnam's.

———. 1951. *After All: An Autobiography.* New York: Farrar, Straus and Young.

Ansolabehere, Stephen, and Shanto Iyengar. 1995. *Going Negative: How Attack Ads Shrink and Polarize the Electorate.* New York: Free Press.

Appel, Joseph H. 1930. *The Business Biography of John Wanamaker, Founder and Builder: America's Merchant Pioneer from 1861 to 1922.* New York: Macmillan.

Arndt, H. W. 1978. *The Rise and Fall of Economic Growth: A Study in Contemporary Thought.* Melbourne: Longman Cheshire.

Ashton, Basil, Kenneth Hill, Alan Piazza, and Robin Zeitz. 1984. Famine in China. *Population and Development Review* 10, no. 4 (December): 613–45.

Autry, James A. 1991. *Love and Profit: The Art of Caring Leadership.* New York: William Morrow.

Axelrod, Robert. 1984. *The Evolution of Cooperation.* New York: Basic Books.

Bailey, Ronald, ed. 1995. *The True State of the Planet.* New York: Free Press.

Bailey, Stephen Kemp. 1950. *Congress Makes a Law: The Story Behind the Employment Act of 1946.* New York: Columbia University Press.

Bairoch, Paul. 1981. The Main Trends in National Economic Disparities since the Industrial Revolution. In *Disparities in Economic Development since the Industrial Revolution,* ed. Paul Bairoch and M. Levy-Leboyer, 3–17. London: Macmillan.

———. 1993. *Economics and World History: Myths and Paradoxes.* Chicago: University of Chicago Press.

Baker, Nicholson. 1994–95. From the Index of First Lines. *New Yorker,* December 26–January 2, 83.

Baker, Russell. 1998. What! No Buster Keaton? *New York Times,* 19 June, A29.

Bakhash, Shaul. 1998. Iran's Remarkable Election. *Journal of Democracy* 9, no. 1 (January): 80–94.

Banfield, Edward C. 1958. *The Moral Basis of a Backward Society.* Glencoe, Il: Free Press.

Barany, Zoltan. 1998. Ethnic Mobilization and the State: The Roma in Eastern Europe. *Ethnic and Racial Studies* 21, no. 2 (March): 308–27.

Barber, Benjamin R. 1995. *Jihad* vs. *McWorld.* New York: Times Books.

Barnum, P. T. 1855. *Life of P. T. Barnum Written by Himself.* New York: Redfield.

———. 1871. *Struggles and Triumphs: Or, Forty Years' Recollections of P. T. Barnum, Written by Himself.* New York: American News Company.

Barr, James. 1987. Biblical Chronology: Legend or Science? Ethel M. Wood Lecture. Senate House, University of London, 4 March.

Barro, Robert J. 1993. Pushing Democracy Is No Key to Prosperity. *Wall Street Journal,* 14 December, A16.

———. 1994. Democracy: A Recipe for Growth? *Wall Street Journal,* 1 December, A18.

Bellah, Robert N., Richard Madsen, William M. Sullivan, Ann Swidler, and Steven M. Tipton. 1991. *The Good Society.* New York: Knopf.

Bennet, James. 1995. A Charm School For Selling Cars: In Class, Making Peace With Buyers; Then There's the Real World. *New York Times,* 29 March, D1.

Bennett, Christopher. 1995. *Yugoslavia's Bloody Collapse: Causes, Course and Consequences.* New York: New York University Press.

Benson, Bruce L. 1997. The Spontaneous Evolution of Commercial Law.

In *Reputation: Studies in the Voluntary Elicitation of Good Conduct,* ed. Daniel B. Klein, 165–89. Ann Arbor: University of Michigan Press.

Berelson, Bernard R. 1952. Democratic Theory and Public Opinion. *Public Opinion Quarterly* 16, no. 3 (Fall): 313–30.

Berelson, Bernard R., Paul F. Lazarsfeld, and William N. McPhee. 1954. *Voting: A Study of Opinion Formation in a Presidential Campaign.* Chicago: University of Chicago Press.

Berger, Peter L. 1986. *The Capitalist Revolution: Fifty Propositions About Prosperity, Equality, and Liberty.* New York: Basic Books.

———. 1996/97. Secularism in Retreat. *National Interest,* Winter, 3–12.

Bergson, Abram. 1984. Income Inequality Under Soviet Socialism. *Journal of Economic Literature* 22, no. 3 (September): 1052–99.

Berke, Richard L. 1994. Victories Were Captured By G.O.P. Candidates, Not the Party's Platform. *New York Times,* 10 November, B1.

Berlin, Isaiah. 1969. *Four Essays in Liberty.* London: Oxford University Press.

Bermeo, Nancy. 1990. Rethinking Regime Change. *Comparative Politics* 22, no. 3 (April): 359–77.

Bernhardi, Friedrich von. 1914. *Germany and the Next War.* New York: Longmans, Green.

Bettmann, Otto L. 1974. *The Good Old Days—They Were Terrible!.* New York: Random House.

Bialer, Seweryn. 1986. *The Soviet Paradox: External Expansion, Internal Decline.* New York: Knopf.

Bittel, Lester R. 1972. *The Nine Master Keys of Management.* New York: McGraw-Hill.

Blakeslee, Sandra. 1998. Placebos Prove So Powerful Even Experts Are Surprised. *New York Times,* 13 October, D1.

Blobaum, Robert E. 1995. *Rewolucja: Russian Poland, 1904–1907.* Ithaca, N.Y.: Cornell University Press.

Boesche, Roger. 1988. Why did Tocqueville Fear Abundance? or The Tension Between Commerce and Citizenship. *History of European Ideas* 9, no. 1: 25–45.

Bradsher, Keith. 1996. Sticker Shock: Car Buyers Miss Haggling Ritual. *New York Times,* 13 June, D1.

———. 1998. At G.M., Can They Get Along? *New York Times,* 29 July, C1.

Brams, Steven J., and Alan D. Taylor. 1999. *The Win-Win Solution: Guaranteeing Fair Shares to Everybody.* New York: Norton.

Brandeis, Louis D. 1934. *The Curse of Bigness: Miscellaneous Papers of Louis D. Brandeis.* Ed. Osmond K. Fraenkel. New York: Viking.

Brearly, Harry Chase. 1997. A Symbol of Safety: The Origins of Under-writers' Laboratories. In *Reputation: Studies in the Voluntary Elicitation of Good Conduct,* ed. Daniel B. Klein, 75–84. Ann Arbor: University of Michigan Press.

Broder, David S., and Haynes Johnson. 1996. *The System: The American Way of Politics at the Breaking Point.* Boston: Little, Brown.

Brody, Jane E. 1997. Personal Health: The Nutrient That Reddens Toma-toes Appears to Have Health Benefits. *New York Times,* 12 March.

Brooke, James. 1990. Colombian Guerrillas Forsake the Gun for Politics. *New York Times,* 2 September, 14.

———. 1993. Governing Party's Candidate Wins Paraguay's Presidential Election. *New York Times,* 11 May, A10.

Brossard, Mario A., and Steven Pearlstein. 1996. Great Divide: Econo-mists vs. Public. *Washington Post,* 15 October, A1.

Bryce, James . 1921. *Modern Democracies.* New York: Macmillan.

Brzezinski, Zbigniew. 1993. *Out of Control: Global Turmoil on the Eve of the 21st Century.* New York: Scribner's.

Buchanan, James. 1990. Socialism Is Dead; Leviathan Lives. *Wall Street Journal,* 18 July, A8.

Buckle, Henry Thomas. 1862. *History of Civilization in England.* New York: Appleton.

Bullock, Alan. 1993. *Hitler and Stalin: Parallel Lives.* New York: Vintage.

Bunce, Valerie. 1985. The Empire Strikes Back: The Evolution of the East-ern Bloc from a Soviet Asset to a Soviet Liability. *International Organi-zation* 39, no. 1 (Winter): 1–46.

Burkhart, Ross E., and Michael S. Lewis-Beck. 1994. Comparative De-mocracy: The Economic Development Thesis. *American Political Science Review* 88, no. 4 (December): 903–10.

Burnham, Walter Dean. 1987. The Turnout Problem. In *Elections Ameri-can Style,* ed. A. James Reichley, 97–133. Washington, D.C.: Brookings Institution.

Burrough, Bryan, and John Helyar. 1990. *Barbarians at the Gate: The Fall of RJR Nabisco.* New York: Harper & Row.

Campbell, Angus. 1981. *The Sense of Well-Being in America: Recent Patterns and Trends.* New York: McGraw-Hill.

Campbell, Angus, Philip E. Converse, and Willard L. Rodgers. 1976. *The Quality of American Life.* New York: Russell Sage Foundation.

Cantril, Hadley. 1965. *The Pattern of Human Concerns.* New Brunswick, N.J.: Rutgers University Press.

Cassidy, John. 1996. The Decline of Economics. *New Yorker,* 2 December, 50–60.

Chandler, Alfred D., Jr. 1977. *The Visible Hand: The Managerial Revolution in American Business.* Cambridge, Mass.: Harvard University Press.

Châtelot, Christophe. 1997. Bulgaria Learns to Live with Its Turks. *Guardian Weekly,* 11 May, 17.

Chernow, Ron. 1998. *Titan: The Life of John D. Rockefeller, Sr.* New York: Random House.

Chodorow, Stanley, and MacGregor Knox. 1989. *The Mainstream of Civilization.* 5th ed. New York: Harcourt Brace Jovanovich.

Churchill, Winston S. 1950. *Europe Unite: Speeches 1947 and 1948.* Ed. Randolph S. Churchill. Boston: Houghton Mifflin.

Clancy, Kevin J., and Robert S. Shulman. 1994. *Marketing Myths That Are Killing Business: The Cure for Death Wish Marketing.* New York: McGraw-Hill.

Cohen, Ben, and Jerry Greenfield. 1997. *Ben & Jerry's Double Dip: Lead with Your Values and Make Money, Too.* New York: Simon & Schuster.

Cohen, Lenard J. 1995. *Broken Bonds: Yugoslavia's Disintegration and Balkan Politics in Transition.* 2d ed. Boulder, Colo.: Westview.

Cohen, Roger. 1997. The Cries of Welfare States Under the Knife. *New York Times,* 19 September, A1.

Collins, Walton R. 1997. Gale Force. *University of Chicago Magazine* 90, no. 2 (December): 16–21.

Conway, M. Margaret. 1991. *Political Participation in the United States.* 2d ed. Washington, D.C.: CQ Press.

Cook, Terrence. 1991. *The Great Alternatives of Social Thought.* Savage, Md.: Rowman & Littlefield.

Crawford, Neta C. 1993. Decolonization as an International Norm: The Evolution of Practices, Arguments, and Beliefs. In *Emerging Norms of Justified Intervention,* ed. Laura W. Reed and Carl Kaysen, 37–61. Cambridge, Mass.: American Academy of Arts and Sciences.

Cringely, Robert X. 1992. *Accidental Empires: How the Boys of Silicon Valley Make Their Millions, Battle Foreign Competition, and Still Can't Get A Date.* Reading, Mass.: Addison-Wesley.

Crook, Clive. 1997. The Future of the State. *Economist,* 20 September, 5–48.

Crozier, Michel, Samuel P. Huntington, and Joji Watanuki, eds. 1975. *The Crisis of Democracy.* New York: New York University Press.

Culhane, John. 1990. *The American Circus.* New York: Holt.

Dahl, Robert A. 1956. *A Preface to Democratic Theory.* Chicago: University of Chicago Press.

———. 1971. *Polyarchy.* New Haven, Conn.: Yale University Press.

———. 1989. *Democracy and Its Critics.* New Haven, Conn.: Yale University Press.

———. 1990. *After the Revolution? Authority in a Good Society.* Rev. ed. New Haven, Conn.: Yale University Press.

De Long, Bradford, and Andrei Shleifer. 1993. Princes and Merchants: European City Growth Before the Industrial Revolution. *Journal of Law and Economics* 36 (October): 671–702.

Deep, Sam, and Lyle Sussman. 1992. *What to Say to Get What You Want.* Reading, Mass.: Addison-Wesley.

Defoe, Daniel. 1727. *The Complete Tradesman in Familiar Letters, Directing him in all the several Parts and Progressions of Trade.* 2d ed. London: Charles Rivington. Repr. New York, 1969: Augustus M. Kelley.

Delli Carpini, Michael X., and Scott Keeter. 1996. *What Americans Know about Politics and Why It Matters.* New Haven, Conn.: Yale University Press.

Denny, Charlotte. 1997. World Bank in Surprise Policy U-Turn. *Guardian Weekly,* 6 July.

Di Palma, Giuseppe. 1990. *To Craft Democracies: An Essay on Democratic Transitions.* Berkeley: University of California Press.

Diamond, Larry. 1996. Is the Third Wave Over? *Journal of Democracy* 7, no. 3 (July): 20–37.

Diener, Ed. 1983. Subjective Well-Being. *Psychological Bulletin* 95, no. 3 (May): 542–75.

Dionne, E. J., Jr. 1991. *Why Americans Hate Politics.* New York: Simon & Schuster.

Dostoyevsky, Fyodor. 1945. *The Brothers Karamazov.* Trans. Constance Garnett. New York: Random House.

Drakulić, Slavenka. 1997. Café Europa: Life after Communism. New York: Norton.

Drescher, Seymour. 1987. *Capitalism and Antislavery: British Mobilization in Comparative Perspective.* New York: Oxford University Press.

Drew, Elizabeth. 1994. *On the Edge: The Clinton Presidency.* New York: Simon & Schuster.

Drucker, Peter F. 1974. *Management: Tasks, Responsibilities, Practices.* New York: Harper & Row.

Dugger, Celia W. Pakistan Premier Prevails in Clash with General. *New York Times,* 20 October, A4.

Dunlap, Albert J. 1996. *Mean Business: How I Save Bad Companies and Make Good Companies Great.* New York: Times Books.

Dye, Thomas R., and Harmon Zeigler. 1988. Socialism and Equality in Cross-National Perspective. *PS: Political Science & Politics* 21, no. 1 (Winter): 45–56.

Easterbrook, Gregg. 1995. *A Moment on the Earth: The Coming Age of Environmental Optimism.* New York: Viking.

Easterlin, Richard A. 1974. Does Economic Growth Improve the Human Lot? Some Empirical Evidence. In *Nations and Households in Economic Growth: Essays in Honor of Moses Abramovitz,* ed. Paul A. David and Melvin W. Reder, 89–125. New York: Academic Press.

———. 1996. *Growth Triumphant: The Twenty-first Century in Historical Perspective.* Ann Arbor, Mich.: University of Michigan Press.

Eckstein, Harry. 1996. Lessons for the "Third Wave" from the First: An Essay on Democratization. Irvine: Center for the Study of Democracy, School of Social Sciences, University of California.

Economist. 1994. Democracy and Growth: Why Voting is Good for You. *Economist,* 27 August, 15–17.

Ellickson, Robert C. 1991. *Order Without Law: How Neighbors Settle Disputes.* Cambridge, Mass.: Harvard University Press.

Ellsaesser, Hugh W. 1995. Trends in Air Pollution in the United States. In *The State of Humanity,* ed. Julian Simon, 491–502. Cambridge, Mass.: Blackwell.

Elshtain, Jean Bethke. 1995. *Democracy on Trial.* New York: Basic Books.

Eltis, David. 1987. *Economic Growth and the Ending of the Transatlantic Slave Trade.* New York: Oxford University Press.

Emden, Paul H. 1939. *Quakers in Commerce: A Record of Business Achievement.* London: Sampson Low, Marston.

Engerman, Stanley L. 1986. Slavery and Emancipation in Comparative Perspective: A Look at Some Recent Debates. *Journal of Economic History* 46, no. 2 (June): 317–39.

———. 1997. The Standard of Living Debate in International Perspective: Measures and Indicators. In *Health and Welfare During Industrialization,* ed. Richard Steckel and Roderick Flood. Chicago: University of Chicago Press.

———. Forthcoming. Capitalism. In *Oxford Companion to United States History,* ed. Paul Boyer. New York: Oxford University Press.

Faison, Seth. 1995. Service With Some Bile. *New York Times,* 22 October, 4-4.

———. 1998. Cry Goes Up: Let a Hundred Garbage Cans Bloom!. *New York Times,* 23 April, A4.

Fenno, Richard F., Jr. 1973. *Congressmen in Committees.* Boston: Little, Brown.

Fischer, Stanley, and Alan Gelb. 1991. The Process of Socialist Economic Transformation. *Journal of Economic Perspectives* 5, no. 4 (Fall): 91–105.

Fishkin, James S. 1995. *The Voice of the People: Public Opinion and Democracy.* New Haven, Conn.: Yale University Press.

Fitzgerald, Frances. 1972. *Fire in the Lake: The Vietnamese and Americans in Vietnam.* New York: Vintage.

FOCUS. 1993. *Current Problems of Slovakia After the Split of the CSFR (October 1993).* Bratislava, Slovak Republic: Center for Social and Market Analysis.

Forster, E. M. 1951. *Two Cheers for Democracy.* New York: Harcourt, Brace & World.

Frank, Robert H. 1988. *Passions Within Reason: The Strategic Role of the Emotions.* New York: Norton.

Franklin, Benjamin. 1856. *The Works of Benjamin Franklin.* Ed. Jared Sparks. Boston: Whittlemore, Niles, and Hall.

French, Howard W. 1996. In One Poor African Nation, Democracy Thrives. *New York Times,* 16 October, A3.

Friedman, Milton. 1962. *Capitalism and Freedom.* Chicago: University of Chicago Press.

Friedman, Milton, and Rose Friedman. 1980. *Free to Choose: A Personal Statement.* New York: Harcourt Brace Jovanovich.

———. 1984. *Tyranny of the Status Quo.* San Diego, Calif.: Harcourt Brace Jovanovich.

Friedman, Thomas L. 1997. Berlin Wall, Part 2: Asia's New Route to Democracy. *New York Times,* 22 December, A21.

Fukuyama, Francis. 1989. The End of History? *National Interest,* Summer, 3–18.

———. 1992. *The End of History and the Last Man.* New York: Free Press.

———. 1995. *Trust: The Social Virtues and the Creation of Prosperity.* New York: Free Press.

Gallagher, David. 1990. Vargas Llosa Pans His Political and Intellectual Peers. *Wall Street Journal,* 6 April, A19.

Ganev, Venelin I. 1997. Bulgaria's Symphony of Hope. *Journal of Democracy* 8, no. 4 (October): 125–39.

Gati, Charles. 1996. If Not Democracy, What? Leaders, Laggards, and Losers in the Postcommunist World. In *Postcommunism: Four Perspectives,* ed. Michael Mandelbaum, 168–98. New York: Council on Foreign Relations.

Gellner, Ernest. 1988. Introduction. In *Europe and the Rise of Capitalism,* ed. Jean Baechler, John A. Hall and Michael Mann, 1–5. London: Basil Blackwell.

Geoghegan, Vincent. 1983. Marcuse and Autonomy. In *Democratic Theory and Practice,* ed. Graeme Duncan, 156–72. Cambridge: Cambridge University Press.

Gerschenkron, Alexander. 1962. *Economic Backwardness in Historical Perspective.* Cambridge, Mass.: Harvard University Press.

Gershman, Carl. 1989. The United States and the World Democratic Revolution. *Washington Quarterly* 12, no. 1 (Winter): 127–39.

Gilder, George. 1984. *The Spirit of Enterprise.* New York: Simon and Schuster.

Goldstein, Judith. 1988. Ideas, Institutions, and American Trade Policy. *International Organization* 42, no. 1 (Winter): 179–217.

———. 1989. The Impact of Ideas on Trade Policy: The Origins of U.S. Agricultural and Manufacturing Policies. *International Organization* 43, no. 1 (Winter): 31–71.

Gordon, Ellen J., and Luan Troxel. 1995. Minority Mobilization without War. Paper Delivered at the Conference on Post-Communism and Ethnic Mobilization. Cornell University, 21–22 April.

Graña, César. 1964. *Bohemian Versus Bourgeois: French Society and the French Man of Letters in the Nineteenth Century.* New York: Basic Books.

Greenhouse, Steven. 1996. Strikes Decrease To a 50-Year Low. *New York Times,* 29 January, A1.

Gregg, Alan. 1956. *Challenges to Contemporary Medicine.* New York: Columbia University Press.

Greif, Avner. 1993. Contract Enforceability and Economic Institutions in Early Trade: The Maghribi Traders' Coalition. *American Economic Review* 83, no. 3 (June): 525–48.

Hardin, Russell. 1991. Trusting Persons, Trusting Institutions. In *Strategy and Choice,* ed. Richard J. Zeckhauser, 185–209. Cambridge, Mass.: MIT Press.

Harding, Harry. 1998. Will China Democratize? The Halting Advance of Pluralism. *Journal of Democracy* 9, no. 1 (January): 11–17.

Harris, Richard. 1966. *A Sacred Trust.* New York: New American Library.

Harrison, David. 1997. Unquenchable Thirst for Freedom. *Guardian Weekly,* 29 December, 20.

Hartwell, R. M. 1995. *A History of the Mont Pelerin Society.* Indianapolis, Ind.: Liberty Fund.

Havel, Václav. 1995. The Responsibility of Intellectuals. *New York Review of Books,* 22 June 1995, 36–37.

Havelock, Eric A. 1957. *The Liberal Temper in Greek Politics.* New Haven, Conn.: Yale University Press.

Hayek, F. A., ed. 1954. *Capitalism and the Historians.* Chicago: University of Chicago Press.

———. 1988. *The Fatal Conceit: The Errors of Socialism.* Ed. W. W. Bartley, III. Chicago: University of Chicago Press.

Heard, Alexander. 1960. *The Costs of Democracy.* Chapel Hill: University of North Carolina Press.

Heilbroner, Robert. 1993. *21st Century Capitalism.* New York: Norton.

———. 1997. Economics by the Book. *Nation,* 20 October, 16–19.

Hellman, Joel S. 1998. Winners Take All: The Politics of Partial Reform in Postcommunist Transition. *World Politics* 50, no. 2 (January): 203–34.

Hess, Stephen. 1987. "Why Great Men Are Not Chosen Presidents": Lord Bryce Revisited. In *Elections American Style,* ed. A. James Reichley, 75–94. Washington, D.C.: Brookings Institution.

Hibbing, John R., and Elizabeth Theiss-Morse. 1995. *Congress As Public Enemy: Public Attitudes toward American Political Institutions.* New York: Cambridge University Press.

Hidy, Ralph W., and Muriel E. Hidy. 1955. *History of Standard Oil Company (New Jersey): Pioneering in Big Business, 1882–1911.* New York: Harper.

Higley, John, and Richard Gunther, eds. 1992. *Elites and Democratic Consolidation in Latin America and Southern Europe.* Cambridge: Cambridge University Press.

Hirsch, Fred. 1976. *The Social Limits to Growth.* Cambridge, Mass.: Harvard University Press.

Hirschman, Albert O. 1970. *Exit, Voice, and Loyalty: Responses to Decline in Firms, Organizations, and States.* Cambridge, Mass.: Harvard University Press.

———. 1977. *The Passions and the Interests: Political Arguments for Capitalism before Its Triumph.* Princeton, N.J.: Princeton University Press.

———. 1986. *Rival Views of Market Society and Other Recent Essays.* New York: Viking.

Historicus [George Allen Morgan]. 1949. Stalin on Revolution. *Foreign Affairs* 27, no. 2 (January): 175–214.

Hockstader, Lee. 1997. Bulgaria Slides Into Economic Collapse. *Guardian Weekly,* 16 February, 19.

Hoggart, Simon. 1997. A Thunderously Adequate Performance. *Guardian Weekly,* 19 October, 8.

Holmes, Stephen. 1993. *The Anatomy of Antiliberalism.* Cambridge, Mass.: Harvard University Press.

———. 1996. Cultural Legacies or State Collapse? Probing the Postcommunist Dilemma. In *Postcommunism: Four Perspectives,* ed. Michael Mandelbaum, 22–76. New York: Council on Foreign Relations.

Holmstrom, Bengt, and David M. Kreps. 1996. Examples for and Questions about: An Economic (?) Theory of Promises. Lionel McKenzie Lecture, University of Rochester, 28 March.

Hood, John M. 1996. *The Heroic Enterprise: Business and the Common Good.* New York: Free Press.

Howard, Michael. 1978. *War and the Liberal Conscience.* New Brunswick, N.J.: Rutgers University Press.

Hume, David. 1955. *David Hume: Writings on Economics.* Ed. Eugene Rotwein. Madison: University of Wisconsin Press.

Huntington, Samuel P. 1984. Will More Countries Become Democratic? *Political Science Quarterly* 99, no. 2 (Summer): 193–218.

———. 1991. *The Third Wave: Democratization in the Late Twentieth Century.* Norman: University of Oklahoma Press.

———. 1997. After Twenty Years: The Future of the Third Wave. *Journal of Democracy* 8, no. 4 (October): 3–12.

Iannaccone, Lawrence K., Roger Finke, and Rodney Stark. 1997. Deregulating Religion: The Economics of Church and State. *Economic Inquiry* 35, no. 2 (April): 350–64.

Inge, William Ralph. 1919. *Outspoken Essays.* London: Longmans, Green.

Inglehart, Ronald. 1997. *Modernization and Postmodernization: Cultural, Economic, and Political Change in 43 Countries.* Princeton, N.J.: Princeton University Press.

Inglehart, Ronald, and Jacques-Rene Rabier. 1986. Aspirations Adopt to Situations—But Why Are the Belgians So Much Happier Than the French? In *Research on the Quality of Life,* ed. Frank M. Andrews, 1–56. Ann Arbor: Institute for Social Research, University of Michigan.

Jäckel, Eberhard. 1981. *Hitler's World View: A Blueprint for Power.* Trans. Herbert Arnold. Cambridge, Mass.: Harvard University Press.

Jefferson, Thomas. 1939. *Democracy.* Ed. Saul K. Padover. New York: Appleton-Century.

———. 1944. *The Life and Selected Writings of Thomas Jefferson.* Ed. Adrienne Koch and William Peden. New York: Modern Library.

Jehl, Douglas. 1997. Persian Gulf's Young Turk: Sheik Hamad, Emir of Qatar. *New York Times,* 10 July, A1.

Jones, E. L. 1987. *The European Miracle: Environments, economies, and geopol-*

itics in the history of Europe and Asia. 2d ed. Cambridge: Cambridge University Press.

———. 1988. *Growth Recurring: Economic Change in World History.* Oxford: Oxford University Press.

Jouvenel, Bernard de. 1954. The Treatment of Capitalism by Continental Intellectuals. In *Capitalism and the Historians,* ed. F. A. Hayek, 93–123. Chicago: University of Chicago Press.

Judt, Tony. 1997. The Longest Road to Hell. *New York Times,* 22 December, A21.

Junn, Jane. 1991. Participation and Political Knowledge. In *Political Participation and American Democracy,* ed. William Crotty, 193–212. New York: Greenwood Press.

Kaeuper, Richard W. 1988. *War, Justice, and Public Order: England and France in the Later Middle Ages.* New York: Oxford University Press.

Kahn, Joseph. 1998. The Latest Asian Miracle: Chaos Without Coups. *New York Times,* 26 July, 4–5.

Kahneman, Daniel, Jack L. Knetsch, and Richard Thaler. 1986. Fairness as a Constraint on Profit Seeking: Entitlements in the Market. *American Economic Review* 76, no. 4 (September): 728–41.

Kamm, Thomas. 1990. Democracy in Argentina Buoyed as Armed Revolt Is Ended Fast. *Wall Street Journal,* 5 December, A13.

Kant, Immanuel. 1952. *The Critique of Judgement.* London: Oxford University Press.

———. 1957. *Perpetual Peace.* Trans. Louis White Beck. Indianapolis, Ind.: Bobbs-Merrill.

Kaufman, Robert R. 1986. Liberalization and Democratization in South America: Perspectives from the 1970s. In *Transitions from Authoritarian Rule: Comparative Perspectives,* ed. Guillermo O'Donnell, Philippe C. Schmitter, and Laurence Whitehead, 85–107. Baltimore: Johns Hopkins University Press.

Keniston, Kenneth. 1960. Alienation and the Decline of Utopia. *American Scholar* 29, no. 2 (Spring): 161–200.

Kennedy, John F. 1964. *Public Papers of the Presidents of the United States: John F. Kennedy, 1963.* Washington, DC: United States Government Printing Office.

Kennedy, Paul. 1987. *The Rise and Fall of the Great Powers.* New York: Random House.

———. 1993. *Preparing for the Twenty-first Century.* New York: Random House.

Kenner, H. J. 1936. *The Fight for the Truth in Advertising: A Story of What Business Has Done and Is Doing to Establish and Maintain Accuracy and Fair*

Play in Advertising and Selling for the Public's Protection. New York: Round Table Press.

Kershaw, Ian. 1987. *The "Hitler Myth": Image and Reality in the Third Reich.* New York: Oxford University Press.

Keynes, John Maynard. 1963. *Essays in Persuasion.* New York: Norton.

Klein, Daniel B., ed. 1997a. *Reputation: Studies in the Voluntary Elicitation of Good Conduct.* Ann Arbor: University of Michigan Press.

———. 1997b. Knowledge, Reputation, and Trust, by Voluntary Means. In *Reputation: Studies in the Voluntary Elicitation of Good Conduct,* ed. Daniel B. Klein, 1–14. Ann Arbor: University of Michigan Press.

———. 1997c. Trust for Hire: Voluntary Remedies for Quality and Safety. In *Reputation: Studies in the Voluntary Elicitation of Good Conduct,* ed. Daniel B. Klein, 97–133. Ann Arbor: University of Michigan Press.

Klein, Daniel B., and Jeremy Shearmur. 1997. Good Conduct in the Great Society: Adam Smith and the Role of Reputation. In *Reputation: Studies in the Voluntary Elicitation of Good Conduct,* ed. Daniel B. Klein, 29–45. Ann Arbor: University of Michigan Press.

Knox, MacGregor. 1982. *Mussolini Unleashed 1939–1941: Politics and Strategy in Fascist Italy's Last War.* New York: Cambridge University Press.

Kraus, Sidney, ed. 1962. *The Great Debates: Kennedy vs. Nixon, 1960.* Bloomington: University of Indiana Press.

Kreps, David M. 1990. Corporate Culture and Economic Theory. In *Perspectives on Positive Political Economy,* ed. James E. Alt and Kenneth A. Shepsle, 90–143. New York: Cambridge University Press.

Kristol, Irving. 1978. *Two Cheers for Capitalism.* New York: Basic Books.

Kunitz, Stephen, and Stanley L. Engerman. 1992. The Ranks of Death: Secular Trends in Income and Mortality. *Health Transition Review* 2 (supplementary issue): 29–46.

Kuteinikov, Andrei. 1990. Soviet Society—Much More Unequal Than U.S. *Wall Street Journal,* 26 January, A14.

Kuznets, Simon. 1961. *Capital in the American Economy: Its Formation and Financing.* Princeton, N.J.: Princeton University Press.

———. 1966. *Modern Economic Growth: Rate, Structure, and Spread.* New Haven, Conn.: Yale University Press.

Ladd, Everett C. 1996. The Data Just Don't Show Erosion of America's "Social Capital." *Public Perspective,* June/July, 1, 5–6.

Laitin, David D. 1995. The Civic Culture at 30. *American Political Science Review* 89, no. 1 (March): 168–73.

Lakoff, Sanford. 1996. *Democracy: History, Theory, Practice.* Boulder, Colo.: Westview.

Landes, David S. 1969. *The Unbound Prometheus: Technological Change and*

Industrial Development in Western Europe from 1750 to the Present. Cambridge: Cambridge University Press.

———. 1998. *The Wealth and Poverty of Nations: Why Some Are So Rich and Some So Poor.* New York: Norton.

Landsburg, Steven E. 1997. *Fair Play: What Your Child Can Teach You About Economics, Value, and the Meaning of Life.* New York: Free Press.

Lea, Homer. 1909. *The Valor of Ignorance.* New York: Harper.

Lebergott, Stanley. 1964. *Manpower in Economic Growth: The American Record since 1860.* New York: McGraw-Hill.

———. 1993. *Pursuing Happiness: American Consumers in the Twentieth Century.* Princeton, N.J.: Princeton University Press.

Leffler, Melvyn P. 1994. *The Specter of Communism: The United States and the Origins of the Cold War, 1917–1953.* New York: Hill and Wang.

Legum, Colin. 1990. The Coming of Africa's Second Independence. *Washington Quarterly* 11, no. 1 (Winter): 129–40.

Lemann, Nicholas. 1996. Kicking in Groups. *Harper's,* April, 22–26.

Lenin, Vladimir I. 1932. *State and Revolution.* New York: International Publishers.

Levin, Murray B. 1960. *The Alienated Voter: Politics in Boston.* New York: Holt.

Levinson, Wendy. 1994. Physician-Patient Communication: A Key to Malpractice Prevention. *JAMA* 272, no. 20 (23/30 November): 1619–20.

Lienesch, Michael. 1992. Wo(e)begon(e) Democracy. *American Journal of Political Science* 36, no. 4 (November): 1004–14.

Lijphart, Arend. 1997. Unequal Participation: Democracy's Unresolved Dilemma. *American Political Science Review* 91, no. 4 (March): 1–14.

Lindberg, Tod. 1996. Ready for Round Two? *Policy Review,* September–October, 38–42.

Lindblom, Charles E. 1977. *Politics and Markets: The World's Political-Economic Systems.* New York: Basic Books.

Linz, Juan J. 1978. *The Breakdown of Democratic Regimes: Crisis, Breakdown, and Reequilibration.* Baltimore: Johns Hopkins University Press.

Lipset, Seymour Martin. 1993a. Reflections on Capitalism, Socialism and Democracy. *Journal of Democracy* 4, no. 2 (April): 43–55.

———. 1993b. A Comparative Analysis of the Social Requisites of Democracy. *International Social Science Journal,* May, 155–75.

Luard, Evan. 1986. *War in International Society.* New Haven, Conn.: Yale University Press.

McAneny, Leslie, and David W. Moore. 1994. Annual Honesty & Ethics Poll. *Gallup Poll Monthly,* October, 2–4.

McCloskey, Deirdre N. 1998. Bourgeois Virtue and the History of *P* and *S*. *Journal of Economic History* 58, no. 2 (June): 297–317.

Macaulay, Stewart. 1963. Non-Contractual Relations in Business: A Preliminary Study. *American Sociological Review* 28, no. 1 (Fall): 55–69.

McCloskey, Donald N. 1990. *If You're So Smart: The Narrative of Economic Experience.* Chicago: University of Chicago Press.

———. 1994. Bourgeois Virtue. *American Scholar* 63, no. 2 (Spring): 177–91.

McCormack, Mark H. 1984. *What They Don't Teach You at Harvard Business School.* New York: Bantam.

———. 1989. *What They* Still *Don't Teach You at Harvard Business School.* New York: Bantam.

McGuire, Martin, and Mancur Olson. 1996. The Economics of Autocracy and Majority Rule: The Invisible Hand and the Use of Force. *Journal of Economic Literature* 34 (March): 72–96.

Machan, Tibor R. 1996. Business Bashing: Why Is Commerce Maligned? *Jobs & Capital,* Winter, 35–40.

Machiavelli, Niccolò. 1950. *The Prince and the Discourses.* Trans. Luigi Ricci. New York: Modern Library.

McInnes, Neil. 1995. Wrong for Superior Reasons. *National Interest,* Spring, 85–97.

———. 1998. Hayek's Slippery Slope. *National Interest,* Spring, 56–66.

Madison, James. 1788. *Federalist Papers, No. 10.* Various editions.

Mahan, Alfred Thayer. 1912. *Armaments and Arbitration: The Place of Force in the International Relations of States.* New York: Harper.

Malkiel, Burton G. 1996. *A Random Walk Down Wall Street.* New York: Norton.

Manion, Melanie. 1996. The Electoral Connection in the Chinese Countryside. *American Political Science Review* 90, no. 4 (December): 736–48.

Mansbridge, Jane. 1997. Normative Theory and *Voice and Equality. American Political Science Review* 91, no. 2 (June): 423–25.

Marody, Mira. 1997. Post-Transitology: Is There Any Life After Transition? *Polish Sociological Review,* 13–21.

Marshall, Alfred. 1890. *Principles of Economics.* London: Macmillan.

———. 1920. *Principles of Economics.* 8th ed. London: Macmillan.

Mason, David S. 1995. Justice, Socialism, and Participation in the Postcommunist States. In *Social Justice and Political Change: Public Opinion in Capitalist and Post-Communist States,* ed. James R. Kluegel, David S. Mason and Bernd Wegener, 49–80. New York: Aldine De Gruyter.

Mayo, Elton. 1933. *The Human Problems of an Industrial Civilization*. New York: Macmillan.

Mencken, H. L. 1920. *Prejudices: Second Series*. New York: Knopf.

Merkle, Daniel M. 1996. The National Issues Convention Deliberative Poll. *Public Opinion Quarterly* 60, no. 4 (Winter): 588–619.

Meyer, Alfred G. 1957. *Leninism*. Cambridge, Mass.: Harvard University Press.

Michnik, Adam. 1997. Gray Is Beautiful: Thoughts on Democracy in Central Europe. *Dissent,* Spring, 14–19.

Milne, Alan Alexander. 1935. *Peace with Honour*. New York: Dutton.

Mises, Ludwig von. 1972 [1956]. *The Anticapitalistic Mentality*. Grove City, Pa.: Libertarian Press.

Moore, Barrington. 1966. *Social Origins of Dictatorship and Democracy*. New York: Basic Books.

Morgan, Edmund S. 1988. *Inventing the People: The Rise of Popular Sovereignty in England and America*. New York: Norton.

Morin, Richard. 1996. Who's in Control? Many Don't Know or Care. *Washington Post,* 29 January, A1.

Morin, Richard, and Dan Balz. 1996. Americans Losing Trust in Each Other and Institutions. *Washington Post,* 28 January, A1.

Morison, Samuel Eliot. 1963. *The Two-Ocean War: A Short History of the United States Navy in the Second World War*. Boston: Little, Brown.

Mosher, Stacy. 1991. Hong Kong: The Governor's Men. *Far Eastern Economic Review,* 3 October, 11–13.

Moynihan, Daniel Patrick. 1975. The American Experiment. *Public Interest,* no. 41 (Fall): 4–8.

Mueller, John. 1973. *War, Presidents and Public Opinion*. New York: Wiley.

———. 1977. Changes in American Public Attitudes toward International Involvement. In *The Limits of Military Intervention,* ed. Ellen Stern, 323–44. Beverly Hills, Calif.: Sage.

———. 1979. Public Expectations of War during the Cold War. *American Journal of Political Science* 23, no. 2 (May): 301–29.

———. 1984. Reflections on the Vietnam Protest Movement and on the Curious Calm at the War's End. In *Vietnam as History,* ed. Peter Braestrup, 151–57. Lanham, Md.: University Press of America.

———. 1985. *Astaire Dancing: The Musical Films*. New York: Knopf.

———. 1986. Containment and the Decline of the Soviet Empire: Some Tentative Reflections on the End of the World as We Know It. Paper given at the Annual Convention of the International Studies Association. Anaheim, Calif., 25–29 March. (http://www.rochester.edu/College/psc/Mueller)

———. 1988. Trends in Political Tolerance. *Public Opinion Quarterly* 52, no. 1 (Spring): 1–25.

———. 1989. *Retreat from Doomsday: The Obsolescence of Major War.* New York: Basic Books.

———. 1991. Is War Still Becoming Obsolete? Paper given at the Annual Meeting of the American Political Science Association. Washington, D.C., 29 August–1 September. (http://www.rochester.edu/College/psc/Mueller)

———. 1992a. Democracy and Ralph's Pretty Good Grocery: Elections, Inequality, and the Minimal Human Being. *American Journal of Political Science* 36, no. 4 (November): 983–1003.

———. 1992b. Theory and Democracy: A Reply to Michael Lienesch. *American Journal of Political Science* 36, no. 4 (November): 1015–22.

———. 1993. The Impact of Ideas on Grand Strategy. In *The Domestic Bases of Grand Strategy,* ed. Richard Rosecrance and Arthur A. Stein, 48–62. Ithaca, N.Y.: Cornell University Press.

———. 1994a. *Policy and Opinion in the Gulf War.* Chicago: University of Chicago Press.

———. 1994b. The Catastrophe Quota: Trouble After the Cold War. *Journal of Conflict Resolution* 38, no. 3 (September): 355–75.

———. 1995. *Quiet Cataclysm: Reflections on the Recent Transformation of World Politics.* New York: HarperCollins.

———. 1996a. Democracy, Capitalism and the End of Transition. In *Post-Communism: Four Views,* ed. Michael Mandelbaum, 102–67. New York: Council on Foreign Relations.

———. 1996b. Policy Principles for Unthreatened Wealth-Seekers. *Foreign Policy,* Spring, 22–33.

Muravchik, Joshua. 1992. *Exporting Democracy: Fulfilling America's Destiny.* Washington, D.C.: AEI Press.

Murray, Charles. 1988. *In Pursuit: Of Happiness and Good Government.* New York: Simon & Schuster.

Nadelmann, Ethan A. 1990. Global Prohibition Regimes: The Evolution of Norms in International Society. *International Organization* 44, no. 4 (Autumn): 479–526.

Nardulli, Peter F., Jon K. Dalager, and Donald E. Greco. 1996. Voter Turnout in U.S. Presidential Elections: An Historical View and Some Speculation. *PS: Political Science & Politics* 29, no. 3 (September): 480–90.

Needler, Martin. 1990. *Mexican Politics: The Containment of Conflict.* 2d ed. New York: Praeger.

Nelson, Michael. 1995. Why Americans Hate Politics and Politicians. *PS: Political Science & Politics,* 28, no. 1 (March): 72–77.

Neuman, W. Russell. 1986. *The Paradox of Mass Politics: Knowledge and Opinion in the American Electorate.* Cambridge, Mass.: Harvard University Press.

Nevaskar, Balwant. 1971. *Capitalists without Capitalism: The Jains of India and the Quakers of the West.* Westport, Conn.: Greenwood.

Nevins, Allan. 1940. *John D. Rockefeller: The Heroic Age of American Enterprise.* New York: Scribner's.

———. 1945. Letter to the Editor. *American Historical Review* 50, no. 3 (April): 676–89.

Niemi, Richard G., John Mueller, and Tom W. Smith. 1989. *Trends in Public Opinion: A Compendium of Survey Data.* Westport, Conn.: Greenwood.

Norris, Pippa. 1996. Does Television Erode Social Capital? A Reply to Putnam. *PS: Political Science & Politics* 29, no. 3 (September): 474–80.

North, Douglass C. 1990. *Institutions, Institutional Change and Economic Performance.* Cambridge: Cambridge University Press.

North, Douglass C., and Barry R. Weingast. 1989. Constitutions and Commitment: The Evolution of Institutions Governing Public Choice in Seventeenth-Century England. *Journal of Economic History* 49, no. 4 (December): 803–32.

Nozick, Robert. 1997. *Socratic Puzzles.* Cambridge, Mass.: Harvard University Press.

Nye, John V. C. 1997. Thinking About the State: Property Rights, Trade, and Changing Contractual Arrangements in a World with Coercion. In *The Frontiers of the New Institutional Economics,* ed. John N. Drobak and John V. C. Nye, 121–42. San Diego, Calif.: Academic Press.

O'Connor, John J. 1994. A Museum That's Its Own Best Exhibit. *New York Times,* 9 September.

O'Donnell, Guillermo, and Philippe C. Schmitter. 1986. *Transitions from Authoritarian Rule: Tentative Conclusions about Uncertain Democracies.* Baltimore: Johns Hopkins University Press.

Olson, Mancur. 1982. *The Rise and Decline of Nations: Economic Growth, Stagflation, and Social Rigidities.* New Haven, Conn.: Yale University Press.

———. 1993. Dictatorship, Democracy, and Development. *American Political Science Review* 87, no. 3 (September): 567–76.

Osler, William. 1932. *Aequanimitas: With Other Addresses to Medical Students, Nurses and Practitioners of Medicine.* 3d ed. Philadelphia: Blakiston.

Page, Benjamin I., and Robert Y. Shapiro. 1992. *The Rational Public: Fifty Years of Trends in American Policy Preferences*. Chicago: University of Chicago Press.

Palmer, R. R. 1959. *The Age of the Democratic Revolution: A Political History of Europe and America, 1760–1800: The Challenge*. Princeton, N.J.: Princeton University Press.

Passell, Peter. 1995. Economic Scene: Battered but Not Broken, the Honey Lobby Is Back and Winning. *New York Times*, 13 April, D2.

———. 1998a. Economic Scene: Socialism and Its Long Lines Are Alive and Well as Disneyland. *New York Times*, 2 April, C2.

———. 1998b. Economic Scene: Salmon Eaters Salute a Victory against the Protectionists. *New York Times*, 22 January, C2.

———. 1998c. Economic Scene: A New Project Will Measure the Cost and Effect of Regulation. *New York Times*, 30 July, C2.

Pateman, Carole. 1970. *Participation and Democratic Theory*. London: Cambridge University Press.

Patterson, Kelly D., and David B. Magleby. 1992. Trends: Public Support for Congress. *Public Opinion Quarterly* 56, no. 4 (Winter): 539–51.

Pei, Minxin. 1998. Is China Democratizing? *Foreign Affairs* 77, no. 1 (January/February): 68–82.

Perlez, Jane. 1990a. East-Bloc's Admirers in Africa Draw Line at Multiparty Politics. *New York Times*, 22 April, 12.

———. 1990b. Is Botswana a Model for Democracies in Africa? *New York Times*, 16 May, A6.

———. 1990c. For Democracy, Just a Nod at an African Meeting. *New York Times*, 10 July, A3.

———. 1993. In East Europe, Kmart Faces an Attitude Problem. *New York Times*, 7 July, D1.

Pessen, Edward. 1984. *The Log Cabin Myth: The Social Backgrounds of the Presidents*. New Haven, Conn.: Yale University Press.

Peters, Thomas J. 1994. *The Tom Peters Seminar: Crazy Times Call for Crazy Organizations*. New York: Vintage.

Peters, Thomas J., and Robert H. Waterman, Jr. 1982. *In Search of Excellence: Lessons from America's Best-Run Companies*. New York: Warner Books.

Pipes, Richard. 1984. *Survival Is Not Enough*. New York: Simon & Schuster.

Plato. 1957. *The Republic*. Trans. A. D. Lindsay. New York: Dutton.

Plattner, Marc F. 1988. Democracy Outwits the Pessimists. *Wall Street Journal*, 12 October, A18.

Plowden, Gene. 1967. *Those Amazing Ringlings and Their Circus.* Caldwell, Idaho: Caxton Printers.

Pogge von Strandmann, Hartmut. 1988. Germany and the Coming of War. In *The Coming of the First World War,* ed. R. J. W. Evans and Hartmut Pogge von Strandmann, 87–123. Oxford: Clarendon.

Pomper, Gerald M. 1974. *Elections in America: Control and Influence in Democratic Politics.* New York: Dodd, Mead.

Popkin, Samuel L. 1991. *The Reasoning Voter: Communication and Persuasion in Presidential Campaigns.* Chicago: University of Chicago Press.

Potok, Mark. 1994. Fear Grips Dallas after Driveway Attacks. *USA Today,* 22 March, 8A.

President's Commission on National Goals. 1960. *Goals for Americans.* New York: Prentice-Hall.

Preston, Samuel H. 1995. Human Mortality throughout History and Prehistory. In *The State of Humanity,* ed. Julian Simon, 30–36. Cambridge, Mass.: Blackwell.

Przeworski, Adam. 1986. Problems in the Study of Transition to Democracy. In *Transitions from Authoritarian Rule: Comparative Perspectives,* ed. Guillermo O'Donnell, Philippe C. Schmitter and Laurence Whitehead, 47–63. Baltimore: Johns Hopkins University Press.

Putnam, Robert D. 1993. *Making Democracy Work: Civic Traditions in Modern Italy.* Princeton, N.J.: Princeton University Press.

———. 1995a. Bowling Alone: America's Declining Social Capital. *Journal of Democracy* 6, no. 1 (January): 65–78.

———. 1995b. Tuning In, Tuning Out: The Strange Disappearance of Social Capital in America. *PS: Political Science & Politics* 28, no. 4 (December): 664–83.

Ramirez, Anthony. 1995. A Crackdown on Phone Marketing. *New York Times,* 10 February, D1.

Reder, Alan. 1994. *In Pursuit of Principle and Profit: Business Success Through Social Responsibility.* New York: Putnam's.

Reeves, Richard. 1993. *President Kennedy: Profile of Power.* New York: Simon & Schuster.

Riker, William H. 1965. *Democracy in the United States.* 2d ed. New York: Macmillan.

———. 1982. *Liberalism Against Populism.* San Francisco: Freeman.

———. 1996. *The Strategy of Rhetoric: Campaigning for the American Constitution.* New Haven, Conn.: Yale University Press.

Riskin, Carl. 1995. Feeding China: The Experience since 1949. In *The Po-*

litical Economy of Hunger, ed. Jean Drèze, Amartya Sen, and Athar Hussain. Oxford: Oxford University Press.

Rohter, Larry. 1996a. To U.S. Critics, a Sweatshop; To Hondurans, a Better Life. *New York Times,* 18 July, A1.

———. 1996b. A Chastened Latin Left Puts Its Hope in Ballots. *New York Times,* 29 July, A6.

———. 1998. Pope Asks Cubans to Seek New Path Toward Freedom. *New York Times,* 26 January, A1.

Romer, Christina. 1986a. Spurious Volatility in Historical Unemployment Data. *Journal of Political Economy* 94, no. 1 (February): 1–37.

———. 1986b. New Estimates of Prewar Gross National Product and Employment. *Journal of Economic History* 46, no. 2 (June): 341–52.

Rose, Richard. 1994. Getting By Without Government: Everyday Life in Russia. *Daedalus* 123, no. 3 (Summer): 41–62.

Rosecrance, Richard. 1986. *The Rise of the Trading State: Conquest and Commerce in the Modern World.* New York: Basic Books.

Rosenbaum, David E. 1997. Against the Current, Republican Senator Is Trying to Block Fund-Raising Restrictions. *New York Times,* 29 September, A12.

Rosenberg, Nathan. 1964. Neglected Dimensions in the Analysis of Economic Change. *Oxford Bulletin of Economics and Statistics* 26, no. 1 (February): 59–77.

———. 1975. Adam Smith on Profits—Paradox Lost and Regained. In *Essays on Adam Smith,* ed. Andrew S. Skinner and Thomas Wilson, 377–89. Oxford: Clarendon Press.

Rosenberg, Nathan, and L. E. Birdzell. 1986. *How the West Grew Rich: The Economic Transformation of the Industrial World.* New York: Basic Books.

Rosenberg, Tina. 1993. Meet the New Boss, Same as the Old Boss. *Harper's,* May, 47–53.

Rosenstone, Steven J., and John Mark Hansen. 1993. *Mobilization, Participation, and Democracy in America.* New York: Macmillan.

Rosenthal, A. M. 1993. New York to Clinton. *New York Times,* 1 October, A31.

Rothenberg, Lawrence S. 1992. *Linking Citizens to Government: Interest Group Politics at Common Cause.* New York: Cambridge University Press.

Rowen, Henry S. 1996. The Short March: China's Road to Democracy. *National Interest,* Fall, 61–70.

Rush, Myron. 1993. Fortune and Fate. *National Interest,* Spring, 19–25.

Russett, Bruce. 1972. *No Clear and Present Danger: A Skeptical View of the United States' Entry into World War II.* New York: Harper and Row.

Rustow, Dankwart A. 1970. Transitions to Democracy: Toward a Dynamic Model. *Comparative Politics* 2, no. 3 (April): 337–63.

Rutland, Peter. 1994/95. Has Democracy Failed Russia? *National Interest,* Winter, 3–12.

Sachs, Jeffrey. 1998. International Economics: Unlocking the Mysteries of Globalization. *Foreign Policy,* Spring, 97–109.

Samuelson, Robert J. 1995. The Price of Politics: Campaign Contributions Haven't Corrupted Congress. *Newsweek,* 28 August, 65.

Sandel, Michael J. 1996. *Democracy's Discontent: America in Search of a Public Philosophy.* Cambridge, Mass.: Harvard University Press.

Saxon, A. H. 1989. *P. T. Barnum: The Legend and the Man.* New York: Columbia University Press.

Scharnhorst, Gary. 1980. *Horatio Alger, Jr.* Boston: Twayne.

Scharnhorst, Gary, and with Jack Bales. 1985. *The Lost Life of Horatio Alger, Jr.* Bloomington: Indiana University Press.

Schemo, Diana Jean. 1997. Ecuador's Military Code: Democracy Is Better. *New York Times,* 11 February, A3.

Schilling, Warner R. 1965. Surprise Attack, Death, and War. *Journal of Conflict Resolution* 9, no. 3 (September): 285–90.

Schleh, Edward C. 1974. *The Management Tactician: Executive Tactics for Getting Results.* New York: McGraw-Hill.

Schlozman, Kay Lehman, and John T. Tierney. 1986. *Organized Interests and American Democracy.* New York: Harper & Row.

Schmitter, Philippe, and Terry Lynn Karl. 1991. What Democracy Is . . . And Is Not. *Journal of Democracy* 2, no. 3 (Summer): 75–88.

Schor, Juliet B. 1991. *The Overworked American: The Unexpected Decline of Leisure.* New York: Basic Books.

Schudson, Michael. 1998. *The Good Citizen: A History of American Civic Life.* New York: Free Press.

Schumpeter, Joseph A. 1950. *Capitalism, Socialism and Democracy.* 3d ed. New York: Harper & Row.

Scitovsky, Tibor. 1992. *The Joyless Economy: The Psychology of Human Satisfaction.* Rev. ed. New York: Oxford University Press.

Scott, Ian. 1989. *Political Change and the Crisis of Legitimacy in Hong Kong.* Honolulu: University of Hawaii Press.

Scott, Robert E. 1959. *Mexican Government in Transition.* Urbana: University of Illinois Press.

Seward, Desmond. 1991. *Metternich: The First European.* New York: Viking.

Shafir, Michael. 1993. Growing Political Extremism in Romania. *RFE/RL Research Report,* April, 18–22.

Sherrill, Kenneth. 1996. The Political Power of Lesbians, Gays, and Bisexuals. *PS: Political Science & Politics* 29, no. 3 (September): 469–73.

Shiller, Robert J., Maxim Boychko, and Vladimir Korobov. 1991. Popular Attitudes toward Free Markets: The Soviet Union and the United States Compared. *American Economic Review* 81, no. 3 (June): 385–400.

———. 1992. Hunting for *Homo Sovieticus:* Situational versus Attitudinal Factors in Economic Behavior. *Brookings Papers on Economic Activity* 1: 127–181, 193–194.

Simon, Julian L., ed. 1995. *The State of Humanity.* Cambridge, Mass.: Blackwell.

Simons, Marlise. 1997. Dutch Take "Third Way" to Prosperity. *New York Times,* 16 June, A6.

Skidelsky, Robert. 1996. *Keynes.* New York: Oxford University Press.

Small, Melvin. 1980. *Was War Necessary? National Security and U.S. Entry into War.* Beverly Hills, Calif.: Sage.

Smith, Adam. 1896. *Lectures on Justice, Police, Revenue and Arms.* Oxford: Clarendon.

———. 1976 [1776]. *An Inquiry into the Nature and Causes of the Wealth of Nations.* Oxford University Press. Oxford.

Smith, Hedrick. 1976. *The Russians.* New York: Quadrangle.

Smith, Sydney. 1956. *Selected Writings of Sydney Smith.* Ed. W. H. Auden. New York: Farrar, Straus and Cudahy.

Smith, Tom W. 1979. Happiness: Time Trends, Seasonal Variations, Intersurvey Differences, and Other Mysteries. *Social Psychological Quarterly* 42, no. 1 (March): 18–30.

Solman, Paul. 1997. Mutual Bet. PBS, *The NewsHour with Jim Lehrer,* 1 October.

Sorauf, Frank J. 1988. *Money in American Elections.* Glenview, Ill.: Scott, Foresman.

Specter, Michael. 1995. Borscht and Blini to Go: From Russian Capitalists, an Answer to McDonald's. *New York Times,* 9 August, D1.

Spencer, Herbert. 1909. *The Principles of Sociology.* New York: Appleton.

Squires, Jim. 1990. Television's Civil War. *Wall Street Journal,* 8 October, A12.

Stanley, Alessandra. 1995. A Toast! To the Good Things About Bad Times. *New York Times,* 1 January, 4-1.

Steckel, Richard, and Robin Simons. 1992. *Doing Best by Doing Good: How to Use Public-Purpose Partnerships to Boost Corporate Profits and Benefit Your Community.* New York: Dutton.

Steinert, Marlis G. 1977. *Hitler's War and the Germans: Public Mood and Attitude during the Second World War.* Athens: Ohio University Press.

Steinhauer, Jennifer. 1998. The Undercover Shoppers: Posing as Customers, Paid Agents Grade the Stores. *New York Times,* 4 February, C1.

Stigler, George J. 1959. The Politics of Political Economists. *Quarterly Journal of Economics* 73, no. 4 (November): 522–32.

———. 1975. *The Citizen and the State: Essays on Regulation.* Chicago: University of Chicago Press.

———. 1982. *The Economist as Preacher and Other Essays.* Chicago: University of Chicago Press.

———. 1984. *The Intellectual and the Marketplace.* Cambridge, Mass.: Harvard University Press.

Stokes, Gale. 1993. Is It Possible to Be Optimistic about Eastern Europe? *Social Research* 60, no. 4 (Winter): 685–704.

Sullivan, Kevin. 1997. Cost of Economic Equality Questioned. *Guardian Weekly,* 8 June, 17.

Summers, Lawrence H. 1992. The Next Chapter. *International Economic Insights,* May/June, 12–16.

Tawney, R. H. 1962 [1926]. *Religion and the Rise of Capitalism.* Gloucester, Mass.: Peter Smith.

Teixeira, Ruy A. 1992. *The Disappearing American Voter.* Washington, D.C.: Brookings Institution.

Thaler, Richard. 1985. Mental Accounting and Consumer Choice. *Marketing Science* 4, no. 3 (Summer): 199–214.

Thucydides. 1934. *The Pelopennesian War.* New York: Modern Library.

Tilly, Richard. 1993. Moral Standards and Business Behaviour in Nineteenth-Century Germany and Britain. In *Bourgeois Society in Nineteenth-Century Europe,* ed. Jürgen Kocka and Allen Mitchell, 179–206. Oxford: Berg.

Tocqueville, Alexis de. 1990. *Democracy in America.* Trans. Henry Reeve. New York: Vintage.

Toner, Robin. 1994. Pollsters See a Silent Storm That Swept Away Democrats. *New York Times,* 16 November, A14.

———. 1995. G.O.P. Gets Mixed Reviews From Public Wary on Taxes. *New York Times,* 6 April, A1.

Trachtenberg, Alan. 1990. Introduction. In *Ragged Dick, Or, Street Life in New York with the Boot Blacks.* by Horatio Alger, Jr. New York: Signet.

Treitschke, Heinrich von. 1916. *Politics.* New York: Macmillan.

Troy, Gil. 1997. Moncy and Politics: The Oldest Connection. *Wilson Quarterly* 21, no. 3 (Summer): 14–32.

Urquhart, John, and Peggy Berkowitz. 1987. Northern Angst. *Wall Street Journal*, 22 September, 1.

Uslaner, Eric M. 1993. *The Decline of Comity in Congress.* Ann Arbor: University of Michigan Press.

Vaill, Peter B. 1989. *Managing as a Performing Art: New Ideas for a World of Chaotic Change.* San Francisco: Jossey-Bass.

Veenhoven, Ruut. 1991. Is Happiness Relative? *Social Indicators Research* 24 (February): 1–34.

———. 1993. *Happiness in Nations: Subjective Appreciation of Life in 56 Nations 1946–1992.* Rotterdam: Erasmus University of Rotterdam Department of Social Sciences.

Verba, Sidney, and Norman H. Nie. 1972. *Participation in America: Political Democracy and Social Equality.* New York: Harper & Row.

Verba, Sidney, Kay Lehman Schlozman, and Henry E. Brady. 1995. *Voice and Equality: Civic Voluntarianism in American Politics.* Cambridge, Mass.: Harvard University Press.

Verba, Sidney, Kay Lehman Schlozman, Henry E. Brady, and Norman E. Nie. 1993. Citizen Activity: Who Participates? What Do They Say? *American Political Science Review* 87, no. 2 (June): 303–18.

Waltz, Kenneth N. 1979. *Theory of International Politics.* Reading, Mass.: Addison-Wesley.

Wang, Hongying. Forthcoming. *Law, Diplomacy and Transnational Networks: The Dynamics of Foreign Direct Investment in China.* New York: Oxford University Press.

Warr, Mark. 1995. Trends: Public Opinion on Crime and Punishment. *Public Opinion Quarterly* 59, no. 2 (Summer): 296–310.

Wasilewski, Jacek. 1998. The Fates of Nomenklatura Elites in Postcommunist Eastern Europe. In *Elites, Crises, and the Origins of Regimes,* ed. Mattei Dogan and John Higley. Boulder, Colo.: Rowman & Littlefield.

Wattenberg, Ben. 1997. Going Ga-Ga over the Golden Age. *Washington Times,* 20 March, A17.

Waugh, Auberon. 1986. *Brideshead Benighted.* Boston: Little, Brown.

Weber, Max. 1958 [1904–5]. *The Protestant Ethic and the Spirit of Capitalism.* Trans. Talcott Parsons. New York: Scribner's.

Weeks, David C. 1993. *Ringling: The Florida Years, 1911–1936.* Gainesville: University Press of Florida.

Weingast, Barry R. 1997. The Political Foundations of Limited Government: Parliament and Sovereign Debt in 17th- and 18th-Century England. In *The Frontiers of the New Institutional Economics,* ed. John N. Drobak and John V. C. Nye, 213–46. San Diego, Calif.: Academic Press.

Weinstein, Michael M. 1997. Dr. Doom Becomes Dr. Pangloss. *New York Times,* 18 August, A18.

Weissberg, Robert. 1998. *Political Tolerance: Balancing Community and Diversity.* Thousand Oaks, Calif.: Sage.

Wells, H. G. 1908. *First and Last Things: A Confession of Faith and a Rule of Life.* New York: Putnam's Sons.

West, Rebecca. 1941. *Black Lamb and Grey Falcon: A Journey through Yugoslavia.* New York: Viking.

White, Michael. 1997. We Care Too, Says Hague. *Guardian Weekly,* 19 October, 8.

Whitehead, Laurence. 1986. International Aspects of Democratization. In *Transitions from Authoritarian Rule: Comparative Perspectives,* ed. Guillermo O'Donnell, Philippe C. Schmitter, and Laurence Whitehead, 3–46. Baltimore: Johns Hopkins University Press.

Whitman, David. 1998. *The Optimism Gap: The I'm OK–They're Not Syndrome and the Myth of American Decline.* New York: Walker.

Wiarda, Howard J. 1976. *Transcending Corporatism? The Portuguese Corporative System and the Revolution of 1974.* Columbia: Institute of International Studies, University of South Carolina.

Wiebe, Robert H. 1995. *Self-Rule: A Cultural History of American Democracy.* Chicago: University of Chicago Press.

Will, George F. 1990. *Men At Work: The Craft of Baseball.* New York: Macmillan.

Williams, Lena. 1990. Free Choice: When Too Much Is Too Much. *New York Times,* 14 February, C1.

Wilson, James Q. 1961. The Strategy of Protest: Problems of Negro Civic Action. *Journal of Conflict Resolution* 5, no. 3 (September): 291–303.

———. 1991. *On Character.* Washington, D.C.: The AEI Press.

———. 1993. *The Moral Sense.* New York: Free Press.

———. 1995. Capitalism and Morality. *Public Interest,* Fall, 42–60.

Woldman, Albert A. 1950. Lincoln Never Said That. *Harper's,* May, 70–74.

Woodward, Susan L. 1995. *Balkan Tragedy: Chaos and Dissolution After the Cold War.* Washington, D.C.: Brookings Institution.

Woolsey, R. James, Jr. 1993. Testimony before the Senate Intelligence Committee. 2 February.

Wright, Richard. 1937. *Black Boy.* Cleveland, Ohio: World.

Wright, Quincy. 1968. War: The Study of War. In *International Encyclopedia of the Social Sciences,* 16: 453–68.

Yang, Alan S. 1997. Trends: Attitudes toward Homosexuality. *Public Opinion Quarterly* 61, no. 3 (Fall): 477–507.

Yardeni, Edward. Forthcoming. The Economic Consequences of the Peace. In *Peace, Prosperity, and Politics,* ed. John Mueller. New York: Westview.

Yergin, Daniel. 1991. *The Prize: The Epic Quest for Oil, Money, and Power.* New York: Simon & Schuster.

Yergin, Daniel, and Joseph Stanislaw. 1998. *The Commanding Heights: The Battle between Government and the Marketplace That Is Remaking the Modern World.* New York: Simon & Schuster.

Zakaria, Fareed. 1997. The Rise of Illiberal Democracy. *Foreign Affairs* 76, no. 6 (November/December): 22–43.

Zweig, Jason. 1997. How to Beat 77% of Fund Investors Year after Year: That's What Indexers Have Done for More than Two Decades. *Money,* August, 136–39.

* Index *